CAMBRIDGE LIBRARY COLLECTION

Books of enduring scholarly value

European History

This series includes accounts of historical events and movements by eye-witnesses and contemporaries, as well as landmark studies that assembled significant source materials or developed new historiographical methods. It covers the social and political history of continental Europe from the Renaissance to the end of the nineteenth century, and its broad range includes works on Russia and the Balkans, revolutionary France, the papacy and the inquisition, and the Venetian state archives.

Illyrian Letters

Although remembered today chiefly for his archaeological discoveries in Crete, Sir Arthur John Evans (1851–1941) became Britain's leading expert on Balkan affairs after publishing his account of travelling through Bosnia in 1875 (also reissued in this series). In 1877 he returned to the region as a correspondent for the *Manchester Guardian*, reporting on the continuing insurrection against Ottoman rule. Evans is at pains to point out that he does not regard himself as a war correspondent, but wishes to introduce 'in a tolerably peaceful fashion the insurgents and their little mountain territory to the English public'. Published in 1878, these letters offer historical, social and religious background to the insurrection. In so doing, they provide a valuable insight into the genesis of more recent conflicts in a region that has always been a melting pot of peoples and cultures.

T0382538

Cambridge University Press has long been a pioneer in the reissuing of out-of-print titles from its own backlist, producing digital reprints of books that are still sought after by scholars and students but could not be reprinted economically using traditional technology. The Cambridge Library Collection extends this activity to a wider range of books which are still of importance to researchers and professionals, either for the source material they contain, or as landmarks in the history of their academic discipline.

Drawing from the world-renowned collections in the Cambridge University Library and other partner libraries, and guided by the advice of experts in each subject area, Cambridge University Press is using state-of-the-art scanning machines in its own Printing House to capture the content of each book selected for inclusion. The files are processed to give a consistently clear, crisp image, and the books finished to the high quality standard for which the Press is recognised around the world. The latest print-on-demand technology ensures that the books will remain available indefinitely, and that orders for single or multiple copies can quickly be supplied.

The Cambridge Library Collection brings back to life books of enduring scholarly value (including out-of-copyright works originally issued by other publishers) across a wide range of disciplines in the humanities and social sciences and in science and technology.

Illyrian Letters

*A Revised Selection of Correspondence
from the Illyrian Provinces of Bosnia,
Herzegovina, Montenegro, Albania,
Dalmatia, Croatia, and Slavonia,
Addressed to the Manchester Guardian
During the Year 1877*

ARTHUR JOHN EVANS

CAMBRIDGE
UNIVERSITY PRESS

CAMBRIDGE UNIVERSITY PRESS

Cambridge, New York, Melbourne, Madrid, Cape Town,
Singapore, São Paolo, Delhi, Mexico City

Published in the United States of America by Cambridge University Press, New York

www.cambridge.org
Information on this title: www.cambridge.org/9781108060967

© in this compilation Cambridge University Press 2013

This edition first published 1878
This digitally printed version 2013

ISBN 978-1-108-06096-7 Paperback

ILLYRIAN LETTERS

Heu micat Illyricum perverso lumine sidus:
  Turcarum referunt patria signa jugum;
Quod prius impositum lunæ, nunc cornubus astrum
  Luna premit: tristes fata dedere vices.
Austriacæ stellam, victrices et sine Marte,
  Restituant aquilæ quo fuit ante polo!

ILLYRIAN LETTERS

A REVISED SELECTION OF CORRESPONDENCE FROM THE ILLYRIAN
PROVINCES OF BOSNIA, HERZEGOVINA, MONTENEGRO, ALBANIA,
DALMATIA, CROATIA, AND SLAVONIA, ADDRESSED TO THE
'MANCHESTER GUARDIAN' DURING THE YEAR 1877

BY

ARTHUR J. EVANS, B.A., F.S.A.

Author of 'Through Bosnia and the Herzegovina on Foot'

LONDON
LONGMANS, GREEN, AND CO.
1878

LONDON: PRINTED BY
SPOTTISWOODE AND CO., NEW-STREET SQUARE
AND PARLIAMENT STREET

'The Inhabitants of any Country, who are descended and derive a Title to their Estates from those who are subdued, and had a Government forced on them against their free Consents, *retain a Right to the Possession of their Ancestors* though they consent not hereby to the *Government*, whose hard *Conditions* were by *Force* imposed on the *Possessors of that Country*. For the first *Conqueror* never having had a Title to the *Land* of that Country, the People who are the Descendants of, or claim under, those who were forced to submit to the Yoke of a Government by Constraint, have always a Right to shake it off, and free themselves from the Usurpation or Tyranny which the Sword hath brought in upon them, till their Rulers put them under a Frame of Government as they willingly and of Choice consent to. Who doubts but the *Grecian* Christians, Descendants of the ancient Possessors of that Country, may justly cast off the *Turkish* Yoke which they have so long groaned under whenever they have an Opportunity to do it? For no Government can have a Right to Obedience from a People who have not freely consented to it; which they can never be supposed to do, till either they are put in a full State of Liberty and choose their own Government and Governors, or at least till they have such standing Laws to which they have by themselves or their Representatives given their free Consent, and also till they are allowed their due Property, which is so to be Proprietors of what they have, that nobody can take away any Part of it without their own Consent; without which Men under any Government are not in the State of Freemen, but are direct Slaves under the Force of War.'

LOCKE, 'Of Civil Government.'

MARBURG

Lake Balaton

R. Mur

STYRIA

CILLI

PART OF HUNGARY

R. DANUBE

OLD
SERBIAN
VOIVODINA

CARNIOLA

C R O A T I A

AGRAM

R. DRAVE

S L A V O N I A

SISCIA
(Sisseck)
PAKRATZ

ESSEK

SYRMIA

NEUSATZ

R. Kulpa

KRAINA

UDBINA

KULEN VAKUF

THE LIKA

R. SAVE

BERBIR

R. Unutz

BANJALUKA

DERBEND

SEMLIN

BELGRADE

B O S N A

TRAVNIK

R. DRINA

S E R B I A

ZARA

D A L

KNIN

R. Kerka

R. Cettina

SEBENICO

SPALATO

BRAZZA

LISSA

LESINA

CURZOLA

LAGOSTA

KISTANJE

L M A

H E R Z E G O V I N A

R. Narenta

LIVNO

SERAJEVO

MOSTAR

Veleč

R. MORAVA

TASLIDJE

R A S C I A

OLD
SERBIA

NOVI BAZAR

R. IBAR

IPEK

A D R I A T I C   S E A

TREBINJE
Sutova

RAGUSA

NIKSIC

MONTENEGRO

CATTARO
Budua

ANTIVARI

DULCIGNO

CETTINJE

PODGORITZA

LAKE OF SKUTARI

SKUTARI

PRISREND

R. Drin

A L B A N I A

MIRIDITES

R. Bojana

C. Pali

DURAZZO

R. Schkumbi

LAKE OF OCHRIDA

Sketch Map
PART OF WESTERN
ILLYRIA

PREFACE.

THE small collection of letters now republished in the present form does not pretend to be a comprehensive history of recent events, even so far as concerns the western part of the Balkan Peninsula, or what may fairly be comprised under the good old term Illyria. It is nothing more than a representative series of observations made in the Illyrian Provinces during the troubled year 1877, throughout which I corresponded, as occasion arose, with the 'Manchester Guardian.'

A previous acquaintance with those lands, some account of which I have already given to the public in my book on Bosnia, and a still earlier acquaintance with their history had led me to conceive an extraordinary interest in their condition, and I had accordingly taken up my abode at Ragusa as a convenient centre for working at the language and antiquities of Illyria and the *Leben und Treiben* of her peoples.

The exciting events of the hour, however, diverted me from these more tranquil pursuits. The deplorable condition of Bosnia, the *fiasco* of the new Constitution, the daily outrages committed by the Irregulars, the unutterable misery of the Refugees, the difficult problems suggested by the internal divisions of the Province ; the Insurrection ; the life-and-death struggle in Montenegro, the movement among the neighbouring Slavonic Provinces of Austria-Hungary, —these and other objects of urgent interest would have been amply sufficient to exhaust the energy of many chroniclers. But while the attention of Europe was centred on the Bulgarian and Armenian battle-fields these in many ways not less important fields of contemplation were almost entirely neglected. While journalists were drawn elsewhere, the temporizing and immoral policy of Austria-Hungary exerted its utmost to shroud the Bosnian Reign of Terror in a veil of diplomatic silence : and false impressions of the Province conceived within the walls of the English Consulate distorted even the scanty information that found its way into the blue-books of our Foreign Office.

Nothing could have been further from my object than to act as a War Correspondent. In so far indeed as the guerilla operations of the Turks and insurgents in Bosnia are concerned it would be a tedious and unprofitable task, even if it were possible, to follow them at length. I have therefore in the Letters now re-published contented myself with introducing in a tolerably peaceful fashion the Insurgents and their little mountain territory to the English public, without attempting in this place to follow the ups and downs of the later course of the Insurrection. The war in Montenegro, indeed, presents a series of more striking pictures, and having been in the Principality at the time of the critical struggle with the Turks, I thought it might be to the convenience of my readers to sub-join in the form of appendices to my letters a brief *résumé* of the chief events of the earlier periods of the war; while a prolonged stay at Nikšić led me to gather together some more minute details of its capture. Happily, so far as Montenegro is concerned, the world may expect a more exhaustive record from a competent military critic, whom hardships and difficulties greater than those of ordinary war could not deter from following step by step the incidents of that brave struggle. Mr. W. J. Stillman, the distin-guished 'Times' Correspondent of whom I speak, may indeed be said to have made the modern history of Montenegro his own, and those who ven-ture on his ground must perforce feel themselves to be intruders.

It has been my own object to take a rather com-prehensive view of all the Illyrian Provinces, and by

extending my observations from the Save to Central
Albania to survey them from a variety of standpoints.
And in so doing I have not considered the scenery
of those countries, their antiquities, and even the folk-
lore and domestic life of their peoples, beside my
purpose. I have often deliberately preferred to lead
up to political conclusions by such apparently indirect
channels. It is practically impossible to separate
peoples as primitive as the inhabitants of those lands
from their surroundings. Where man is ignorant,
Nature still is his mistress. The broad distinctions
between politics and the relations of domestic life that
exist among civilized nations are out there non-exis-
tent, and even the nymphs and dragons that haunt
the Bosnian caves and forests may, in their way, play
as real a part in the affairs of men as Insurgents or
Bashi-bazouks. Nor should any one who desires to
present the 'Illyrian Question' adequately before the
world fail at least to touch upon the antiquities of
those historic lands, where the monuments of the Past
present the weightiest protest against Present ruin,
and form the true mirrors of the Future. My letter
about Durazzo is thus largely occupied by antiquarian
suggestions and historical reminiscences which point
their moral : yet, while glancing at these topics I have
purposely reserved for other occasions any disquisitions that might be called archæological.

Thus it will be seen that my Letters are rather side-lights on the Eastern Question than an attempt to exhibit an act of the Russo-Turkish war. They have, indeed, little to do either with Turks or Russians. In Bosnia, the province of the Ottoman Empire with which I am chiefly concerned, even among the native Mahometans there are, strictly speaking, no Turks ; and, on the other hand, Russia has deliberately resigned the province to the sphere of Austrian Interests.

As far as I can see all that I have related in these letters points to one conclusion, the conclusion typified in the heraldic device on the title-page, and explained by the Latin lines that I have ventured to append to it,[1] namely, that in the interests of the populations that lie between the Save and Adriatic, in the interests of the Hapsburg Monarchy itself, in the interests of Europe and of humanity, Austria should incorporate Bosnia in her dominions, and restore the lapsed suzerainty of the Hapsburgs over the whole of Illyria. I do not love Austria, and I cannot be said to have dealt too leniently with her in the course of this book. I have been led to these conclusions with great regret. But I confess that, so

---

[1] The device on the Illyrian escutcheon previous to the Turkish Conquest was an eight-rayed star above a crescent. The Turkish device, as every one is aware, is the same star to the right of the crescent. This curious heraldic coincidence suggested the epigram.

far as I can see ahead, the extension of Austria to the South and East, and the ultimate reconstitution of the monarchy on an Illyrian or South Slavonic basis, is the only consummation that can prevent Russia from ultimately advancing to the shores of the Adriatic..

CONTENTS.

————•◦•————

LETTER IV.

THE CLOUDLANDS OF FREE BOSNIA.

LETTER V.

FEUDAL CASTLES AND INSURGENT HUTS.

LETTER VI.

THE DEVASTATION OF BOSNIA AND MR. CONSUL HOLMES' REPORTS.

LETTER VII.

HOW THE NEW CONSTITUTION WAS PROMULGATED IN BOSNIA.

LETTER VIII.

THROUGH THE LIKA.

LETTER IX.

ON THE SCENE OF TURKISH OUTRAGES.

NOTE.

a

CONTENTS.

NOTE.

A SHORT REVIEW OF THE WAR IN MONTENEGRO

PAGE

LETTER XV.

PEACEFUL SKETCHES OF MONTENEGRO IN WAR TIME.
(I.) FROM CATTARO TO CETTINJE.

LETTER XVI.

PEACEFUL SKETCHES OF MONTENEGRO IN WAR TIME.
(II.) IN THE VILLAGE CAPITAL.

LETTER XVII.

THE FALL OF NIKŠIĆ.

MAPS.

KEY TO THE PRONUNCIATION

of the SERBO-CROATIAN ORTHOGRAPHY *adopted for Illyrian names in this book.*

Serbo-Croatian Letter.		Approximate Sound.
ć	=	like *ch* or *cs*, before a vowel *ty*
č	=	German *tsch*
j	=	*y*
lj	=	Italian *gl*
nj	=	Italian *gn*
š	=	like *sh*

SKETCH MAP OF SOUTHERN BOSNIA,
Showing the Insurgent District in that part of the Province.

London, Longmans & Cº

The material originally positioned here is too large for reproduction in this reissue. A PDF can be downloaded from the web address given on page iv of this book, by clicking on 'Resources Available'.

ILLYRIAN LETTERS.

—◆—

LETTER I.

REFUGEE AND INSURGENT BOSNIA.

Impossibility of peaceful settlement in insurgent provinces. Extent of Bosnian insurrection. Reign of terror in country districts. A quarter of a million refugees. Inadequacy of official relief. Corruption of 'patriots.' Miss Irby and Miss Johnston's work.

Knin (on the Dalmatian-Bosnian Frontier), *February* 8, 1877.

THERE seems to be a general impression in England that though the Conference has ended in smoke, matters are much smoother now than they were a few months ago. Russia, we are told, will only bluster and threaten a bit; Serbia is already negotiating terms ; and as to Bosnia and Bulgaria— after all, what is the lot of the Christian inhabitants of Turkey when weighed against the peace of Europe ? The oil of diplomacy has been poured upon the troubled waters, and somehow *ça s'arrangera.* The refugees will return ; the insurgents will see the propriety of laying down their arms the instant that Russia fails them ; and as to the condition of the rayah, well, we must trust to the good sense of the Turks to 'ameliorate' it themselves.

Now I do not profess to be in the confidence either

B

of Russia or the Principalities, but so far as the Bosnian refugees and the Bosnian insurgents are concerned, and I may add the Bosnian Mahometans, I have set myself to examine personally the true state of affairs, and in the course of a somewhat difficult journey have seen and heard enough to open the eyes of those who indulge in these comfortable speculations. I will even venture to assert that so far as concerns those very countries where the present troubles originated, the prospect of a settlement was never more remote than it is at present.

The Bosnian refugees will not return.

The refugees, driven forth from Bosnia by deeds of savagery (which, though unreported by English newspapers, almost surpass the horrors of Bulgaria), are dying by tens and hundreds, starved and frozen in the inhospitable gorges of the Dinaric Alps ; but they will not return.

The insurgents will not lay down their arms.

The Bosnian insurgents hold already in their possession mountain strongholds, embracing over 1,000 square miles, are fairly armed, and, as I believe, capable not only of holding their own without foreign assistance, but ultimately, perhaps, unless thwarted by foreign intervention, of forming a new free State—a little Bosnian Montenegro—in the north-western angle of the province.

The new Constitution stillborn in Bosnia.

Finally, as to Turkish promises and paper constitutions, the fall of Midhat will have already prepared your readers for the intelligence that the Turkish Government has not dared to promulgate the new Constitution in Bosnia in the native language, and that, so far at least as Western Bosnia is concerned, the Government of Stamboul has practically ceased to exist. The country not in the hands of the insurgents is terrorized over by the dominant caste of native Mahometan fanatics, the begs and agas, and their (in Bosnia still half-feudal) train of murderous Bashi-Bazouks, who have cast off the last semblance of obedience to the Central Government. In the country about Travnik and Banjaluka, the worst horrors of Bulgaria are repeating themselves at this very moment. I have before me the following details from a source on which you may absolutely rely. The outburst of fanaticism at present desolating that already desolated part of Bosnia, had its origin among the dregs of the Mahometan population of Travnik, the ex-capital of this country. One gang of these ruffians numbering about a hundred made its way to Banjaluka, and since the end of last month robber bands of these fanatics have been making inroads into the Christian villages whose inhabitants had not fled the country. As to the number of persons actually murdered, it is impossible at present to obtain exact details. In a single village, however—Zupa, by Banjaluka—there were six such assassinations; many have been cruelly beaten, and other outrages have been committed of which I cannot write. The worst is, that in the depths of winter a large and peaceful population have been scared from their homes, and are either hiding in the forests or have crossed the frontier. The Agram papers raise the number of this fresh exodus of refugees to 5,000, but this is probably an exaggeration, and I have been careful to accept nothing on the authority of Croatian or Dalmatian journals. The fact which I wish to impress upon my readers is that, so far from the refugees returning to their burnt homes, their numbers are rather augmenting; and even while I write this, news reaches me of fresh arrivals of refugees at this place from Glamoš; these, however, on their own showing, were driven forth by no particular act of barbarity, but simply by hunger and misery.

The total number of the refugees amounts at present to

LETTER
I.
Reign of Terror in Bosnian country districts.

Fresh arrivals of rayah fugitives.

about a quarter of a million, some of whom are at present in Serbia, some in Montenegro, and the rest in the Austro-Hungarian provinces of Dalmatia, Croatia, and Slavonia.   Of those here in Dalmatia the last official account gives the following number :—In the district of Bencovatz, 1,779 ; of Sebenico, 13 ; of Knin, 10,490 ; Curzola, 4 ; Ragusa, 17,094 ; Cattaro, 2,200 ; Sinj, 2,300 ; Macarsca, 300.   The real numbers, however, will be found considerably to exceed these figures.   The Austrian authorities have refused to register many who live too near the Bosnian frontier ; others, but a very small minority, have means of their own ; and others again have been supported by friends across the border.   The two English ladies—Miss A. P. Irby and Miss Johnston, who, in pursuance of their great work of relief, have stationed themselves here at Knin, as the head-quarters of human misery—have the best reasons for believing that, so far as this district is concerned, 12,000 would be nearer the mark ; while if the fugitives in the mountains on the other side of the border be reckoned, the numbers in this neighbourhood would be raised to nearer 17,000.

The Austrian Government professes to give ten kreutzers daily, or rather less than twopence, to every adult, and half that amount to children ; but, as I have already intimated, many in the more remote and mountainous districts receive nothing at all ; and even where it is given, I am sorry to be obliged to add that even this pittance is cut down by the villany and corruption of the official underlings who distribute it, so that many adults have received no more than three kreutzers a day.   If we remember the past history of Knin, the centre of a wild Morlach population—robbers driven seawards from the interior, pirates driven inland from the sea, repressed and corrupted later by Turkish, Venetian, and Austrian despotism—it is the less to be wondered at that though the population of this place have many amiable characteristics—as what Dalmatian has not?—truth and honesty are not to be reckoned among their conspicuous virtues. The history of the *Comitato*, formed here professedly to aid the oppressed rayahs beyond, and the refugees on this side of, the border, is a history of peculation and intrigue. The 'patriots' are quite as corrupt as the officials, and sums collected in Serbia and elsewhere to aid the refugees have been perverted to very different purposes by men in whom the old predatory instincts of the Morlach and the super-subtlety of the Venetian are perpetually triumphing over all nobler impulses. I could point to men here who have grown rich on the misfortunes of those they professed to aid. I may have to allude to still blacker charges; and, indeed, it adds not a little to the difficulty of one's position here, that one is forced to refuse the Dalmatian kiss of peace from thieves and even would-be murderers.

Private charity and official relief having in this district fallen into such hands, the state of the refugees has been most deplorable. Small-pox and famine-typhus have wrought terrible ravages among the weaker portion of these unfortunates; and though the disease has now somewhat abated since October last, over 2,000 have died in this district alone. The arrival of the two English ladies has been, indeed, a godsend to the Bosnians in this part. In Slavonia and Croatia they have been working over a year, and besides distributing enormous supplies of food and clothing, they have founded eighteen [1] day schools, where the destitute

---

[1] Now (January 1878) twenty-two.

LETTER I.

Corruption of Knin 'Comitato.'

Miss Irby and Miss Johnston's work.

children have been both fed and taught. Since their
arrival here their energy has been unflagging ; they have
performed long and weary journeys in the rough carts of
this country to seek out those who stood most in need of
help ; and besides distributing Indian corn and blankets
and clothing in the most judicious and methodical
manner, they have had the satisfaction of setting on foot
a new school for refugee children at Plavno, about two and
a half hours' drive from here. They are also carrying
out an admirable plan—much appreciated by the
Bosnians—of providing the women with flax to make
their own clothes. By the local committee their pro-
ceedings are viewed with characteristic jealousy, but by
the simple Bosnians they are held in a kind of veneration,
and natives have come from afar to see the two English
queens—' Kralitzas,' as they call them. Great, however,
as their exertions have been, the need here is scarcely to
be measured in words, and there are districts among the
mountains where no one has yet penetrated, and where
the distress is still more awful.

LETTER II.

THE FUGITIVES IN THE CAVERNS.

Bosnian Border, *February* 9.

IN order to explore some of the more inaccessible haunts of misery, as well as to obtain a personal acquaintance with the position and prospects of the Bosnian insurgents, I set forth on an expedition among the wild and snow-capped highlands of the Dinaric Alps that lie beyond what is still known as the Turkish frontier.

I left Knin under very good auspices, in company with a native gentleman who has been doing his best to help the two English ladies in their difficult work of relief. Uzélatz, of whom I speak, was born of Bosnian parents, though on Dalmatian soil, and, though a man of culture and independent means, took the command of the insurgents of this part of Bosnia during the first year of the revolt. During his year of leadership he gained several important successes against the Turks, and there can be little doubt that, had he remained in command, the insurgents would at present be in possession of a larger area of country. He was, however, wounded, and forced by reasons of health, as well as by the intrigues of

Start on expedition.

Uzélatz.

the Comitato, to give up his command, which was taken
up in turn by a brave but illiterate Bosnian, the Vojvode
Golub, and finally by the Serbian Colonel Despotović,
who at present commands.   Like the other few honest
men in Knin, Uzélatz has been forced by the transactions
of the Comitato to hold himself aloof from it; but he
has not ceased to do all in his power for the unfortunate
Bosnians, and his intimate acquaintance with the country
and exhaustive information on all the present phases of
Bosnian history, qualify him to speak on these subjects
with some authority.   It is much to his credit that,
sympathising as he does with the present movement, his
feelings are absolutely untinged with religious fanaticism.

During the year of his command he did all in his power
to conciliate the native Slavonic Mahometans of Bosnia,
and with some partial success—nay, he carries his
religious indifference so far that he has more than once
exclaimed in my hearing, ' Oh, if the Christians of
Bosnia would only turn Mahometans, that would be
better than these miserable feuds.'

As to priests—even of the Pravoslav or Orthodox
profession—the ex-insurgent leader had a most whole-
some and cordial aversion to them: indeed, one of the
chief grievances of the rayah is the state to which the
Turks have succeeded in reducing the Pravoslav Church
in the province.   The Metropolitan at Serajevo and the
Eparchs buy their offices from that faithful servant and
nominee of the Divan, the 'Greek' Patriarch at Stamboul, and the single idea of the new 'Spiritual Pasha,' on
his arrival amongst his flock, being how to make the
speculation pay, the state to which the inferior clergy
are reduced may faintly be imagined.   The more ignorant the village popes are, the less capable are they of

withstanding the exactions of their superior ; so their spiritual overseer resigns them to their pristine state of ignorance, and is rather pleased than otherwise when he finds a priest who cannot read the liturgy ! 'None of your new-fangled heretical learning for me,' remarks the fat Metropolitan as he pockets the fees, which the wretched village priest has had in his turn to screw out of his congregation.　But the Fanariote hierarchy, I am happy to say, has rather over-reached itself here, as it did in Bulgaria ; the yoke of the foreign Turcophile bishops has tended very strongly to knit together the village popes and their flocks in a common opposition, and has only brought out the more that democratic spirit always so strong in the lower grades of the Orthodox Church, and itself a still surviving influence of the old Greek republics, just as Roman Catholic centralisation perpetuates the organization of the fourth century Empire.

Uzélatz whiled away our journey by telling me many merry tales about village popes and the Fanariote bishops, one or two quite worthy of Boccaccio.　A late Metropolitan, who rejoiced in the curiously appropriate name of Dionysos, for he was of a Bacchanalian turn, used to find it profitable to take with him on his visitations a goodly assortment of 'icons,' which he disposed of to the faithful at prices varying from a ducat apiece, the episcopal benediction being thrown into the bargain. As, however, Dionysos added gambling to his numerous accomplishments, and as indeed he did succeed on one occasion in 'rooking' one of his brother bishops of a considerable sum, we need not be surprised if the venerable Metropolitan, in addition to the holy images, sometimes added to his luggage a pack of cards.　Now it so chanced that, having on one occasion driven a more

than usually profitable trade in icons, the bishop was
asked by a pious rayah whether he had yet an image of
St. George for sale. The Metropolitan looked into his
bag, there was not so much as an icon to be seen ; he
fumbled among his vestments—anathema ! he must have
sold them out; but here his eye rested on a familiar piece
of pasteboard—it was a happy thought ! . . . Do my
readers know the Venetian cards in use in these regions ?
—probably not. . . . 'Yes,' replied the bishop, 'I have
yet an image of the holy St. George, but indeed it is an
image of such great price that it were sacrilege to part
with it.' ' Your grace,' said the man, ' I will give ten
grosch for such an image.' ' Ten grosch for such an
icon !' quoth the holy man, 'I would not part with it
for less than half a ducat.' The poor man reluctantly
handed the coin to the Metropolitan and went away
rejoicing, with *the king of spades* in his wallet ! They
say that after the success of this first experiment the
bishop made the pleasing discovery that if a queen of
hearts were passed for Our Lady, or knaves were chris-
tened angels, heaven might yet smile upon the pious
fraud. Of the whole story I will say, *Se non è vero è
ben trovato!*

Uzélatz told me that when he was an insurgent
leader he was resting one day in a small Bosnian hut,
divided into two rooms by a small partition, and two
priests, who did not know that he was there, were
drinking in the further compartment. Suddenly a Bosnian woman came in in a great hurry : ' Your Reverence,
my father is dying, and needs your comfort; pray make
haste or it will be too late !' ' Oh ! I can't be bothered !'
said the pope addressed. 'I'll come,' said the other, ' if
you'll give me a ducat.' ' We are very poor, your Reve-

rence—we have not so much in the house. Here are
three grosch, only pray be quick !' 'But you've got coins
enough on your dress,' was the brutal rejoinder (the
Bosnian women adorn their fez and breast with Turkish
paras) : 'just snip them off and hand them me if you
want me to come.' The poor woman cut off her barbaric ornaments and handed them to the priest. 'You
are surely coming now, father?' 'I'm going to have a
drop of something, I can tell you, and eat my dinner
before I budge ;' but here he was interrupted by a well-
directed blow from Uzélatz, who had vaulted the partition
at this point of the dialogue—and his Reverence lay
sprawling on the ground. The woman received her money
back, together with some involuntary contributions from
the pope's privy purse ; the other pope hurried off
double quick, to administer ghostly comfort free, gratis,
and for nothing ; and his Reverence himself got a good
sound drubbing, at the conclusion of which Uzélatz took
care to cut his beard off. Alas ! in Bosnia a beardless
priest is no better than a layman.

'Always the best thing to do with priests,' remarked
my ex-insurgent friend, oracularly—'cut their beards off.'

'Have you done it more than once?' I inquired. It
appeared that Uzélatz *had* performed that operation on at
least one other occasion. Priests in Bosnia are invited at
times to sprinkle houses with holy water for the regu-
lation fee of one grosch for each house. One fine day a
pope conceived the happy idea of inviting himself to
perform the lucrative lustration. He appeared accordingly in a village then occupied by the insurgents, and
unfolded to the eyes of the astonished villagers a document, which he professed to have received from the
Vojvode Uzélatz, authorizing him to sprinkle every house.

The villagers, who could not read, had no choice but to believe his story, and, as water is cheap and there were over fifty houses in the village, the pope was in a fair way to make a pretty penny. He had already visited several houses, and, it being customary on such occasions to offer his Reverence a cup of arrack, was beginning to get a little unsteady on his legs, when who should appear on the scene but Uzélatz himself. Of course the villagers all wanted to know why he had sent the pope to sponge on them. 'Where is he?' said the Vojvode. 'Drinking "raki" at So-and-so's.' Uzélatz hurried to the house, but no sooner did his Reverence catch sight of him than he found his legs in a moment and was off, 'like a wolf.' 'Stop!' shouted Uzélatz, but as the pope only ran the faster, he pretended to take aim at the runaway and fired off his gun. This had the desired effect, and the pope was cringing at the Vojvode's feet like a whipped hound. 'What is this precious document that you have been showing to the people? Out with it!' shouted Uzélatz. 'Oh! pray have mercy on me,' cried the pope, unfolding a ragged piece of newspaper. 'The fact is I picked this up, and I thought a little holy water would hurt nobody.' Uzélatz sheared the shepherd.

Here you have—rather an unfavourable specimen, perhaps—a village pope as he exists in Bosnia; tutored in avarice and resigned to ignorance by his ecclesiastical superiors, but withal very much of 'a man and a brother.' Cut off his beard and there he is, a layman like the rest. Many Pravoslav priests have actually become insurgent leaders. The village pope is the natural ally of the insurgent, just as his Fanariote bishop is the natural ally of the worst among the pashas.

I must not forget my other companion on this

journey, old Lazar, a brave, simple old Bosniac, who
has dealt the Turks many a hard blow in his day, and
who is at present a most trusty henchman of the English
'Kralitzas,' for whom he distributes corn in the more
inaccessible localities, and, not being able to read or
write, checks his accounts by cutting notches on sticks,
after the manner of our old English tallies. He is honesty
itself. The natives say you might trust him anywhere
with a thousand florins, and his reverent affection towards the English ladies was delightful to witness. Even
to me, as their friend, his devotion has been most touching; he has offered to go with me among the Turks
themselves, and would do it too, though to him it means
tolerably certain death.

While Uzélatz has been recounting these merry
tales of popes and metropolitans we have left far behind
us Knin, with its ancient peak stronghold,—with its rich
expanse of plain, overgrown at a later season of the year
with luxuriant vines and golden maize, but as yet bare
and wintry enough,—with its crystal Kerka that dashes
headlong, like a fugitive spirit, in spray and foam from the
rock wilderness a few miles above the town, and, gliding
through the soft champaign and under the town bridge,
hides itself once more in endless rock-gullies,—up which
only yesterday the Bora—the true Boreas of antiquity, the
wild storm-wind for which Illyria is noted—was whistling
and shrieking, flinging itself upon the water with the
swoop of a sea-eagle, and such fierce might that the whole
surface of the river was momentarily lost in a curling
mist of spray, as when some parched highway is shrouded
in a dust-cloud by our milder gusts! Knin is left behind
us as we ascend the romantic valley of the Butišnitza;
but not the winter, not the snow which clings to the

mountain sides, towering above us on either hand, and glistens on the loftier peaks of Mount Dinara beyond,— not the Bora which howls ominously through the gorges and hurries to us from the snowfields above with an icier breath.

We approached the Bosnian frontier by way of the village of Stermnitza, about which as many as 6,000 refugees are crowded. I had already been present at one of Miss Irby's distributions of corn to the fugitives near Knin, and had shuddered at the half-starved swarms as they clamoured for a piece of English blanket to cover their rags : but such misery as was here I had never in my life seen, nor imagined to exist before. It was pitiable. They thought we had brought food for them all. They crowded round us, these pinched haggard faces, these lean bony frames, scarred by disease and bowed down with hunger ; they followed till it seemed a dreadful dance of death. There was one lad of twelve, as pale and frail as one of the little snowdrops on our path; we could see that he could not live many hours—and who could wish him to?—yet to him, as if for protection, clung another younger child, whose only clothing was a few rags tied together and eked out by the long tresses of a woman's hair. Some English help has already reached Stermnitza, but in many cases it had come too late, and in this village alone over six hundred have died in the last few months.

A little further on the mountain side we came upon a new graveyard already well tenanted. We now crossed the Bosnian frontier, and followed a path which Uzélatz himself had constructed along a precipitous mountain steep, passing the *débris* of a stupendous landslip, and beneath some extraordinary rock pinnacles called the ' Hare Stones ' by the Bosnians, because, according to the local legend, a hunted hare had once leaped from one rock-column to another across an enormous chasm. Near here we saw the first signs of Turkish ravages—the village of Zaseok, burnt by the Turks at the first out-break of the insurrection ; and presently found an old Bosnian, who guided us by more difficult mountain paths to a lonely glen, where a torrent divides the Austrian from the Bosnian territory, and where, in the Christian side, we descried a series of caves in the rocky mountain side, to which we now made our way. Then indeed broke upon my sight such a depth of human misery as it has perhaps fallen to the lot of few living men to witness.

We crossed a small frozen cataract, and passed the mouths of two lesser caverns, toothed with icicles three feet long and over, and then we came to the mouth of a large cave, a great black opening in the rock, from which, as we climbed up to it, crawled forth a squalid and half-naked swarm of women, children, and old men, with faces literally eaten away with hunger and disease. A little way off was another smaller hole outside which leant what had once been a beautiful girl, and inside, amidst filth and squalor which I cannot describe, dimly seen through smoke and darkness, lay a woman dying of typhus. Others crowded out of black holes and nooks, and I found that there were about thirty in this den. In another small hole, going almost straight down into the rock, I saw a shapeless bundle of rags and part of the pale half-hidden face of another woman stricken down by the disease of hunger ; another den with about a dozen, and then another more horrible than any. A black hole, sloping downwards at so steep an angle as made climbing up or down a task of some difficulty, descended thus abruptly about thirty feet, and then seemed to disappear into the bowels of the earth. The usual haggard crowd swarmed out of the dark and fœtid recesses below and climbed up to seek for alms. A woman seated on a ledge of rock half way up burst into hysterical sobs ; it was the sight of old Lazar. The good old fellow had already discovered these dens of destitution, and had brought them some food from the 'Kralitzas' all the way from Knin. They had tasted nothing then for three days, and would have all died that day, she said, if he had not come.

Then, slowly tottering and crawling from an underground lurking place at the bottom of the pit, there stumbled into the light an old man, so lean, so wasted, with such hollow sunken eyes, that he seemed nothing but a moving skeleton—it was the realisation of some ghastly mediæval picture of the resurrection of the dead ! He seemed to have lost his reason, but from below he stretched out his bony hands towards us as if to grasp our alms, and made a convulsive effort to climb the rocky wall of his den. He raised himself with difficulty a few feet, and then fell back exhausted, and was caught by a girl in her arms. Poor old man ! It was not hard to see that he would never leave that loathsome den alive ; nay, I dare not say that those horrible recesses

were not catacombs as well. Not far off we passed another cave. Not a soul crawled forth from its dark recesses ; not a sound, save the patter of an icicle just reached by the noonday sun, broke the sepulchral silence of its vaults. We had come too late. The bodies of women and children lay within.

Strange as it may seem, amidst all this horror and misery, the old Slavonic Zadruga, or family communism, has been preserved. Every cavern has its house-father and house-mother, and they have carried their little constitution underground! I availed myself of these microcosms of representative government to distribute among the cave constituencies sufficient for their present wants. We then passed on to another mountain gorge, where about 180 more of these unfortunates were crowded in rude and insufficient shelters on the mountain side, and while halting near here a pretty little girl came up and told us how the Turks had fired at her but had not hit her, which the little person thought great fun.

Here for the present I must pause.[1]

Another Refugee colony.

---

[1] My readers will be glad to learn that the refugees in the caves who still survived were rescued from their awful condition by Miss Irby and Miss Johnston's exertions. They have been housed in wooden huts, for which Mr. W. R. Mitchell, who visited them in July and was struck by their wretched condition, supplied the funds.

c

LETTER III.

AT INSURGENT HEAD-QUARTERS.

LETTER
III.

Czerni Potuk, Free Bosnia, *February* 9.

*The camp
at Czerni
Potuk.*

FTER quitting the scenes described in my pre-vious letter, we made our way up the course of the Czerni Potuk, or Black Brook, above which the present commander of the insurgents, Colonel Despotović, has pitched his head-quarters. Uzélatz here left me, having the best reasons of his own for not putting himself in the power of the present chief, who is in close league with the Knin Comitato ; and under the guidance of old Lazar I ascended a difficult mountain steep towards a gap in the rocks, which forms a kind of natural gateway to the impregnable gorge in which the low wooden sheds of the insurgent stationary camp are built.

The position is splendid, and from the heights about opened out a glorious panorama of the now snow-strewn mountains of free Bosnia. The heights are singularly bare of vegetation, like the neighbouring rock wilderness of Dalmatia and the Dinaric Alps in general; but for purposes of defence they are admirable. Here and there the precipitous ascent to the camp and the rocky ridges around are flanked with breastworks of stone, but such artificial defences are evidently a work of supererogation.

Nothing, indeed, is wanting to the Bosnian insurgents but a leader. The present commander was appointed originally last August by the Serbian Government (which from the beginning has assumed a peculiar patronage over the Bosnian insurrection), on the plea that the stout old Bosnian Vojvode who then commanded, Golub Babić, could not read or write—not a serious disqualification for guerilla leadership over mountaineers as illiterate as himself. There was nothing in the previous career of Despotović to justify the choice. Originally in the Russian army, he joined the Serbians, but got into hot water with Tchernayeff, and was despatched to Bosnia as the place where he could do the least mischief. He signalized his arrival here by writing a despatch to the Government at Belgrade in which he asserted that he had taken Glamoš, Kliuč, and other strongholds from the Turks—the fact being that since he took the command not a single district has been added to the insurgent possessions. On the contrary, his despotic manner has so thoroughly disgusted this most *égalitaire* of peoples that several bands have already broken away from his authority, and only a couple of days ago a deputation from the insurgent camp arrived in Knin to consult on the best means of getting rid of him.

Affairs have been brought to this pitch by an act of harshness the more unwise that if it was committed in the

*Different
ways of
preserving
discipline
among Bos-
nians.*

name of discipline it had all the appearance of an act of private vengeance.

One of the most popular men here, Vranić, who was regarded with peculiar veneration by the Bosnians as a martyr of the Christian cause, for which he had spent twelve years in a Turkish dungeon at Widin, appears to have shown some dissatisfaction at the small amount of the rations meted out, and to have hinted that the men would like to know what became of all the money sent from Serbia, Russia, and elsewhere. The same man was not long afterwards tempted by hunger to take an ox from a village, telling the villagers that the colonel would pay for it.

Uzélatz during the days of his command had dealt with a similar offence in an original but effective manner. One evening one of his men had made off with a portion not his own. The savoury mess was already simmering over the fire, and the purloiner and his friends were smacking their lips at the prospect of a good supper, when who should walk in upon them but the Vojvode. ' So the goose is *there*, is it, my lads?' he observed grimly, ' well, I'll pepper it for you !' and he discharged his gun into the pot.

Despotović, however, who has the makings of a petty autocrat about him, behaved less leniently, eagerly seized the occasion, and, disregarding the entreaties of his men or the past services of one who had suffered for the cause, shot him in the camp. It needs a thorough acquaintance with the Bosnian character and the peculiar relations of chiefs and followers in the insurgent camp to understand the feelings of horror and indignation which this stern act has roused among the Bosnians. Old Lazar sits for hours at a time brooding over the death of Vranić, who was his friend, and the disaffection against Despotović is general.

Knowing all this, it was with very mixed feelings that I found myself in the presence of this potentate, a man of spruce but bovine presence, who swaggered up clinking his spurs, and welcomed me in a loud voice in French. He took me a small stroll along the mountain edge, and after venting his spleen against Uzélatz, against whom even he admitted that he had no specific charges, launched forth on his own prowess against the Turks.

Pointing to a line of snowy mountains from which Hannibal himself might have recoiled, he observed casually that up there he had beaten 12,000 Turks.

I looked unaffectedly surprised.

'Beat them!' resumed the Colonel, twirling his moustache and clinking his spur against the rock. 'Beat them! Why, I cut them to pieces!'

'Well, now, Colonel,' I observed, maliciously, 'I have always wondered why you did not occupy Kliuč'—the strong Turkish rock-fortress to the west of the insurgent territory, on the capture of which see Despotović's famous despatch. The Colonel muttered something about the Austrians seizing all his powder, and changed the subject. We shortly returned to his quarters, where I was served with tea *à la Russe* and spongecake *glacé* (within an hour or so's distance from those starving denizens of the caves); after which the General—I cannot call him Colonel!—had in some of his rank and file, and bullied them apparently for my special delectation. After supper, served on a Turkish *tepshia* and washed down with a choice variety of Dalmatian wine, the General waxed still more candid in his confidences. 'Voyez-vous,' he remarked, with a magnificent flourish, 'que je

ne suis pas seulement commandant de l'armée bosniaque
—je suis chef du peuple bosniaque.'

'In fact,' I said, 'this is your Montenegro, and you
are its Nikola.'

'Precisely,' said our ex-Russian officer; 'j'y suis le
Prince Régnant.'

*A Maho-
metan
Effendi.*

During the evening I was pleased to make the
acquaintance of a Mahometan Effendi, who had been
captured by the insurgents, and, in return for his freedom,
has consented to remain here as Despotović's secretary
for Turkish correspondence. He was quite a different
stamp of man from the surrounding rayah insurgents.

*Refining
influence
among
Bosnian
Maho-
metans.*

His manners were distinguished from those of the more
rugged warriors around by that peculiar Oriental polish
which in Bosnia marks off the Mahometan Slavs so decisively from their oppressed Christian kinsmen.   Perhaps
it is that among the dominant caste in Bosnia the stately
influence of Asiatic civilization has been engrafted on
some still surviving relics of Western chivalry—inherited
together with much of its barbarism and caste tyranny—
from the days of the feudal kingdom.   In that case this
polish, which has something of the gloss upon the tiger's
skin, is a speciality of the Bosnian Mahometans ; indeed,
I would note that as early as the seventeenth century
the Imperialists and subjects of the Serene Republic,
whose acquaintance with Turkey surpassed that of other
Europeans, had already made the observation that (to
quote the words of an old chronicler) 'the Turks of
Bosnia be far more courteous and polite than the other
Turks : forasmuch as these latter are wont to be of a high
and mighty spirit, neither friendly nor accommodating.'[1]

---

[1] See *Der Neu-eroffneten Otto-
manischen Pforten Fortsetzung,*   Augspurg, 1701, p. 128, sub anno
1671 : 'Die Innwohner (von Bos-

My Effendi was endowed with a peculiar address in his conversation with his captors and employers, and supported rather a difficult position with an easy grace that excited my admiration. I don't think any courtier of Stamboul could have surpassed the deferential grace, the consummate stateliness, of the 'temena' with which he saluted the insurgent commander! It was flattery in gesticulation, an elaborate compliment spun out in dumb show,—and to see the Colonel stroke his whiskers after it! 'C'est un homme d'esprit, tout-à-fait spirituel,' he remarked to me, complacently.

Not less strange was the origin of our interview. I had been trying to find what traditions of the mediæval kingdom of Bosnia might linger on among the natives of this district, the scene of the final overthrow of the Bosnian kingdom. The insurgents knew little. They had historic traditions indeed, but they all belonged, not to ancient Bosnia, but to ancient Serbia. The heroes they recalled were all Serbian, and not Bosnian ; till at last one of them suggested that they should call in the Mahometan Effendi, for the Mahometans know something of Bosnian history; and sure enough the Effendi was ready with strange local legends which the Christians had lost. It is the descendants of the renegade nobility of this country who inherit its history, while the orthodox Greeks, as the insurgents of this district all are, hardly had a share of it in the past. The Roman Catholics, on the other hand, who divided with the heretic forefathers of the present Mahometans the past history of Bosnia, have also their traditions still ; but the Orthodox Church

LETTER
III.

*A stately
' temena.'*

*National
traditions
among Ma-
hometan
Bosniacs.*

nien) den Ruhm haben dass sie viel höflicher und politer seyen als die andere Türcken : dann diese letztere seyn gemeiniglich eines hochmüthigen Geists, unfreundlich und unerträglich.'

LETTER
III.

*Non-pro-
vincial
character of
Pravoslav
Church in
Bosnia.*

seems to have crept into Bosnia from the East since the Turkish conquest. In days of captivity it, as the more communistic confession, has been perpetually gaining ground in the house-communities of the rayah; it has imported with it national heroes, Slav, it is true, but from beyond the old Bosnian area; and to-day even in Bosnia the thoughts of its votaries turn to Dushan and Lazar, and not to their provincial kings.

This silent advance of the Orthodox Serbian Church, borne onwards on a tide of nationality, at the present moment invading Dalmatia, Croatia, and Slavonia simultaneously,[1] is fraught with pregnant consequences, and a few generations hence may make the dreams of South Slavonic union, vain to-day, easier of realization than they were in the days of the greatest Serbian Czar.

[1] Since this was written a most striking landmark of the increased numbers and influence of the Orthodox Church has made its appearance in Dalmatia. On October 21st (1877) the first Pravoslav Church ever permitted within its walls was opened at Ragusa, and the opening ceremony was attended by deputations and clergy from Zara, Cattaro, and the other Dalmatian cities, as well as from Montenegro and towns in the Herzegovina. The Archimandrite Dušić attended from Belgrade. The erection of this church and the demonstration of the opening ceremony derive additional significance from the fact that the Roman Catholic hierarchy had striven tooth and nail to prevent such a 'scandal,' as they called it, in 'Catholic Ragusa.' The good-tempered and even sympathetic attitude of the Ragusan citizens during the day formed a marked contrast to that of their priests.

LETTER IV.

THE CLOUDLANDS OF FREE BOSNIA.

Extent of insurgent territory. Start to explore it. Turkish ravages. Up Mount Duillitza. Illyrian poljes or mountain plateaux. Their value in defensive mountain warfare. Two more insurgent camps. Entertained by Vojvode. Finer type of men in this part. To what due. Monstrosities of barbarism. Old Castle of Aleksia. On the track of the Bashi-bazouks. Massacre of Vidovosélo. Chasm of the Gudaja. Vale of Unnatz. Insurgent 'chéta.' A Homeric evening.

Tišovo, Free Bosnia, *February* 10.

THERE are some five hundred insurgents encamped in the neighbourhood of Despotović's head-quarters : those I saw were fairly clad, some in Montenegrin fashion, well armed, and seemed to want for nothing. The insurgents, however, under Despotović's command are scattered at present over a wide area of country, forming an irregular mountainous triangle between the Austrian frontier and the Turkish fortresses of Kulen Vakup, Kliuč, and Glamoš, the chief bulwark of which to the east is the great mountain mass of Czerna Gora, or the Black Mountain ; so that there literally exists at the present moment a little Bosnian Montenegro.

It was to exploring the whole of this difficult country and to visiting the other principal insurgent camps that I

LETTER
IV.

*I start to
explore
'Free
Bosnia.'*

*Indigna-
tion against
England
among Ma-
hometans
in Bosnia.*

had resolved to devote the following days; and I was lucky in securing the services of the ex-commander Golub Babić, who is still chief Vojvode of the insurgents and their most trusted leader, as my guide and escort. I was also accompanied by Atanasija Smilianić,[1] a young but exceedingly brave warrior, of a famed and noble Dalmatian race, and who spoke German tolerably well.

I was mounted on a sure-footed Bosnian pony, and, with no more deadly weapon than a walking-stick, set forth with my escort armed to the teeth to explore a country as little known to Europeans as the wilds of Asia; the Mahometan Effendi, of whom I took leave, grimly expressing a hope that I would call on some friends of his at Petrovatz, as they had vowed a vow to hang the first Englishman they set eyes on! Obviously we are losing our popularity in Bosnia, and indeed the Effendi explained that among the Bosnian Begs, who have lost a good deal of property during the present troubles, the English are peculiarly hateful, many of them declaring that they would never have fought against the insurgents at all if they had not been sure of English help. This is to be regretted, as the fanatical raids of these Begs on the Christian population of this part have been attended with terrible havoc and ferocious deeds of cruelty.

*Turkish
ravages.*

Not long after leaving the camp of Czerni Potuk I passed by the ruins of the Christian villages of Poduillitza and Dolovi, and further on of Stozišta, burnt and entirely razed to the ground by the Turks. There was a church, of which only the foundations were traceable. We now followed a mountain path, coasting and gradually ascending the great mass of Mount Duillitza, whose lower flanks

---

[1] Killed five months later in leading an assault on a Turkish position near Livno.

were covered with a stunted growth of small beeches.
The path was very difficult, being in places covered with
snowdrift ; but some hours of tedious progress up a pass
brought us to a mountain plateàu divided by a central
ridge into two plains, which, shut in on all sides by the
mountain, looked like the beds of two large lakes.

These 'poljes,' as they are called, are the characteristic
feature of the limestone mountains of Illyria, and are the
oases of this vast desert, for whereas the mountains themselves are strewn with fragments of calcareous rock and
usually extremely barren, the surface of these 'poljes' is
quite flat and covered with soil, at times of great fertility.
Thus it is that here the villages congregate, and the fields
and pasture lands of the peasants are circled like a fortified
town by mountain walls, and are often approachable, as
in this instance, only by difficult mountain portals. When
this fact is appreciated you will understand the great
capabilities of defence possessed by a country whose
mountain strongholds contain fertile fields where corn
may be sown and harvest gathered in.   Against the
Turkish towns the insurgents may show themselves weak,
but with arms and ordinary leaders they could defy the
invader for generations in these mountain fastnesses.

They are themselves beginning to appreciate their
defensive strength and the importance of dividing their
energies between agriculture and defence ; but during
the period when the insurrection on this side was confined
to a few villages on the Dalmatian frontier the Turk had
penetrated into these secluded uplands, and the village
of Resanovce, to the right, from which the neighbouring
'polje' derives its name, had been burnt, as also Petchi,
the village of the 'polje' to the left.

Further on were two villages that had been spared

LETTER
IV.

*Received by
armed
demonstra-
tion.*

by the destroyer. On enquiry I found that they belonged to a Beg of Livno, who had harried this part of the country, but had had the wisdom not to destroy his own property, though his tenants were rayahs. He burned the Christian villages of another landowner instead ! The first of these unburned villages was Ispodisek ; the second was Mala Čevce, which is at present a *chéta*, or camp, of the insurgents; and here, as we approached, we found about two hundred armed men drawn up in a regular line with fixed bayonets, who saluted the chief Vojvode as he rode up. In this village and the other the women and children still remained.

*A lonely
ride.*

We now made our way between Mounts Prokus to the right and Jedovnik to the left, and ascended to a plateau covered with a beech forest, containing some respectable timber, in parts of which the snow lay deep, and then set to crossing another frozen ' polje.'

I have been in many wild places, but I think I never experienced a stranger sensation of being out of the world than while riding for hour after hour through this vast snow-laden forest and across the white icebound mountain plateau,—alone with my two insurgent companions, in a silence only broken by the clatter of our horses' hoofs, as we penetrated deeper and deeper into the unknown, unrecognized, undefined cloudland commonwealth—shall I call it? or principality?—in the Turkey of diplomatists—in the Christendom of patriots.

It was already twilight when we caught sight of our day's destination, the village of Veliki Tišovo, perched on a rocky knoll on the side of the ' polje.' Here is another insurgent camp containing over four hundred armed men who, as we approached, formed in line and received us with another military demonstration.

Here, as elsewhere, the men are hearty and hopeful and are armed with serviceable breechloaders, and the village they occupy lies in such a secure position that it has never been visited by the Turks. Amongst them I noticed a young hero of thirteen with a fine yataghan taken from the Turks. We were received into the hut of Péro Kréča, the local Vojvode, and glad enough I was to seat myself before his blazing pine-logs, for the cold on these uplands is intense. We were feasted with excellent broth and mutton, and a very jovial evening was enlivened with some songs about the Sultan by no means complimentary in their character.

I am much struck at the difference between the men here and the Bosnian rayahs that I remember still under the Turkish yoke. They are incomparably less degraded, whether that so short an enjoyment of freedom has already elevated their character, or that the mountaineers of this part have always been superior in physique to those of the more central districts and of the Possavina, or lands about the Save, where the inhabitants are a smaller race and are contemptuously spoken of by the Bosniacs themselves as 'frogs.' The people about here are Pravoslav in their religion to a man, whereas in the more central and northern districts, with which I had been previously better acquainted, the population was largely Catholic; and it has often been remarked that the Pravoslavs or Orthodox in Bosnia are more manly and moral than the Latins. The Pravoslav pope grasps his congregation by the hand; the Romish priest leads them by the nose. The Orthodox pope is obliged to be a married man, which itself is a good thing, for it is to be observed as an odd coincidence that the only regions in Bosnia in which prostitutes

LETTER
IV.

*Monstro-
sities of
barbarism.*

are to be found are those where Romish priests are
plentiful.

Here I heard an instance of those revolting practices
which, with many other evil relics of mediæval feudalism
or importations of Asiatic barbarism, still survive among
the Slavonic Begs of Bosnia.   Mili Kotor, a peasant of
Grahovo, near here, was captured by one of the Mahometan landlords and his Bashi-bazouk retainers, and forced
to swallow large quantities of salt and water.   In a mill
at Stermnitza may be seen any day by those who are
curious as to these monstrosities of barbarism a man who
was tied face foremost to a tree and worried by dogs
while the Beg sat by and smoked his chibouk.

Unnatz, in Free Bosnia, *February* 11.

We left Tišovo about 6.30 this morning, and following another mountain pass, leaving on our left the great
forest of Chator, a two hours' ride brought us to another
'polje' and the village of Préodatz.   The Turks had never
penetrated here, and one half of the village was still
occupied by its inhabitants ; the other half, however, had
left, having no corn to sow, and are now among the refugees at Stermnitza.   So the cottages are empty and half
ruined, for the fugitives have carried with them part of
the wooden roofs for firewood.   There are turbine mills
over the little stream, but the millers have gone.   In this
village was an ancient graveyard, and an old cross overthrown and half buried in the earth.   The people
said that when the Turks first conquered Bosnia a
marriage was going on here ; that the Turks rushed in,
killed the wedding guests and bridegroom, and carried off
the bride, and that this cross was set up in memory of the
tragedy.   I had the cross raised, and discovered on its

*Deserted
half of
Préodatz.*

under side a very ancient Bosnian inscription; but
though I have not yet succeeded in deciphering the runes,
they are hardly likely to throw much light upon the
legend. Beyond this was another monument of ancient
Bosnia, the foundations of a church long destroyed ; and
on a peak above, perched as if by magic on almost inaccessible rocks, overlooking on one side a stream at the
bottom of a stupendous chasm, stand the fine ruins of a
castle dating from the feudal days of the Christian kingdom.   Its massive tower looked down at present on
wasted fields and deserted homesteads, and brought home
to one in a singular way what the wretched serfs of
Bosnia have suffered both in the present and the past.
Aided by some ancient footsteps cut into the rock-wall, and
worn away in mediæval times by long-forgotten warders,
I climbed up and explored the interior, but snow and ice
made the rock so difficult to descend that I should probably be a prisoner in the Castle of Aleksia at this
moment, had it not been for one of the insurgents, who
scaled the precipice and showed me a more practicable
descent.

But I must pass on to monuments of more modern
tyranny.   Descending on another 'polje,' we stopped at a
wretched hut at a village called Podić.   Villages here
are often scattered, as in this instance, over a large area
of country, so that in a map it is often impossible to
localize a name with any precision.   In this instance, the
district of Podić runs apparently in an undefined manner
into that of Vidovosélo, to the north-west of this 'polje,'
and the whole of this district has been ravaged by the
Turks in a most atrocious manner.

As I have no wish to indulge in loose and unsubstan-
tiated charges, I may say that I have taken down the

LETTER
IV.

*Witnesses
of outrages
examined
by me.*

accounts of three sets of witnesses. First, of the peasants, a man and woman, at the hut at Podić; secondly, of two peasants of Vidovosélo, by name Stoian Vasovic and Gavran Tadić, whom I saw at Unnatz, and who actually witnessed what occurred from a wood above the village where they had hidden themselves; and lastly, from Boian Sterbatz, who was horribly cut in the neck by a blow from a yataghan and his left hand nearly severed, and who lies at present in the insurgent hospital at Knin, where I saw him, and whose deposition and extraordinary signature I have before me.

All these accounts agree in the minutest particular, and I do not think that even the Turks themselves would call them in question.

*The mas-
sacre of
Vidovosélo.*

On the 12th of July last year, about two in the afternoon, the peasants of this district were peacefully engaged in their fields, when a large band of Bashi-bazouks from Glamoš, under the leadership of Ahmed Beg Pilipović of that place, broke into the 'polje.' They hunted down and killed—some on the plain and some in the houses—twenty-three unarmed peasants, nine of the village of Podić and fourteen of Vidovosélo. I have the names and families of all the victims before me. Among them were two children, one of five years old and the other about ten. The village pope, Damian Sterbatz, was hacked to pieces; his wife, Stana Sterbatz, was cut with yataghans about the breast; and his daughter, Militza, was wounded in the arm. The villages were first plundered and then burnt, and the Turks made off to Glamoš, carrying with them the heads of most of their victims.

The hut we were in was saved from burning by the timely appearance of an insurgent band on the height above. A party of Bashi-bazouks were engaged in plundering the cottage when they caught sight of the enemy, and as unarmed peasants and women were their game, and not armed men, they decamped in a hurry.

After paying a visit to the graves of the victims, we crossed the 'polje' and made our way towards the valley of the Unnatz, the most important stream in the insurgent territory, by a pass which showed the wonderful capabilities of defence possessed by this country. It was a narrow cleft between the mountains of Tešainovatza and Poinatz, through which the Gudaja torrent poured its waters towards the Unnatz. The channel of the torrent formed the only path, and above on either side two sheer walls of rock, in places not three yards distant from each other, towered several hundred feet. Such a pass as this could be defended against hundreds by ten resolute men.

Emerging on the valley of the Unnatz, I found a more fertile and friendly country than any I have yet seen in the liberated district of Bosnia. The beech trees were finer and the soil richer, and the village of Lower Unnatz itself, to which we now made our way, was as flourishing as any in this part of Bosnia before it was burnt and harried by the Turks. As it is, the devastation is cruel; the fields lie waste, and only a few huts, where the 'chéta,' or insurgent camp, is pitched, are still unburnt and surrounded by a little cultivation. On our way we made a slight *détour* to visit the remains of an ancient church that once rose on the other side of the valley, and the architectural fragments which I there discovered showed that in days before the Turkish conquest something of a higher civilization had penetrated into this remote valley.

About eleven hours from our morning's start we arrived at the 'chéta' of Unnatz, where we were received, as elsewhere, with military honours by a troop of about one hundred and fifty insurgents.

We were now welcomed into the hut of the local Vojvode, Simo Kralj, and here I passed an evening which carried one back to Homeric times. The evening meal was served, as elsewhere, on a round board, on which was first set a great bowl of boiled Indian corn, from which the assembled chieftains and their guest helped themselves by means of curiously ornamented wooden spoons. This was succeeded by lumps of mutton, which we picked off the board with our fingers, one at a time, and at intervals the host handed to each in turn a silver drinking cup of curiously antique shape filled to brimming with thick Dalmatian wine. The women and children, and those of less consequence, ate afterwards, and during the meal two women held torches of resinous pinewood above our heads. Then the 'ghuzla,' the national lyre, was brought out, and a venerable minstrel played and sang the songs of free Bosnia, for amongst this highly poetic people the insurrection has already its unwritten epics.

Then I stretched myself with the others on the hay that had been strewn, as an unusual luxury, for our common couch, and, with my feet towards the embers, prepared to pass from cloudland into dreamland ; and last of all the chieftain, with patriarchal ceremony, spread a sheepskin over me against the small hours of the night.

LETTER V.

FEUDAL CASTLES AND INSURGENT HUTS.

Ermanja, Free Bosnia, *February* 12.

NEXT morning I was guided up a mountain above Unnatz to see an old castle, called Vissovića Grad, of extraordinary interest, as, according to the local tradition, the refuge of Helena, one of the last Queens of Christian Bosnia; others, however, told that a certain Black Queen, of more mysterious origin, lived here. The ruins[1] were even more magnificent than those of the Castle of Aleksia, and so difficult of access that the insurgents brought up a ladder to aid us in climbing the rocks. Even with this aid, the approach to the castle is a

---

[1] The castle and the other ancient remains that I saw in this district were absolutely unknown even to Slavonic antiquaries.

D 2

LETTER
V.

*Old Castle
of
Vissovića.*
matter of considerable difficulty, for it rises on an isolated peak of rock, separated from the main body of the mountain by a chasm, and on the other side towering sheer above the Vissovića torrent which, hundreds of feet below, leaps in a score of little waterfalls, foaming and roaring through the dark gorge towards the Unnatz. The most perfect part of the castle was the octagonal tower which crowned the whole stronghold, and outside which, near the very summit, I discovered another old Bosnian inscription. Below the tower was what apparently had been a great banqueting hall, with a curious moulding round one of the windows, and the remains of a great stone chimney, a relic of civilization quite unexpected. Under the tower I observed a small hole going down into the rock, half choked with earth, but with the aid of my insurgent guides I cleared away sufficient to afford a passage for my body, and regardless of the entreaties of the Bosniacs, who thought the enterprise uncanny, I disappeared below and found myself in an ancient dungeon, hewn apparently out of the solid rock. I wondered what grim scenes had been enacted there in the Black Queen's days!

But I cannot stop to describe old castles at present. My guides now directed me across a bare mountain plateau to an object of more living interest—a wretched *A colony of
starving
fugitives.* settlement of rayah fugitives who had fled from near Stari Maidan, in Turkish Bosnia, the scene of terrible atrocities. At this spot there were about thirty in all, but, from the lamentable state in which they were, many must have died before this letter reaches you. Seven or eight of them were children—such little old faces, pinched, and wrinkled and distorted with famine and disease, some scarcely able to stand. They had been living through the winter on what they could beg of the villagers of

neighbouring 'poljes' almost as destitute as themselves. I distributed some paper florins among them, which they received with stupid wonder; what did they know of Austrian paper money?—they wanted bread ! There are hundreds of such groups, from what I can hear, among these mountains, to whom no one can hope to penetrate with aid.

LETTER V.

Starving fugitives in the mountains.

We now descended once more to the valley of the Unnatz, in which I discovered what I take to be the remains of a large Roman building, a great mound from which protruded large, finely-squared blocks, some of which had been used in mediæval times as tombstones, but on one of which I discovered to my delight a bas-relief of Mercury standing, caduceus in hand, in a singularly graceful attitude, which evidently dated from the best period of Roman art.   Beyond were the ruins of a house belonging to Ali Beg Kulenović.   We had seen another such at Unnatz, burnt as reprisals after the harrying of this valley by the Beg and his hordes.

Bas-relief of Mercury and remains of Roman buildings.

Most of the unarmed inhabitants of Unnatz itself succeeded in escaping before the Turks came, but five were murdered.   I was told by a man here who had seen the bodies—and his evidence has since been corroborated by that of others—that among the slain were two old women ; one, Jeka Pećianska, said to have been aged eighty-five, and the other Simeona Mihailović, of whose age I could get nothing more definite than that ' she was old, very old, about one hundred.'   This great age is not, however, intrinsically improbable, as there are instances of extraordinary longevity to be found among the Bosnian refugees.   One about whom Miss Irby made inquiries is reported to be 107.   No children were killed here.

Two old women murdered by Bashi-bazouks.

LETTER
V.

*Strange
bedfellows.*

We followed a side stream up a romantic gorge to a hovel called Panšavoda, where we passed the night. The former homestead had been burnt by the Turks, and its blackened site lay on the other side of the rivulet. The inmates, however, had escaped to the forest above, and seemed to have carried off most of their property, as they were now very well off, having about fifty sheep and some half-dozen cows, which latter passed the night with us. One meets with strange bedfellows in these regions! The peasant family here as well as the insurgents were very curious to know why I took such pains to explore the ancient ruins. Of course they were firmly convinced that I had come to hunt for treasure. 'Ay,' said one old fellow, 'folks say there is gold enough under Vissovića tower, if you only dig deep enough.'

*The gold-
hoards and
dragons of
Free
Bosnia.*

'Ah!' I replied, laughing, 'I've been down already under Vissovića tower—but if you want to do the same I advise you to look out for the dragon!'

'There are always dragons where there are gold hoards,' was the sage reply, 'or else the treasure would have been dug up long ago, you may be sure.'

I had recourse to Æsop and told them the fable of the man who bade his sons dig in their vineyard for gold, which greatly pleased the Bosniacs.

Next morning at daybreak we started once more on our way, and ascended a mountain plateau, where was a small 'polje,' and many more burnt houses, the fences round the fields still standing, except where they had been hacked and trampled down by the authors of this havoc.

*Ermanja
Minster.*

A few more hours through a beech forest, where snowdrops grew, and down a steep incline, brought us to Ermanja, which derives its name from Hermann of Cilli, whose massive round tower still stands amidst the black-ened ruins of what till a year ago was a flourishing Christian village. There was also a famed Pravoslav monastery, now destroyed, and a church, to which I made my way. It had been restored a few years ago and newly whitewashed, for its frescoes have long dis-appeared; but it is at present little short of a ruin. The Turks, who paid it a visit in September 1875, have cer-tainly done their worst. They have torn up the floor, smashed and overthrown the sacred furniture, broken in the roof and parts of the wall, and riddled the whole inside with bullet holes. It was on September 15, 1875, that Tahir Beg Kulenović came here with a horde of 3,500 Bashi-bazouks and burnt this and the neighbouring villages of Great and Little Svietnić, cutting down three old men, six women, and four children who had not es-caped in time. The rest of the inhabitants took refuge on the mountain plateau of Osjenitza, which we had passed above Unnatz On May 14, however, of last year they were hunted out even there by a gang of Bashi-bazouks from the direction of Kulen Vakup, Bielaj, and Petrovatz, and twenty-four more were massacred, in this case, as in the other, all of them old men, women, and children.

At the 'chéta' here I noticed certain Croatian ele-ments among the men, showing that we are now on a more northern part of the frontier. Croatia is, in fact, only separated here from Bosnia by the Unna, which at this point, after a beautiful fall, joins the Unnatz. The insurgents here, as elsewhere, seemed in good spirits and to want for nothing; and indeed, after visiting five in-surgent camps, I am inclined to take a far more favour-able view of the prospects of the insurrection than is

LETTER
V.

A dese-crated church.

Massacre of Osjenitza.

usual outside Bosnia. Among the Slavs of the border countries there is at present a certain amount of dejection, owing chiefly to the corrupt transactions of many of their own committees and *soi-disant* patriots ; and in Croatia especially subscriptions have latterly fallen off. But once on the free soil of liberated Bosnia one breathes a purer air, and I do not doubt that the men I have met would shed the last drop of their blood rather than lay down their arms. No one here dreams of peace. The number of insurgents under arms, even during the armistice, amounts to nearly 2,000, and when the armistice expires this can be raised to between 4,500 and 5,000 men—a force amply sufficient to defend these alpine strongholds against any odds.[1] Every man amongst them is a born cragsman, and their leaders know every stock and stone of these almost unexplored mountains.

Serb, Bosnian-Croatian Frontier, *February* 13.

At Ermanja I was present at a little 'Skupština,' or assembly for debate, of some insurgent Vojvodes. The

---

[1] The camps then under Despotović's command were at Czerni Potuk, under Despotović's immediate supervision; at Peulje, under the monk Ilija Bilbija ; at Marinkovce, under Peter Krečo ; at Upper Unnatz, under Simo Kralj ; at Ermanja, under Trifan Stoikovič; at Osredke, under Paul Babić ; and at Mala Čevce, Veliki Tišovo, and lesser detachments at about twenty other spots. In these accounts the insurgents of Northern Bosnia, in Mounts Germetz and Kosaratz, the detachment in Mount Prolog, under the Roman Catholic, Fra Buonaventura ; those under Mussić on the Herzegovinian frontier near Ragusa, and the Herzegovinian insurgent bands along the whole northern and eastern borders of Montenegro are not reckoned in, as owning no allegiance to Despotović. The same general distribution of the insurrection continues now (February 1878) unaltered, except that the Upper Herzegovinian clans are more thoroughly merged in Montenegro.

speakers were assembled in a ring inside an insurgent hut. I was much struck at the real parliamentary capabilities of these simple armed peasants in discussing their affairs. Each speaker in turn said what he had to say in a straightforward, business-like manner, without any oratorical vagaries, and yet with a ready flow of speech which never hesitated. I cannot believe that a party of English farm labourers could have discussed their affairs with equal readiness. These people, it is true, cannot read or write, but they have in their rude way a kind of civilization, and even education, of their own. In this part of Bosnia what is known as the 'Zadruga' system prevails—that is, the people live in large family communities, holding all things in common, and choosing a 'house-father' and a 'house-mother,' generally the elders of the family, to direct these. Thus what is really a group of families becomes one household, whose members discuss their affairs in common in the common hall where they meet for meals, and it is natural that, practising every day the forms of parliamentary government in miniature, the faculty of debate should be more developed in the rayah of Southern Bosnia than in an English Hodge. The people about here are, in fact, educated in many practical ways by the hardest of all task-mistresses—necessity. Every man here is capable of building his own house, though it is true he does not aspire to a high style of architecture; and every woman can make her own clothes. At the wretched hovel of Panšavoda I was much struck with the neatness of a set of earthenware pots which the family had just been making for themselves.

Nor is the more æsthetic side of education altogether wanting. The music is rude, but everybody is a musi-

Marginal notes: LETTER V. / *Faculty of debate among Bosniac rayahs.* / *The Zadruga or family community.* / *Domestic education among rayahs.*

*Domestic
culture
among
Bosniac
rayahs.*

cian. Literature is altogether wanting, but the poetic
lore of the Bosniacs and other Southern Slavs surpasses,
perhaps, in extent that of any other European people.
Historians these simple Bosniacs have not, but the past
lives in their heroic lays, and has not history some need to
be idealized among the children and great-grandchildren
of bondsmen ? In much of their dress these people display
great taste ; and, speaking generally of South Slavonic
peasants, I should say that the beauty of their costume
and the brilliance of its colouring are not anywhere surpassed. But what strikes the stranger perhaps most is the
extraordinary elegance of the devices with which the peasants here adorn their tombstones.   Compared with the
neighbouring population of Dalmatia I have even noticed

*Traits of
cleanliness.*

traits of cleanliness, traceable no doubt to a good influence of Islâm among the warriors and peasants of free
Bosnia. Thus they washed their hands by pouring water
on them, Turkish fashion, from a tin vessel before and
after meals ; and, though the floor was only of earth,
they swept away the crumbs and fragments after every
repast with a fir branch that serves as a broom in these
establishments.

*The upper
valley of
the Unna.*

The path from Ermanja to Serb, where I left the
territory of Free Bosnia, lies along the upper valley of the
Unna, the right bank of which belongs to the insurgents,
the left being the Austro-Hungarian frontier. This tract,
through which I rode about four hours, was the most
fertile I had yet seen. It was entered by a narrow and
difficult gorge, through which the blue waters of the Unna
burst their way in a series of beautiful cascades, and
where, on the rocks above, keeping watch and ward for
stray cattle, we saw a fine wolf, at whom my escort fired
ineffectually. Thus this oasis of fertility, being bordered

by Christendom on the only accessible side, offers every
possible facility for defence, and should never be allowed
to come once more into the hands of the Turk.   Many
refugees now across the border might, no doubt, be
induced to return here if only supplied with seed corn ;
and the soil is so good that, judging from what is possible
in some of the neighbouring Dalmatian valleys, I should
say that on the southern slopes vines and olives might be
profitably cultivated.   At present it is the usual scene of
devastation, contrasting forcibly with the opposite (Austrian) bank of the river.

At a small Bosnian hovel opposite the Croatian village
of Serb I took leave of my escort, the Chief Vojvode
Golub and Smilianić, and found myself once more on
Austrian soil.   Here, from Uzélatz and others, I have
learned the particulars of a plot concocted by Despotović
against his life.   It seems that the colonel, having learned
from me that the ex-insurgent commander was on his
way to the valley of the Unna, sent five of his most trusted
henchmen to seize Uzélatz in the Bosnian hamlet of Serb
and shoot him.   I saw the gang set out on their errand
on horseback, but had no idea of their mission ; and I
have since discovered that he offered old Lazar, in whose
company I had arrived at the camp of Czerni Potuk, a
large bribe if he would betray the confidence he enjoyed
with Uzélatz to decoy him to his doom.   The gallant old
Bosniac refused the offer with indignation, but the other
myrmidons set forth on their errand, and found Uzélatz
at Serb, surrounded by a party of insurgents and peasants,
amongst all of whom Uzélatz is extremely popular.   The
emissaries of Despotović came up and told Uzélatz
that they were very sorry, but they had their orders, and
he was to accompany them.   Uzélatz, who had no

weapon with him, simply raised his stick, and about forty of the insurgents then at Serb stepped forward and surrounded the emissaries of their own colonel! The captors were taken captive, but were set free and allowed to return to head-quarters, there to report on the result of their mission.

LETTER VI.

THE DEVASTATION OF BOSNIA, AND MR. CONSUL HOLMES' REPORTS.

Sinj, on the Bosnian-Dalmatian Frontier, *February* 20.

T Ermanja, as I have already mentioned, as also at Unnatz, there was a kind of debate among the insurgent chieftains on the present crisis and the attitude of Serbia and the Great Powers, especially England. It is a great misfortune at the present crisis that the English representative in Bosnia should be the object of almost fanatical abhorrence among the rayah population of the province. The peculiar position of Serajevo, the general alienation even of the Christian *bourgeoisie* of that city from the lot of the oppressed peasantry of the country districts, and the inherent necessity of the consul of a friendly power maintaining friendly and even intimate relations with the powers that be, combine to render it extremely difficult for Mr. Holmes to maintain an *entente cordiale* with the rayah and malcontent

LETTER
VI.

*Difficulties
in the way
of an
English
Consul in
Bosnia.*

elements of the country. An English consul cannot
resort to those underhand sources of information which
lie at the disposal of less scrupulous governments. The
sources of information which our representative in Serajevo
has at his disposal are either those of the official Osmanli
or those of that peculiar class of Christians (with whom
all visitors to the Levant are well acquainted), who,
having grown rich under the protection, and often in the
service, of the ruling caste, are usually, for reasons of their

*Consul
Holmes'
statements
necessarily
'ex parte.'*

own, more Turcophile than the Turks themselves. It is
certainly too much to expect that Mr. Holmes should
have been informed by the Turks themselves and their
friends of the horrors which have desolated the greater
part of Bosnia. So long as we are content to see English
interests represented in a barbarous country weighed
down by a corrupt and despotic government, so long
must this unfortunate state of things continue. The real
mistake lies not so much in the conduct of English consuls,
which is imposed on them to a great extent by their
position, but with our Foreign Office and an uncritical
portion of the English public when it accepts as gospel
truth reports prepared under auspices so unfavourable.
To have overcome the difficulties in his path, our consul in
Bosnia must have possessed tact, vigour, and the critical
faculty in no ordinary degree. He must have been able
to converse with the natives of his province in their own
language. He must have been continually in the saddle
in a province where travelling of every kind is a severe
physical strain. If Mr. Holmes possessed none of these
qualifications, some of the obloquy with which he has

*Foreign
Office 'tra-
ditions.'*

been covered must be shared by the Foreign Office, which
appointed him to duties beyond his power of fulfilling.

So much in fairness must be said ; but, at the same

time, I must enter the strongest possible protest against the consular reports received by our Government from the capital of Bosnia ; and when, as has already often happened, Bosnian rayahs have inveighed against their partiality, I must confess that my tongue was tied.[1] Here, at Ermanja, and elsewhere the insurgent speakers accused our consul of going to Constantinople to deny the fact that the devastation in this province is anything like what the Christian fugitives make out. Now I do not know what Mr. Holmes may have said or done at Constantinople, but considering the Turkish and philo-Turkish sources of his information, considering that the towns at which he has resided have been protected by the presence of regulars from the unutterable outrages which have desolated the country districts, considering that the highroads by which he may have left the country have been also held by the Nizams, and that in these exceptional localities the burnt villages are happily few, it is *à priori* extremely probable that he carried optimist views of the situation of the province with him to Stamboul. The insurgents here accused our consul of lending all the weight of his authority to discredit a report on the devastation of Bosnia which Uzélatz had drawn up and presented to the Conference.   Having a copy of this report before me, I have done all in my power to test it in the part of Bosnia that I have visited, and I am bound to say that, so far as my experience goes, I have found it fully borne out by testimony collected on the spot, and the evidence of my eyes.

The number of villages burnt or partly burnt in the part of Bosnia that lies along the Dalmatian border and

---

[1] See note at the end of Letter IX.

LETTER
VI.

*Uzélatz's
report on
devastation
verified by
my observa-
tions.*

extends inland towards Banjaluka, and is generally
known as South Bosnia, amounts, according to my
friend's report, to 145. In the district that I have visited
I have verified fifteen of these, and have besides seen two
burnt hamlets, Poduillitza and Dolovi, which had not
been reckoned. On the other hand, Préodatz I had set
down as among the unburnt villages, and the houses that
I saw there, though partially deserted, were certainly
unburnt, but villages here are scattered over so many
miles of country that it is quite possible that a part of it
was burnt, and in that case the discrepancy is explained.
The statistics for this part of Bosnia were prepared by
Uzélatz himself almost entirely from his own personal
observation, and you may rely upon their honesty. The
villages of this part contain, as a rule, between 20 and
100 houses, and their population varies between 150
and 1,000 souls, though it is generally nearer the lower

*The wast-
ing of
Southern
Bosnia by
the Turks.*

figure. Assuming an average population in each village
of only 200 souls, the number of rayahs burnt out in
Southern Bosnia would amount to 29,000, a number
which falls short by about 1,000 souls of that of the
refugees along this part of the frontier. The number of
churches burnt in this part of Bosnia alone amounts
to 81.

*The wast-
ing of the
Save
Valley.*

Now, these figures relate to the poorest and most
rocky district of the province, and the proportion of
desolation and destruction in the more populous tracts,
such as the rich plains of the Save Valley, far exceeds
that of Southern Bosnia. The accounts I have received
from English sources of the havoc wrought by the Turks
in the Herzegovina and on the Serbian border fully bear
out the terrible statistics that I have before me.

According to the doleful domesday book of Christian

Bosnia, no less than 2,600 villages and scattered hamlets have been wholly or partially burnt by the Turks in Bosnia and the Herzegovina since the outbreak of the present revolt. The number of old men, women, and children butchered in cold blood amounts to over 6,000. The number who have died in the interior of the country from hunger and exposure will probably never be known; the number of refugees on Christian soil I have already stated to be at least a quarter of a million.

E

LETTER VII.

HOW THE NEW CONSTITUTION WAS PROMULGATED IN BOSNIA.

LETTER
VII.

*Still subsisting ties between Mahometan and Christian Bosniacs. Ease
with which re-conversion takes place. Instance of Udbina. Sworn
brotherhood between Christians and Mahometans. Promulgation of
Constitution at Kulen Vakup. Style of new Constitutional Sovereign
of Bosnia. 'Most comfortable words.' The seven subject kings of
Europe. Equality before the law at Gradiška. Forcible conversion
to Islâm. How a Christian memorial was got up by a Turkish Effendi. Different aspect of affairs in larger Herzegovinian towns.
Constitution not disagreeable to Osmanlì bureaucracy. A new form
of electoral intimidation. Mahometan refugees at Ragusa.*

Ragusa : *February* 26.

 AM able to send you some details as to the
promulgation of the new Turkish Constitution
in Southern Bosnia. The source of my information oddly illustrates the peculiar position of the
Mahometans in Bosnia and the relations which, in spite
of differences of creed, still subsist between the dominant
caste and their Christian kinsmen. In Bosnia, as my
readers are no doubt aware, there are, strictly speaking,
hardly any Turks. The Turkish language is only spoken
by a small body of Osmanlì officials and soldiery, the
native Mahometans being as full-blooded Slavs as the
rayahs they oppress, and speaking the same Serbian dialect.

The native Mahometans belonged originally for the most part to a persecuted Puritan sect who, on the Turkish invasion, welcomed the then more tolerant Turks, and afterwards renegaded in a body. Yet they have never forgotten that their forefathers were once Christians, and, fanatics as they are, they seem to become easy converts to Christianity when once they see that destiny is against them.

LETTER VII.

Survival of Christian traditions among Mahometan Bosniacs.

' Kismet,' for instance, has been decidedly against the Mahometan population of the old Bosnian district of Udbina, which has now been long under Austrian dominion, and forms part of Croatia. And what has taken place?

The inhabitants, who were formerly all Mahometans, are now Christians to a man, and only betray their Moslem antecedents in such family names as Osmanić, Abdulić, and others. *En passant*, I may observe that the instance of Udbina is extremely suggestive of a possible reconversion of Mahometan Bosnia should it fall once more into Christian hands ; but, what more concerns my immediate purpose, I should never have been able to give you some rather curious details as to the manner in which the new Turkish Constitution is interpreted among the Bosnian Mahometans, were it not for the peculiar history and relations of the border villagers under notice

Instance of Udbina proves possibility of reconversion.

The inhabitants of Udbina, though they have changed their creed, have never ceased to keep up the closest intercourse with their Mahometan friends and relatives across the Bosnian frontier, and in many cases are bound to them by that most sacred and binding of all Slavonic ties—the ' Pobratimstvo,' or ' Sworn Brotherhood.' Thus a friend of mine who is a native of Udbina is ' sworn-brother' to a Mahometan merchant of the neighbouring

Bosnian town of Kulen Vakup, and these friendly relations have not been interrupted even by the present civil
war.   During a recent visit to my friend's house the
Bosnian merchant gave the following naïve and unvarnished account of the promulgation of the Turkish Magna
Charta at Kulen Vakup, and the official explanation of
the Conference and its results.

*Reading of
new Constitution.*

The reading of the Constitution took place opposite
the Konak, in the presence of the inhabitants; but, lest
they should understand a word of it, it was read by a
Turkish Effendi in Osmanlì, which is as intelligible to the
native Bosnian Mahometan as so much Chinese.

The preamble and Sultan's title were, however, read
in the native language, and the grand old Bosnian imperial style was retained, of which I give you a literal
translation.

*Titles of
new Constitutional
Sovereign.*

The new constitutional sovereign of Bosnia, though
he does not vouchsafe to his subjects any information as
to their new liberties, is careful to remind them in their
own tongue that he is ' Brother of the Sun, Uncle of the
Moon, Sworn-brother ('pobratim') of all the Stars, the
Friend of Allah, the Kinsman of Mahomet, the Son of
Osman, Emperor of Emperors, King of Kings, Prince of
Princes, and Lord of the Earth unto the Sky.' [1]

During the reading of the Osmanlì document some of
the bystanders were inconsiderate enough to ask for an
explanation of some of his longer paragraphs, but the
Effendi only condescended to details so far as to inform
them that ' these were most comfortable words, that the

---

[1] In the original Bosnian:
'*Brat sunca stric mjeseca, pobratim
sviju zviezda, priatelj Alaha, rod-
jak svetca Muhameda, sin Osma-* *nov, Car Careva, Kralj Kraljeva,
Knjaz Knjazeva, i Gospodar od
Zémlje do neba.*'

Sultan had given them new roads and new bridges and new schools,—and that these were, indeed, most comfortable words.' The Mahometan inhabitants of Kulen Vakup heard nothing that could raise the susceptibilities of the most orthodox believer, and interrupted the vague and soothing responses, which their inquiries from time to time elicited, with shouts of ' Peki effendum ! ' (Hear, hear, Effendi).

When the Constitution had been read, however, a great native landowner of this part and commander of the native irregulars, the Beg Tahir Kulenović, who at the head of his Bashi-bazouk retainers has been guilty of some of the worst atrocities committed against the rayahs of this neighbourhood, and who, in the complete collapse of the Turkish bureaucracy in Southern Bosnia, is at present almost as much an independent feudal chieftain as was his remote ancestor the mediæval Bosnian Ban Culin, volunteered some more pointed commentaries on the new Constitution and the Conference, which to any one who does not know the extraordinary ignorance as to the outside world displayed by the Bosnian Mahometans would seem hardly credible.

The Beg informed the assembled people that the ' Emperor of Emperors, King of Kings, Prince of Princes, and Lord of all the Earth unto the Sky' had called together the seven subject kings of Europe—(who was the seventh ?)—to Stamboul, there to signify to them his sovereign will and pleasure as to the disturbers of the peace in his dominions, and more especially those rayah dogs who had fled from their lawful lords and masters ; that he had bidden the Swabian Czar (the Emperor of Austria) to slay all those rayah dogs who refused to return ; that the Swabian Czar had promised to do his

LETTER VII.

' *Most comfortable words.'*

Some pointed commentaries on the new Constitution.

The seven subject kings of Europe.

bidding; and that, furthermore, condign justice should be executed on those who did return for having presumed to leave their lawful lords and masters.

Grotesque as this account of the Conference and its results will seem to my readers, it agrees exactly with the accounts given by the Begs in other towns of Southern Bosnia; as, for instance, by the powerful Beg Filipović at Glamoš, and the agreement can hardly be purely accidental. Many of the Begs openly assert that a general massacre of the Christians still remaining in the country forms one of the provisions of the new charta, and that ' that is the only way of rooting out rebellion from among us.' It is an ominous coincidence that a recrudescence of Mahometan outrage should have followed immediately on the so-called promulgation of the new Constitution in Bosnia; and the proclamation of equality of both Christian and Mussulman before the law finds a curious commentary in the fact that the ears of several of the rayahs lately massacred near Banjaluka have been publicly exhibited in the Law Court of Turkish Gradiška. Another direct result of the Constitution and Conference seems to be the mania which is setting in among the Turks of Southern and Western Bosnia for forcibly converting rayahs to Islâm. At Gradiška alone several instances of this have just occurred. I may mention the names of Ilija Visteka, a servant of Sali Effendi, and his wife. The new name imposed on him is Ali; of Djuro Ketzman, forcibly Moslemized to Méchmet; and Jovo Popović, now Selim.

Recrudescence of outrage follows promulgation of Constitution in Bosnia.

You are aware that a few months ago a sham petition was got up in Bosnia for transmission to Stamboul to protest in the name of the Christian population of Bosnia that no government could be more beneficial than the

Sultan's and no subjects more contented than the Bosnian rayahs when not goaded to revolt by foreign agitators.

On that occasion about a hundred Christians of Banjaluka refused to set their signature to a lie. Thereupon a certain Féim Effendi, one of the most powerful and ferocious of the Bosnian landowners, a man who has done on a smaller scale in Northern Bosnia what Ahmed and Chefket did in Bulgaria, seized on the recalcitrant memorialists, locked them up, and subjected them to every form of insult and intimidation till they consented to set their signatures to the precious document which was to gladden the eyes of Sir Henry Elliot. And this Féim Effendi—whose very name is a word of terror to the hapless Bosnian fugitives—has just been 'elected' to represent Banjaluka in the Constitutional Assembly of regenerated Turkey.

In the Herzegovina, on whose frontier I continue this letter, affairs wear a different aspect. The Osmanli troops are massed at Stolatz and Mostar, in view of future Montenegrin operations, and so it happens that at these larger towns and at Trebinje the authority of the Central Government, which in Southern Bosnia is in absolute abeyance, still prolongs itself in a fashion under the protection of its regular troops.

The Osmanli acts in a very different manner from the native Mahometan of Bosnia. Your true Turk would never dream of imitating the indiscreet and inflammatory utterances of the Bosnian Begs. It is a mistake to suppose that the new Constitution is altogether disagreeable to the Osmanli bureaucracy. Detested alike by the Bosnian Mahometans and the Bosnian Christians, these alien officials hope to prolong their rule in the province,

Féim Effendi and the recalcitrant memorialists.

Different aspect of affairs in larger Herzegovinian towns.

LETTER
VII.

*The
Osmanli
bureau-
cracy and
the new
Constitu-
tion.*
as they have done hitherto, by adroitly manipulating the divisions of the natives. *Divide et impera* is the motto of the Turkish bureaucrat in Bosnia, who knows that if Greek, Latin, and Mahometan were to patch up their differences he would be hounded out of the country to-morrow. And the Stamboul officials are shrewd enough to perceive that a sham constitutionalism, which perpetuates in the law courts and imposes, as a *sine qua non* of office, the use of a language 'not understood of the people,' may be manipulated to the advantage of officials whose mother tongue is Turkish. And so it happens that the Osmanli bureaucracy is jubilant over the new Constitution, and that, under the protection of the bayonets of the Nizam at Mostar and elsewhere, this precious document has been promulgated even in the native language. At Mostar, where consular supervision has also to be taken into account, these enlightened *employés* of the Turkish Government have seized on and forcibly elected a Christian merchant as deputy for the capital of Herzegovina. The unfortunate Bilić, who was anything but ambitious of this unexpected honour, was so far intimidated that he dared not refuse it at Mostar, and was accordingly packed off to Stamboul by way of Ragusa. The instant, however, he set foot on Christian soil he despatched a letter to Mostar resigning his seat, and, fearing to return, is at present a refugee at Ragusa.[1] Truly, it remained for the Turks to discover this new form of electoral intimidation !

Meanwhile the Mahometan population of Herzegovina are becoming more and more dissatisfied with the first fruits of the new *régime*. Among the merchants of the towns

---

[1] He was, however, afterwards induced to continue his journey to Constantinople.

ruin has been sown broadcast by an enormous influx of paper money ; the little town of Trebinje alone has been flooded with a new paper currency to the amount of 100,000 piastres.   In the district of Trebinje, indeed, nothing but the neighbourhood of the Turkish Nizam has prevented Mahometan discontent from bursting into open revolt. According to the law the heads of families are exempted from military service, but the Kaimakam of Trebinje has been attempting to extort large sums of money, in some cases as much as 1,000 florins, from the heads of the richest Mahometan families in lieu of military service. Upon their appeal, the tyrant tried to seize and imprison them, but has not been able to set hands on more than a dozen.   The rest, to the number of over a hundred, and among them several Begs and influential landholders, have fled, and during the last few days no less than seventy Mahometan refugees have arrived at Ragusa. Even as I write I hear of fresh arrivals.   They are appealing to Stamboul for redress.

LETTER
VII.

*Mahometan
discontent
in Herze-
govina.*

LETTER VIII.

THROUGH THE LIKA.

 HAVE already sent you a telegraphic summary of the deplorable outrages perpetrated by the Turks on the unfortunate Bosnian refugees who were driven by misery to make a trial of Turkish promises, and rebuilt their burnt houses at Očievo. I write this on my way to penetrate, if possible, to the scene of the massacre, as well as personally to obtain the evidence of the witnesses of the outrages who have succeeded in finding their way back to Christian soil. I have accompanied to the frontier village where I write this a relief expedition which the unflagging energy of the English ladies (Miss Irby and Miss Johnston) has despatched to bear food and clothing to the hitherto terribly neglected Bosnian refugees of this part of the Croatian frontier; and I am sorry to have to add that I

*Start with
a relief
party of
Miss Irby's.*

have been a witness to an act of official barbarity which has gone far to render the efforts of English charity unavailing.

A weary eight hours' drive from Zara brought me to Obbrovazzo, in Dalmatia, from which place our party started to ascend the snowy ridge of Mount Velebić, which forms the barrier between Dalmatia and Croatia, and between the Austrian and Hungarian divisions of the Hapsburg monarchy.

Just before descending from the cold plateau of this wildest and nakedest of mountains, our wagons, containing the clothes and coverings for the refugees, were stopped at the truly alpine Custom-house which here marks the Hungarian frontier and bars the main pass between Dalmatia and Croatia.

You are aware that it has long become a principle of the comity of nations in the presence of great and national distress for civilized Governments to forego those customs' regulations which stand in the way of foreign assistance to the sufferers. Acting on this principle, the Austrian Government has allowed the clothes and woollens sent from England for the Bosnian refugees to pass free of customs. But in the Hungarian half of the monarchy it is far otherwise. The Magyars, in their blind hatred of the Slavs, whose eventual freedom threatens to stand in the way of their own domination, seem to have forgotten —I will not say the received usages of civilized nations, but the most ordinary dictates of humanity. My readers know by this time how Magyar officers and officials consented to remain silent as to impalements and other atrocities of which they had themselves been witnesses, and which were only at length exposed by the chance experience of English travellers. But my readers do

not know that only the other day, when fresh Turkish
atrocities, of which I have already given some account,
drove new bodies of Bosnian rayahs across the Hungarian
frontier by Novi and elsewhere, the few cattle that these
homeless fugitives had succeeded in taking with them
were seized by the Magyar officials on the plea that they
must have stolen them from the Turks! And so it is
that, in spite of the example set by the Austrian half of
the monarchy, and in spite of the most urgent entreaties
and representations, the Government of the Magyar continues to exact the uttermost farthing of a protectionist
tariff at the expense of its naked and destitute Bosnian
suppliants.

To judge by what took place on this occasion, the
officials have orders to be peculiarly rigorous in their
treatment of goods sent for the benefit of the refugees;
at least it is hardly credible that their manner of investigation was normal in its character.

*Humanity
of the
Hungarian
Govern-
ment!*

Our wagons, containing clothes and woollens from
England, were overhauled in the most ruthless manner
conceivable. Any one who had come up during the
process would have supposed that we were being plundered by a gang of brigands! The scene almost baffles
description. Every sack was ripped open, and prodded
and pierced besides in a most barbarous fashion by
pointed instruments of iron. Shirts, flannels, blankets,
clothes of every kind were flung about the road; and,
after a weary process of weighing and calculating, a sum
so exorbitant was demanded for the warmest clothes
despatched from England, that, in the impossibility of
paying it, seven hundred woollen articles that were to
have clad the shivering women and children who have
sought refuge in the mountainous borderlands of Christen-

dom had to be sent back down the steeps of Mount
Velebić into Dalmatia !

And here it is still winter—snow mountains on either
side, and this evening a cruel *bora*, that chills one to the
bone through warmer clothing than the wretched fugitives
could ever hope to wear.

Winter—and what winter ! The blue sky and bluer *The*
sea, the waving palms and budding myrtles, the fragrant *Croatian*
jonquils, rosemary, and wallflowers, just beginning to *Siberia.*
perfume the rocky shores of Ragusa and the Dalmatian
islands, are already a dream of the past! This Lika
district on whose mountainous margin I had arrived has
well been called the 'Croatian Siberia'! You may like
to hear how I was snowed up in a little hut, which serves
as a kind of hospice on the Croatian side of Velebić. The
snow began overnight and continued all day, shrouding in
a cold sheet of white the lilac crocuses that had ventured
too trustingly to woo the eye of spring on the mountain
lawns. Towards evening a change took place in the
storm ; the snow turned into a kind of sleet, which, freezing as it fell, sheathed every branch and twig in over
half an inch of ice. The hut I was in was in the middle
of a forest, and as the sleet continued during the night
one branch gave way under the weight of ice and then
another, till crash followed crash in such quick succession
that it sounded like the roar of artillery around, interrupted as the lesser branches gave way with sharp,
snapping, explosive noises, like pistol shots at close
quarters. The spectacle next morning was stupendous! *A forest*
The whole forest was wrecked! There is no other *wrecked.*
word that will describe it. The whole ground was
covered waist-high with poles of fallen branches ; spread-
ing forest queens had been stripped till they were mere

naked trunks—mutilated torsos. Fragile trees had been crushed—Tarpeia-like, but with a girdling weight of crystal. Tender saplings and trees of more elastic growth had been simply bowed down, like weeping willows, their slender sprays poured down towards mother earth in taper icicles, till every tree looked like a frozen fountain! Or here and there at turns on the mountain-side the wind had curved, and clawed, and twisted the crystal fingers in fantastic bends, and sometimes seemed to have spun them out in as many graceful waves as the river rack takes in the current of a stream, but these quite motionless. When the sun shone out through the clouds and the frozen fountains glittered in its light and twinkled with a myriad prismatic hues—then, indeed, it was a vision of enchantment!

But I have descended from the mountains whose ridge acts as a wall between such opposite climates and holds South and North 'in eternal divorce.'

I reached Udbina, where I write this after a day's journey through a strange, wild land, part of the great Illyrian desert, with its scattered oases of fertility, its chaotic rocks, underground rivers, and mysterious caverns; a country—as everywhere in Illyria—presenting the most startling contrasts of nakedness and cultivation, and rich in folk-lore and romance, which seem to reproduce the alternating grimness and beauty of the landscape.

Every churchyard we pass is haunted with those ghostly creations of Slavonic and Oriental phantasy, the

Vukodlaks, or vampires. But the local mythology takes in turn a more airy and enticing form. At St. Roch we passed a little roadside spring welling from a stone basin known to the Lika folk as the 'Fountain of Wisdom,'

and paused to refresh ourselves with the Waters of Know-
ledge.   On a mountain side to the south of Udbina
another fountain—of healing—springs from the snow, and
the peasants say that once upon a time the angels danced
the 'kolo' (the national Slavonic dance) on the snow above,
and that next morning was seen the circle of celestial
footprints.   So every year the sick of Udbina and the
neighbourhood make a pilgrimage thither on the eve of
July 24, bathe in the holy stream, and pass the night
beside it.   Next morning comes the Greek priest and
says mass, and the cure is perfected.

On a peak to the south rises the ruined stronghold of
the Counts of the Lika, the last of whom, John of Kar-
lovitz, was chased away by the Turks in the seventeenth
century ; and the peasants tell still of strange fruits and
flowers that grow where once their lord's garden smiled.
To the west stretch the forests of the Kuk Planina ; and
on a peak beyond, known as the 'Green Mountain,' the
foundations of another ancient castle are traceable, as to
whose origin even tradition fails.   Beetling above this
looms a mysterious rock, under which explosions as of a
pistol shot have been heard from time to time by
frightened shepherds.   Woe indeed to the flocks and
herds that stray too near that ill-omened spot!   The
shepherds say that a dragon is coiled below keeping
watch and ward over the gold hoard which beyond doubt
lies hidden within, and that every living creature that
approaches the monster's den is blasted by his poisonous
breath.   Sheep or oxen, they say, that have strayed too
near the rock have often been found next morning stiff and
stark.   And, should any one wish to peer beyond the dra-
gon's rock still further to the west, he may catch a glimpse of
an even more uncanny mountain-hollow, where lies the

*LETTER
VIII.*

*Haunted
springs.*

*Castle of the
old Counts
of the Lika.*

*The
dragon's
rock.*

Czerno Jezero, or Black Pool, whose depths no mortal
man has fathomed.

Nor is it only from its haunted hollows and dragon-
guarded peaks and fairy legends that this neighbourhood
is profoundly interesting. Udbina lies in the Lika division of the old Military Frontier which Hapsburg Em-
peror-Kings formed centuries ago as a kind of political
sea-wall against the then encroaching tide of Islâm. A
few years ago commenced that process of transition which
soon will cause this old military organization, which converted every peasant into a militiaman, to be numbered
among the institutions of the past. The days of
Mahometan conquest are over, and while the Austrian
watch-houses on this side of the frontier fall to rack and
ruin, it is the Turks who are building new ones on the
Bosnian side in fear of Christian encroachments.

But though the Military Frontier has passed or is passing away with the circumstances that necessitated it, one
is reminded at every step that one stands on land reclaimed from the Crescent.

On the peak above Udbina Church rise the ruins of
a Turkish 'kula,' or fortress. Below Udbina Hill is a
small rakish-looking Roman Catholic chapel, which at
once excites suspicions as to its antecedents, and, in fact,
parts of it once belonged to a mosque. Near it is a heap
of stones upon a slight mound overgrown with thorns,
and one of the village elders assured me that it was
Bajazet's tomb. The Turks, it seems, still hold this spot
in peculiar veneration, and, extraordinary as it may seem,
Mahometan pilgrims still come from beyond the Bosnian
border to pray at the reputed tomb of their warrior-saint,
interred in what is now the soil of Christendom. The
villagers told me that in old times a head was preserved

in the chapel which was the cause of great strife among the adherents of the three creeds who dispute for mastery in these lands. The Catholics said the head was St. Mark's, the Pravoslavs claimed it for St. Paul, and the Bosnian Turks swore by the beard of the Prophet that it was Bajazet's !

LETTER VIII.

The Udbiners themselves are, as I have already mentioned in a previous letter, mostly descendants of Mahometan families who, on the Christian re-conquest of the district at the end of the seventeenth century, consented to submit to the rite of baptism—just as, two centuries before, the forefathers of the same villagers had consented to receive the faith of Islâm from the Turkish conqueror. They still retain in many cases their Mahometan family names; they still keep up friendly relations with a few Mahometan connections beyond the border. But their sympathies, like those of all true Likaners, are entirely with the rayahs. Among the people of the Lika generally the memories of Turkish rule are still fresh, and their hereditary hatred of the oppressor still intense. Many a brave band of these borderers has crossed the frontier to aid the insurgents at a pinch—ay, and if occasion offers, many are prepared to do so again.

Re-conversion of Mahometan Udbiners to Christianity.

Hereditary hatred of Turks among Slavonic border population.

Nor is it easy for the Hungarian Government to prevent such incursions when the whole border population is in league with these practical sympathisers. Any one who wants to realise how intense are the passions which the wrongs of their brothers beyond the border rouse among the neighbouring Slavonic populations; how mighty are the silent forces at work in favour of South Slavonic unity and liberation; how vain is the legerdemain of diplomacy and the sand-ropes of statesmen, who see Governments and nothing beyond Governments; and,

LETTER
VIII.

*Silent
forces at
work in
favour of
South
Slavonic
unity.*

lastly, how artificial and unstable is the present political organisation of the Austro-Hungarian monarchy, and this precious dualism, devised by Count Beust to divide the empire between a minority of Germans and Magyars, and to exclude that Slavonic majority which gains every day in numbers, wealth, and culture—any one, I say, who wishes to realise all this should wander as I have wandered amongst these border populations, and should talk as I have talked with peasant, burgher, and soldier.

Even in Agram, the capital of Croatia, it is easy for the foreigner to deceive himself, for there is a portion of the Croats proper who, owing partly to historical causes, partly to the fact that they are Catholics and under the denationalising influence of the Romish priesthood, hold themselves aloof from the aspirations of their Serbian kinsmen of the Greek Church.

But—and I have never yet seen this most pregnant fact pointed out—over half the ' Grenze,' the old military frontier of Croatia, containing the most warlike and not the least civilised part of the population, is peopled by what is, in fact, a separate and purely Serbian nationality,[1]

[1] By Serbian nationality is meant rather a difference in political tendencies and religion than in blood or language. The Croats themselves belong to the Serbian branch of the Slavs, and their language is almost identical with that spoken in the Serbian States beyond the border. Three dialects are, however, to be noted among them, and their language has been divided into three divisions, according to the word employed for the interrogative 'what?' which is variously pronounced ' *Kai*,' ' *Ča*,' and ' *Što*, the divisions being named *Kajkavština*, *Čakavština*, and *Stokavština*. The 'langue de Kai' lies to the north-west, and approaches the Slovene area and language, its prevalence being due to earlier Slovene settlements in these districts; the counties of Agram, Varasdin, Kreutz, and Belovar are its strongholds. Generally to the east of this is the area of the 'langue de Što;' to the south, that of the 'langue de Ča.'

mostly adherents of the Greek Church, descendants of
Serbian refugees who at different times have fled from
the Serbian provinces—Bosnia, Herzegovina, and Rascia
—under Turkish yoke. Even when, as sometimes happens, this immigrant population professes Roman Catholicism, their Romanism takes a peculiarly national form.
Mass is read, not in Latin, as among the Croats proper,
but in their own vernacular; their priests are free from
offensive sacerdotalism, and resemble more the Greek
' popes.' Here at Udbina are some of these ' national'
Catholics. Yesterday was a great feast-day among them,
the merry-making being preceded by mass; but I was a
little surprised and not a little amused to see his Reverence bustle out with his congregation, form a ring for
the national 'kolo' dance, seize two buxom lasses by the
waist, and join, as lustily as ecclesiastical vestments would
allow, in the merry-go-round!

What I have said of the political relations in Croatia
is to a great extent true of Dalmatia, except that in
Dalmatia there is a small so-called ' autonomous' party
in some of the coast cities, who speak Italian, dream of
union with Italy, and eschew everything Slav. But these
are a small and insignificant minority. Of the Slavonic-
speaking population, which, with this small exception,
occupies the whole country, the majority is certainly
Catholic; and a certain proportion of the Catholics are
here, as in Croatia, lukewarm towards the South Slavonic
cause, and content themselves with aiming at the union
of Croatia, Slavonia, and Dalmatia, and the formation of
some small kingdom which they could call Catholic and
Croatian.

But in Dalmatia, as here in Croatia, it is the Serbs—
the Greek Church or Pravoslav population—who hold

LETTER
VIII.

That the
Serbs alone
hold the
future of
Illyria in
their hands.

the future of the country in their hands.   There, as here,
it is the Serbs, and the Serbs alone, who are inspired by
those motives and passions that are capable of deciding
the destinies of nations.   Call it patriotism, call it Panslavism, call it faith, or call it fanaticism, the motive force
is there, and it is irresistible.   Roman Catholicism damps
the patriotic aspirations of its adherents in these parts as
much as possible ; the Greek Church fans them and
intensifies them.   The Catholic Croats and Dalmatians
have little beyond a negative policy—vague and halting.
The Serbs are animated by every sympathy of race and
religion, and their object is as definite as it is grand—the
eventual union of all South Slavonic peoples in a free
State of their own.   The Catholic Croats have no allies,
even among their own kinsmen and co-religionists ; the
Serbs of Dalmatia and Croatia look not only to their
brothers of the Black Mountain, of free Serbia, and of the
former Serbian Vojvodina in Hungary, and to the Serb
populations still under the Turkish yoke—but to their
Catholic kinsmen, the Chesks of Bohemia and Moravia,
and the Slovenes of Styria, Carinthia, and Carniola, who,
unlike the Croats, forget religious differences in common
Slavonic patriotism.   And there is another ally in the
north more powerful than these, and united by ties of
religion as well as blood.

Austria
and the
Serbs.

People here are already privately discussing the possibilities of a Serbian revolt in Dalmatia, the Bocche di
Cattaro, and the Croatian mountains in the event of a
war between Austria and Russia.   That such a war is at
present imminent seems to me extremely unlikely.   That
Austrian interests must eventually clash with Russian
seems to me certain.   Till that day arrives the final
solution of the Eastern Question is by mutual accommo-

dation postponed. And when that day arrives it will be well for Austria, and well for Europe, if she has made her peace with her own Slavonic subjects, and sapped by con ciliatory means the solidarity to-day existing between the Serbs and Russians. Meanwhile, however, I should like to ask the Austrian ambassador at the court of St. James's and the gypsy premier of Hungary one seemingly trivial question,—why it is that so many of the loyal subjects of his Imperial, Royal, and Apostolic Majesty in Dalmatia and Croatia wear caps on which the initials of Prince Nikola of little Montenegro are embroidered in golden letters?

LETTER VIII.

Bitter re pugnance of Serbian population to Austrian govern- ment.

No! *those* dreams at any rate are vain. Montenegro is too small even to become the nucleus of a great South Slavonic state. Austria, it must be confessed, is the only Southern state at present existing that can weld into unity that perplexed array of petty principalities and rival pro- vinces, with their sub-nationalities and antagonistic reli- gions. It does not require a prophet's eye to perceive that Austria can only exist as a Slavonic power; but if her statesmen wait till they are summoned to surrender, as surrender sooner or later they must, their German pro- vinces, before they retreat upon the south and east, then they will have waited too late. Her Slavonic provinces— what the German had left of them, that is—might aggre- gate themselves indeed to some vague Confederation of the Danube or the Balkan, but what paramount power could give that political union which must be the pre- lude to national unity? In ten years Russia might be on the Adriatic as well as the Ægean, and the Serbian Con- federation have become another Poland! And yet what Austria is asked to do to-day is no light thing. If the Hapsburgs wish to take up the Imperial crown of Serbian Czars, they must break with their Roman Catholic

Montenegro too small to become nucleus of South Slavonic Power.

Will Austria?

traditions, they must quarrel with the aristocratic minority of Magyars which forms the ruling caste in Hungary,— although for the Magyars one thing is certain, they can obtain better terms from a South Slavonic state than from Russia.   All this requires political self-abnegation such as few governments could practise.   Will Austria accept her destiny ?   Will she stoop to conquer ?   These are questions about which no patriotic Englishman who desires the consolidation of a strong South Slavonic power as a bulwark against our rival in the East, can afford to be unconcerned.

LETTER IX.

ON THE SCENE OF TURKISH OUTRAGES.

Lapatz, Bosnian-Croatian Frontier : *April* 12.

 HAVE succeeded in penetrating to the scene of the worst outrages that during the last few weeks have been committed by the Turks on returned and returning refugees in Southern Bosnia, as well as on other peaceful rayah villagers who had never left their homes. Besides visiting the burnt and plundered homesteads, I have spent several days in hunting up the fugitives themselves, part of whom have found shelter in the mountain villages beyond the Croatian frontier, and part within the hospitable limits of Free Bosnia. And let it be well understood, for the Turks and their admirers will not be slow to seize on any imaginary palliation for their villany, that all the outrages of which I write have been committed outside the limits of the district held by the insurgents ; that they have been committed solely on unarmed men and helpless women and children ; and, further, that they cannot be looked on as a retaliation for any violence committed by the insurgents, inasmuch as the insurrection has during the whole winter, and, in fact, ever since Despotović took the command, remained strictly on the defensive.

Evidence taken of 21 rayahs.

I have taken down the evidence of twenty-one of the victims, choosing generally fathers of families for the purpose; and as I saw these at different places, some on Austro-Hungarian and some on insurgent territory, and as on all material points the evidence is singularly corroborative, I think you may rely on the accuracy of my report.

I will leave what new experiences I gained of the insurgents and their territory for another letter, and will proceed at once to the end and object of my personal investigation—the burnt villages of Great and Little Očievo. After examining several of the refugees at Serb, on the Croatian frontier, and others at different places among the mountains of Free Bosnia (among which with this object I have made a four days' march), I started from Sienitza Grad, the extreme outpost of the insurgents in this direction, to make my way, if possible, to the actual scene of the Očievo outrages.

Difficulties in my path.

As there was a spice of adventure about this undertaking, it may interest my readers to know some of the straits to which I was reduced.

In the insurgent camp at Sienitza Grad every one conspired to dissuade me from my project. They said that, though the ruins of Očievo were deserted by the Turks, marauding bands of Bashi-bazouks still lurked in the neighbourhood, and that only two days ago some haystacks on a height above the villages, which had

hitherto escaped, had been burnt by these gentry. Then
the elements were unfavourable. It was necessary to
enter the Turkish parts of Bosnia to cross the Unnatz,
but the rain and melting snow had so swollen the river,
always rapid, that the fords had become impracticable,
and to try to swim it was, in the opinion of all the assembled Bosniacs, sheer madness.

However, go I must and go I would; so, climbing
down the somewhat precipitous rocks to the river, I
divested myself of the greater part of my apparel, put a
notebook and a few necessaries in my hat, and, leaving
clothes, revolver, and other impediments to the charge of
the astonished Bosniacs, made the fatal plunge. The
intense cold was far more dangerous than the current;
but Father Unnatz was propitious, and I did succeed in
reaching the opposite shore; and after a period of en-
forced inactivity on the bank, started without guides or
guards, and in a singularly primæval condition, to find my
way as best I might to the burnt villages, over the mountains of Bashi-bazouk-land.

As often happens to travellers on such occasions, I
lost my way, and was stumbling on among rocks and
stunted pinewoods, pretty well exhausted, when I heard
something very like a war-whoop below, which under the
circumstances was hardly reassuring. However, on re-
connoitring I found that the sounds proceeded from a
brave Bosnian rayah, a native of Očievo, who had been
roused by my example to swim the Unnatz and volunteer
his services as a guide to the burnt villages.

After a weary ascent and partial descent of a mountain neck, we arrived at the scene of the outrages, and I
found that all that the various witnesses had described to
me touching the destruction of property was strictly true.

A more hideous scene of havoc I have never seen and never wish to see again. Two homesteads alone remained unburnt, saved from destruction, it is supposed, by their Mahometan landlords ; but even these were partially wrecked and entirely gutted. All the other houses were burnt to the ground, though here and there one or two of the wickerwork storehouses for maize usual among the Bosnians had been merely rifled of their contents, and not further destroyed ;—the Turks had providently left a few of the hives to be refilled !

What made the havoc even more melancholy was its twofold character. There were first the blackened foundations of the homesteads burnt the other day with the fresh smell of fire upon them ; and side by side with these the *débris* of the former village, burnt by Turks on the 24th of June of last year. The foundations of the former homesteads were larger as well as more numerous than those of the huts which the returning refugees had ventured to rebuild, and formed a striking commentary on the straitened circumstances of these unfortunate people. In the former village there were, if my information is correct, over forty families. In the village, or rather two villages, just destroyed I reckoned twenty one burnt huts and two unburnt, which agrees with the number of families mentioned to me by name by a variety of witnesses.

The havoc was of the most thoroughgoing kind. Every little article of domestic use that had not been carried off—pots, pans, rags of sacking and clothes—were scattered about pell-mell, broken, torn, and trampled under foot. Here and there maize or beans had been scattered on the ground in the process of carrying the plunder off. To discover the little hoards of money which the rayah families might possess, the pillagers had in many cases grubbed up the earth-floor of the huts, and in one I saw the actual hole from which the hoard of the most well to-do family—amounting, so my guide declared, to 8*l*. in paper money, but this is probably an exaggeration—had been grubbed out by the Bashi-bazouks.

We had already explored the ruins of the upper village, or Greater Očievo, and were surveying those of the lower village from a height above, when my Bosnian guide, with the quick instinct of a savage, sank down on hands and knees behind a rock, and, pointing to a partially wooded mountain side beyond, whispered to me, 'Turski! Turski!' ('The Turks, the Turks!'). From the nature of the ground there was no difficulty in concealing ourselves, but we thought it wise to effect a retrograde motion, and pursued the same path which the fugitive villagers had taken on a similar but more urgent occasion. I found here plenty of traces of the stampede of the unfortunate villagers; on a thorn-bush part of a woman's clothing, and the remains of a family chest thrown down in the hurry of flight, but rifled now of its contents, whatever they may have been. I also picked up some Turkish cartridges—like all the ammunition that has fallen into the hands of the insurgents at different times, of American fabric; and, nearing the river, the hoof-marks of the pursuing Bashi-bazouks were still visible on the turf We then followed the Unnatz river to a point higher up where the Bosnian thought there might be a ford practicable from this side; and in one way or another, after about a quarter of an hour's struggle through the torrent and over the shallows, finally found ourselves once more on the left bank.

I will now give you the results of the evidence I have

LETTER IX.

Investigations in Little Očievo interrupted by appearance of Bashi-bazouks.

Traces of stampede villagers.

collected from the victims as to the actual occurrences at Great and Little Očievo and two other hamlets situated in the neighbouring Cerljevitza mountains—namely, Klekovatza and Vaganatz.

Names of witnesses.

Regarding the Očievo outrages I have examined thirteen witnesses. Three of these—David, Militza, and Anja Karanović—I saw at Serb, on the Croatian border; one, Gregor Pavičić, at Lapatz, also within the Grenze; nine—namely, Lazar Šipka, Vid Rodić, Giuro Šipka, Milan Rodić, Milan Karanović, Jovan Tankosić, Stefan Karanović, Mihailo Rodić, and Blaž Karanović—at Sienitza Grad, in Free Bosnia ; and the wife of the murdered Vaso Karanović, at Boboljuša, also in Free Bosnia.

The story of Očievo.

On the approach of the Turks on June 24 of 1876 the villagers fled mostly to Austrian soil, leaving their homes to be burnt and pillaged. The extreme misery, however, of the refugees on this part of the Hungarian frontier, the approach of winter, and the impossibility of procuring fodder for the cattle they had succeeded in carrying with them induced the fugitives to crave permission to return from their Mahometan landlords—namely, Mujo Kurtaghić, Osman Aga Andjić, and Nedjim and Ismail Begs Kulenović, all resident in Kulen Vakup.

The Begs, who are beginning to suffer severely from the want of serfs to supply their needs, promised the Očievers that if they returned they should be unmolested, and accordingly most of the families actually did return, and rebuilt their burnt cottages.[1]

---

[1] The names of the heads of the various families who returned and the numbers of each family were given me, as follows:—David Karanović, 17; Damian Karanović, 19: Djuro Karanović, 4 ; Vaso

On Saturday, March 10, a body of Bashi-bazouks, estimated by the villagers at about a hundred, under the leadership of Ali Beg Trovka, Mujo Beg Bibanović, and Ali Beg Kulenović (who, however, arrived rather late in the day), made their appearance in the lower village. They plundered the house and barn of David Karanović, seized all his corn, the clothing they found in the house, and, if his deposition made to me is correct, took from him and his house-community 45 goats. about 50 sheep, 18 oxen, and one horse. They robbed in the same way three other families. They then proceeded to the house of the village elder or Knez, the elected representative of the community, who receives a kind of official seal from the Turkish authorities. What follows I have from his wife. A Bashi-bazouk seized him on either side, while a third despatched him with pistol shots. Another member of the family, Teto Karanović, was wounded in the arm, but escaped. The head of the murdered Knez, Vaso Karanović, was then cut off and carried away. The women and girls were stripped of the girdles and other ornaments that they possessed, and the irregulars were proceeding to outrages of a more shameful kind when stopped by the timely arrival of Ali Beg Kulenović, who succeeded on this occasion in restraining his retainers. The Turks then made off with their booty to Kulen Vakup, carrying with them in triumph the head of the village elder.

Another of my witnesses, Gregor Pavićić, of Boriće-

LETTER IX.

Očievo attacked by Bashi-bazouks.

Murder of a village elder.

Karanović, 7; Parro Karanović, 8; Mili Karanović, 7; Ilija Karanović, 6; Blaž Karanović, 11; Trifan Šaratz, 13; Péro Šaratz, 2; Mihailo Rodić, 11; Vid Rodić, 27; Marko Sipka, 17; Obrad Šipka, 10; Djuro Šipka, 6; Nikola Šipka, 12; Pero Šipka, 6; Luka Rodić, 8; Milan Tankosić, 11; David Tankosić, 8; Mili Tankosić, 5; Blaž Sténić, 8; Mili Sténić, 8: total, 231.

vatz, who, though a Christian, is employed on various errands across the Croatian border by the Turks of Kulen Vakup, happened to be there when the murderous gang returned. The Mudir said that it was no use kicking the head about the streets, and that they had better give it to the Giaour to bury, which he accordingly did.

Meanwhile it was mooted that night in Očievo whether to fly at once or not; but the weather was bitterly cold. A fierce 'bora,' the tempestuous nor'-nor'-easter of Illyria, was blowing, and the snow lay deep; so it was decided to put off their departure.

Second arrival of the Turks.

Next day, Sunday, the Turks appeared again, but in larger numbers. According to all accounts, there were from 200 to 300 Redifs, and from 400 to 500 Bashi-bazouks. The leaders were the Kaimakam of Petrovatz, the Turkish Prefect, and the supreme Government official of the district; while Ali Trovka and Ali Kulenović represented the Begs. The troops came from Kulen Vakup, Petrovatz, and Bielaj.

The village given up to indiscriminate plunder and rapine.

Then followed a scene of indiscriminate plunder and rapine. An attempt was made to seize the house-fathers of the village, but, warned by the fate of their Knez, they all succeeded in escaping. Many of the girls and women, however, fell into the hands of the marauders; the girdles and ornaments were torn from those who still possessed them; the more youthful among them were set apart for

Girls and women outraged.

a worse fate. According to the lowest estimate, ten of them fell victims to Turkish lust; according to the wife of the village elder, who probably knew more than the men, who on this subject were very reticent, about fifteen. Pity and shame made the men loth to mention the names, and I would not press this point.

The Turks pursued the refugees to the Unnatz, firing

on them on the way; and the cartridges that I picked up formed a striking corroboration of this part of the evidence. The river was happily then low and easily fordable, but the pursuers came up with some women and children on the bank, and flung Simeona Šipka, a young woman, and a child, Vid Šipka, into the water. Both of them, however, were saved. Another woman, with child, was seized, and was so terrified that she gave birth prematurely. The Turks did not attempt to pursue beyond the Unnatz, fearing to enter insurgent territory. After burning the two villages, they made off laden with all the stores and movables on which they had been able to lay their hands, and with large droves of cattle also taken from the villagers. The total number of animals carried off by them, as nearly as I could arrive at it, was 450 sheep and goats, 55 oxen, and 27 horses.

The villagers took refuge partly on Austrian and partly on Free Bosnian territory, and some of the men have gone to swell the ranks of the insurgents. The day after the flight two small children of Vid Rodić, by names Jovan and Sargen, were missed, and were sought for next day among the ruins of the now deserted village. They were found at last, dead and frozen on the snow.

At Boboljuša, on a mountain on the left bank of the Unnatz, I found a miserable family of refugees from Očievo, or rather a family community, for there were three families there, but only one house-father—seventeen of them crowded into a wretched shed. Seven or eight of them were children, and in the middle lay a little lad of about five prostrate with small-pox. They had only provisions for a few days. I was able to give them a reprieve from hunger from a small fund at my disposal —but what could save the other children from infection?

LETTER IX.

Women and children thrown into the river.

Two children found afterwards frozen in the snow.

As I have already said, the recent outrages in this district have extended to two other hamlets besides Očievo. To gain further evidence about these I went to Unnatz, in the insurgent district, and to Osredke, on the Croatian border, where I had heard that some of the victims had taken refuge. Vaganatz, the scene of one of these outrages, was simply an isolated farm inhabited by Stephen Rodić, his two daughters (Djorgia and Sava), and his boy Obrad. The Turks, numbering about a hundred, arrived here a fortnight ago, broke into the house, shot the father, tortured one of the little girls to try to extract information as to the whereabouts of insurgents, who have no camp in this district, and threw the other girl, who was sick, out of doors. They burnt the house after first pillaging it, and made off to Petrovatz with twelve oxen and four horses, part of which belonged to Rodić himself and part to a certain Nikola Morača. The boy, aged eleven, escaped, and, after wandering about four days without food or shelter, found his way to Unnatz, which the girl Djorgia and her sick sister also succeeded in reaching. At Unnatz I saw three men, Jovan Skakić, Damian Turitza, and Obrad Baić, who had visited the burnt homestead and found the headless body of Rodić. His head had been carried by the Turks to Petrovatz. They had also seen the boy Obrad and heard his account of the tragedy, which agreed with that which I took down from the lips of Djorgia Rodić, whom I succeeded in finding at Osredke. Several witnesses there testified that when she arrived she was bruised all over owing to the cruel treatment she had received at the hands of her father's murderers ; but when I saw her, which was a fortnight later, she bore no marks of violence, at least on her hands and face.

The little maiden gave her evidence very well. She said she was about thirteen, but seemed rather uncertain as to her age. She saw her father shot and his head chopped off ; he was at home ill when the Turks came. She thought there were over a hundred. She had seen Redifs and Bashi-bazouks before, and both were there. Pašitza Kulenović was the leader ; she had seen him before in Unnatz. The Turks asked her whether she knew where the insurgents were. She said she lived at home with father and sister and Obrad, and she knew nothing. They then beat her with their guns, but she could say no more. She had no mother, and now she had no father.

As to the atrocities perpetrated on the peaceful inhabitants of Klekovatza, in this same district, I have obtained the most direct and convincing testimony. My witnesses are Pope Lazar Ketzman and his wife, Sava Ketzman, whose arms still bore marks of injuries received in defence of her chastity, both of whom I examined at Osredke ; Spiro Ketzman, examined at Unnatz ; and Jovo Voivodić, at Serb.

The inhabitants of Klekovatza had all originally fled from the village of Drinić, near Petrovatz, burnt by the Turks last year. Some had fled to Austrian soil, and returned this spring to the number of about thirty. On April 20 about two hundred and fifty Turks fell on the village, which, like Očievo, was perfectly peaceful, and, as I know from evidence collected before these deplorable events took place, quite beyond the limits of the insurgent territory. The leaders of the Turkish horde were Murad Beg Kulenović and Méchmed Berizović, and there were present, besides Bashi-bazouks, Redifs under a 'Kolash.' The usual scenes took place. The houses, five in all,

G

were first pillaged and then burnt. Three brothers of the pope—namely, Vučim, Péro, and Ilija Ketzman—and Toreta and Vučim, kinsmen of the same family, five in all, were murdered. Cattle was lifted to the number of over 200 goats and sheep, 50 oxen, and 10 horses. The women and girls suffered the usual fate. The pope, who was less reticent on this matter than the Očievo witnesses, mentioned to me five of the Ketzman family—Militza, Maria, Smiliana, Rushitza, and Mara— who had been thus outraged. The heads of the murdered men were cut off and taken to Petrovatz.

*The above to
be regarded
as a sample
of what has
been occur-
ring in
Bosnia.*

These events, which I have done all in my power to investigate and make public, are but a sample of what on a greater or lesser scale has been occurring, and is still occurring, throughout the length and breadth of Bosnia and Herzegovina. In a single small district of the province, in the month succeeding the promulgation of the new Constitution, three peaceful villages have been burnt and plundered, over 800 head of cattle have been taken from their Christian owners, eleven men and three children murdered—and indirectly how many more?—and at least a score of girls and women outraged. Multitudes are now cowering suppliants for charity on Christian soil, the indignation of neighbouring Slav populations has been fed, the Bosnian insurrection has been swelled by desperate men, and, what is more, the Turkish Government is absolutely powerless, even if it had the will, either to punish the ringleaders, or to give redress to the victims, or to guarantee them security for the future.

In face of facts like these it is monstrous to babble of protocols and diplomatic amenities, or even of consular commissions. Every mild interference at Stamboul or Serajevo only irritates the dominant caste in the provinces to new deeds of horror. It is iniquitous to ask the refugees to return, or to express bland hopes that the brothers and husbands of the murdered, the robbed, and the ravished will lay down their arms. There is only one remedy for the state of things in Bosnia—an immediate Austrian occupation of the province, to be followed either by final incorporation with the monarchy or the prolonged administration of the province by an European commission.

NOTE.

THE BRITISH FOREIGN OFFICE AND THE OUTRAGES IN BOSNIA.

FOREIGN
OFFICE
AND
BOSNIAN
OUTRAGES.

*Questions
asked in
Parlia-
ment.*

ON March 9th, Sir George Campbell asked in the House, in reference to my previous correspondence in the *Manchester Guardian*, whether it was true 'that owing to the continued gross oppressions of the Mahometans, a large proportion of the Christian inhabitants of Bosnia were passing the winter in caves and holes and other wretched asylums, on the Austrian frontier, in the most miserable manner;' and also, 'whether Bosnia was not still the scene of obstinate insurrection.'

Mr. Bourke, who does not appear at that time to have mastered the geography of the question, replied vaguely, not about Bosnia, but about Nikšić and the Montenegrin border of Herzegovina. 'He had reason to hope, however, that when peace had been concluded between the Porte and Montenegro, tranquillity might be restored in the adjoining provinces.' *Solitudinem faciunt, pacem appellant!*

On March 23rd, I sent the first information of the outrages at Očievo and the neighbouring villages, in a telegram to the *Manchester Guardian*; and in a more detailed form on March 26th. On April 10th, information as to these outrages was asked for in the House of Commons by Mr. E. Jenkins.

Mr. Bourke replied that after Sir G. Campbell's question in the House on the 9th, a telegram had been sent (March 13th) to Mr. Consul Holmes, and that three despatches, from which he proceeded to read extracts, had been received in reply, dated March 14th, 16th, and 29th. From the last of these, dated March

29th, nearly three weeks after the occurrence of the outrages under notice, it appears that no breath of them had reached consular ears at Serajevo ; and Mr. Holmes is still assuring the Government ' that there is no truth whatever in the assertion that there is an increase of murders and outrages in the province.' Mr. Holmes is quite right : nobody who knows anything about Bosnia ever supposed that the state of things marked by the outrages at Očievo and elsewhere was abnormal in its character. For three years it has become chronic.

The amenities of consular diction permit Mr. Holmes in these despatches to speak of the insurgents impartially as ' filibus-ters ' and ' brigands ; ' and he does me the honour to quote a few extracts from my letters to the *Manchester Guardian,* amongst others, my experience as an eye-witness to the misery of the refugees, ' just to show,' as he puts it, ' how incorrectly what passes in Bosnia is represented by Slavophiles, who, from their vicinity and facility of correspondence, ought to be better informed, if they desired to be so.' It is to be observed that our Consul, residing in a province where, with the exception of a small bureaucratic clique of Osmanlìs (by whom he was surrounded), the whole population Mahometan as well as Christian is Slav, uses ' Slavo-phile ' as an epithet of contempt.

As regards the insurgents, Mr. Holmes writes to Lord Derby : ' I am at present confined to my room by an indisposition ; but I in-tend to take an early opportunity of urging the Vali to take steps at once, if possible, to sweep these bands of brigands out of Bosnia.' Of this 'sweeping out' anon. Mr. Holmes further states that he is aware that he is ' represented as a passionate Turcophile ; ' and pro-ceeds to enumerate the great disadvantages under which he labours ' in common with the few who have any knowledge of affairs in Bosnia, in having to contend against the great majority of uninformed and prejudiced speakers and writers on the state of affairs in these countries.'

The better, perhaps, to illustrate his ' knowledge of affairs in Bosnia,' and in order to satisfy the natural desire of his ' superiors,' as he calls the Foreign Office, for information from his own unexceptionable sources, Mr. Consul Hòlmes takes up a ten-days-old copy of the *Times* ; and having cut out an extract from a letter of the Austrian Correspondent (whose Turco-Magyar sympathies

FOREIGN OFFICE AND BOSNIAN OUTRAGES.

Mr. Consul Holmes' Reports.

Mr. Holmes' sources of informa-tion.

FOREIGN
OFFICE
AND
BOSNIAN
OUTRAGES.

*Mr. Consul
Holmes' Re-
ports.*

are well known), despatches it to the Foreign Office with all the
pomp and dignity of a State paper ! Thus we have the extraordinary
spectacle of an English Consul in Bosnia, reduced to obtain his
information as to his own province from Vienna, through London !
The information obtained by this lengthy process is very much what
might have been expected. It is the 'inspired' Austrian 'view'
of the insurrection as it ought to be represented ; but that Mr.
Holmes should have endorsed such a tissue of misrepresentation,
without having in any way tested its accuracy, is as astonishing as
the ignorance of the current history of his province which this
document displays. In it Despotović's command is placed in a
district to which he never, I believe, paid so much as a flying visit !
The refugees are described as chiefly driven forth by their insurgent
brothers—the fact being that the little mountain-tract which I
have called ' Free Bosnia ' is one of the few districts in the province
where rayah villages still exist. The insurgents, as I satisfied
myself by visiting seven of their camps, are native Bosniacs almost
to a man ; but Mr. Holmes lends the weight of his consular authority
to such a perversion of fact as the following :—' The so-called
insurrectionary movement is but a brigandage on a large scale,
being kept up, not by the people themselves, but for the most part
by adventurers from other Slav districts.'

I will remark *en passant* that at the present moment the country
in the hands of the insurgents is the only part of Bosnia where a
stranger may wander without arms or passport secure from the
insults of fanatics or the assaults of robbers or assassins, and secure,
wherever he arrives, of meeting with a kind and hospitable reception,
and of finding food and shelter, for which the men whom it has
pleased our Consul to stigmatize as 'brigands' will accept no pecuniary compensation. Mr. Holmes accounts for the fact that (with
the best of wills) he was unable to report Christian atrocities which
should act as a set-off to those perpetrated by Bashi-bazouks by the
sublime consideration ' that the Turks have thought it more dignified
to revenge than to complain.' Silent assassination ! The dignity of
revenge ! Strange language for the English representative in Bosnia
to be using on the eve of new massacres ! As to the maxim itself,
Mr. Holmes does not seem to be aware that it is after all not new,
and has indeed been shared by a large proportion of the cut-throats

and assassins of all ages. But society with singular unanimity has restrained this noble spirit of individual vindictiveness, by various modes, but most frequently with a hempen halter ; and when it has ceased to do so it has generally ceased to be society.

As to the outrages about which the question had been put by the member for Dundee, it was not to be expected that anything should be known about them at the British Consulate three weeks after their occurrence. On Mr. W. E. Forster asking whether the Government had taken means to obtain information as to the particular outrages in question, Mr. Bourke replied that no such steps had been taken, and that, really, the great expense of telegrams had to be considered.

On April 25th, Mr. E. Jenkins inquired whether attention had been called to the fact, that the account of murders and outrages upon refugees who had returned to their homes at Očievo, in Bosnia, had been fully confirmed by inquiry on the spot as reported in the *Manchester Guardian* of Saturday. Mr. Bourke acknowledged the receipt of a short report or *résumé* of the results of my investigations which I had forwarded to the Foreign Office through our Consul at Trieste ; and further, that this information had been telegraphed to Mr. Consul Holmes, who had immediately telegraphed to Vice-Consul Freeman, then at Mostar, to make an inquiry into the outrages which I had reported.

On May 12th, in the adjourned debate, Mr. Shaw Lefevre again called attention to the despatch of Mr. Consul Holmes, describing the state of Bosnia in glowing terms.

On June 21st, Mr. Vice-Consul Freeman's report on the outrages at Očievo was received by the Foreign Office ; and on July 10th Mr. Shaw Lefevre brought the despatch and the general conduct of our Consul in Bosnia before Parliament. Mr. Shaw Lefevre pointed out the substantial agreement between Mr. Vice-Consul Freeman's report and my correspondence ; and the extraordinary contradictions between the report of Mr. Freeman and his chief. Mr. Bourke stoutly denied that there was any substantial discrepancy between Mr. Holmes and Mr. Freeman ; but Mr. Dillwyn and Mr. James supported Mr. Shaw Lefevre's allegations, Mr. James pointing out that at the very time that Mr. Consul Holmes was denying 'the astounding statements' about impalement and other atrocities perpetrated in Bosnia, and asserting that 'neither the Turkish authorities nor the Consuls nor the people have ever heard of anything resembling the cruelties mentioned,' (see Mr. Holmes' despatch, October 5th, 1876), he had a report dated the 17th of the previous March in his possession, *from his own Vice-Consul, Mr. Freeman,* to the effect that a man had been impaled at Novi, in full view of an Austrian village ; and that four other persons had been killed and their heads exposed on stakes ; and that the master of the Orthodox school at Priedor had been butchered, and his head paraded about the streets with drums and bands of music.

Mr. Vice-Consul Freeman contradicts Mr. Holmes' reports.

Mr. Vice-Consul Freeman in his report on the Očievo outrages rectifies, in fact, a whole string of mis-statements to which his superior, Mr. Consul Holmes, had committed himself.   He denies that the insurgents are mere brigands, and asserts on the contrary that ' Colonel Despotović maintains the strictest discipline among his men.'   He comes to the conclusion that so far as Očievo is concerned, the Christian villages were burnt with circumstances of atrocity ; he bears out all that I had stated as to the misery of the refugees, and adds his testimony to the fact that the Turks have converted a large part of Bosnia into a desert.

As to the outrages at Očievo, Mr. Vice-Consul Freeman examined thirteen men and twenty girls and women, among the refugees from the burnt villages, and the evidence he obtained from these harmonizes in most particulars with that which I had previously taken down, viz., that the refugees had been invited to return by the Mahometan landlords and had been promised security by them ; that the inhabitants were peaceful villagers and not insurgents ; that the Turks, besides burning and plundering the villages of Očievo and murdering some of the inhabitants (according to Mr. Freeman's rayah evidence five, according to mine only one), had outraged girls and women.   Mr. Freeman complains that the evidence was vague and unsatisfactory ; and I must add that I found the same difficulty in getting these people to descend to particulars, but this is much what would be found among any people in the same stage of barbarism as the Bosniacs.   I will also observe that some individual cases of horror, the details of which were related to me, were not borne out by Mr. Freeman's evidence ; and I have therefore willingly omitted them in my account.

Mr. Freeman laboured under the disadvantage of making his inquiries three weeks later than mine, and when the memory of events was not so fresh. To this I suppose is due the fact that he does not distinguish between the two days on which the outrages were committed, and that he confuses the order of events. Mr. Freeman did not visit the actual ruins of the villages themselves, and therefore had no opportunity of testing the accuracy of the witnesses by the mute evidence of the things destroyed; nor did he examine the refugees from the burnt villages whom I hunted up in obscure mountain retreats in the country which I have called 'Free Bosnia.' Had he done so he would have been less ready to accept some of the counter-statements made to him by the Turks at Kulen Vakup, such as the allegation that the whole affair was brought on by a battle between them and the insurgents at Očievo; that the Kaimakam only burnt four guard-houses of the insurgents that he found there; and the further insinuation that the insurgents or the refugees must have burnt their own village, and, I suppose, plundered and outraged themselves! I know from evidence derived before these unfortunate events took place that Očievo was quite beyond the limits of the insurgent territory on this side; and that the Unnatz was at this point recognised as a well-defined boundary, the overstepping of which was most sternly prohibited by the insurgent commander—true to the defensive strategy resolved on from the beginning. Indeed, if Očievo were an insurgent stronghold, how does Mr. Freeman explain the fact that the Mahometan Begs invited the refugees to return there? As to the statement of the Kaimakam about the 'guard-houses,' I can only say that the charred remains of the villages that I saw were those of the very small peasant huts of this part of Bosnia. One act of humanity on the part of this Kaimakam, according to all my accounts the chief ringleader in the outrages, ought to be mentioned, as Mr. Freeman heard it from a rayah woman. Dosta Karanović said that this officer prevented the burning of her house because she had sick children there.

As to the outrages and massacres at Vaganatz and Klekovatza, which were among the worst mentioned in my report, Mr. Freeman is altogether silent, not having visited those districts.

I must, while adding my homage to the painstaking character of Mr. Freeman's report, protest very strongly against some sweeping

FOREIGN OFFICE AND BOSNIAN OUTRAGES.

Mr. Vice-Consul Freeman too ready to accept Turkish counter statements.

FOREIGN
OFFICE
AND
BOSNIAN
OUTRAGES.

statements which he makes as to the morality of the Bosnian rayahs. After observing that ' the excesses and outrages,' to quote our Vice-Consul's words, ' committed by the Bashi-bazouks last year, all over the country, were beyond description,' and mention ing that even respectable Turks had admitted to him that every possible horror had been perpetrated during the last two years,— Mr. Freeman further regrets to state that the Mahometan landlords of this part of Bosnia, ' according to common report, have but little respect for the wives and daughters of their dependents ;' but adds as a comment of his own, ' In a country, however, like Bosnia, where morality is at such a very low point, this last grievance, I should say, is not their greatest.' Now this statement as to the morality of the Bosnian rayah is cruelly untrue. Mr. Freeman has been doubtless misled by generalizing from the state of society in Serajevo, which is very different from that of the country districts. By travellers so well acquainted with Bosnia as Ami Boué, Thoemmel, and Roskievié, the peculiarly rigorous morality of the Bosnian rayahs, those at least belonging to the Orthodox Church, has been made the object of special eulogy. I will add that all that I know myself of Bosnian country life, and all that I know from residents in the country, whose experience of Bosnia is far greater than my own, bears out the evidence as to the purity of their family life. Not a grievance indeed ! Has Mr. Freeman never seen those sad, dull faces ? I commend to his notice the following description, written by Miss Irby, and referring to the Turkish inroad into the insurgent territory, that took place in this same neighbourhood shortly after our Vice-Consul had concluded his report on the earlier outrages perpetrated at Očievo and else- where :

*Vice-
Consul
Freeman's
attack on
the morals
of Bosnian
rayahs
rebutted.*

' I have seen several peasants from the plundered villages of Tišovo and Préodatz, and have conversed at leisure with three of the four women who were carried off by the Turks, and who escaped on Saturday night into Austrian territory. On Thursday afternoon the cry reached the villagers of Tišovo, " The Turkish soldiers are coming ! " Before the Turks reached the village all the inhabitants had run away except an old man of eighty and a few women and children. . . . Then these four women were questioned as to where were the men of the village and where was the insurgents' camp, and were threatened with the soldiers' knives to make them answer. They were carried off by the troops, driven with cruel force on the march by day and spending the nights in the tents with the soldiers. In speaking of those two nights in the Turkish tents they hid their faces and said, ' Better it would have been that we had perished ! If there had been fire we would have sprung into it, or if there had been water we would have drowned ourselves ; but there was neither fire nor water.' Their fear now is that God is angry with them, and will send them to hell for what they have suffered. The poor girl Stoja, whose figure bespoke despair, hid her tear-swollen face on the shoulder of the older woman. Their terror and confusion on arriving here are not to be described, but they were reassured by kindness. They are simple, modest, peasant women of the better class. But for their costume they might have been English cottagers. . . . On Saturday evening, in the dark, the women escaped to the woods. The fourth, a girl of fifteen, had suffered so terribly that she sank down in the flight. On reaching the frontier the other three found the mother of this girl, who had escaped previously. When she was told of the bitter sorrow of her daughter, the poor woman rushed back into the woods to seek her. No tidings have been heard of them since.'

The troops into whose power these unfortunate women fell were despatched into this district at the special instance of Mr. Consul Holmes—now Sir W. R. Holmes.

FOREIGN OFFICE AND BOSNIAN OUTRAGES.

Some effects of Mr. Holmes' 'urging the Vali.

LETTER X.

INTERVIEWS WITH THE BOSNIAN BEGS.

St. Roch, Croatia: *April* 17.

 HAD resolved to visit the Bosnian Begs and learn their opinions on the present situation from their own lips. Their head-quarters, and at the present moment the fountain-head of all the fanatical elements in Bosnia, is Kulen Vakup, of the promulgation of the Turkish Constitution at which place I have already given my readers some account.

To Kulen Vakup, therefore, I resolved to go. The Croats of the frontier at Lapatz and elsewhere assured me that it would be considerably easier to pay a visit to another world—to go to Bihać or to Livno was just possible ; but as to Kulen Vakup, no Giaour from beyond the borders had ventured there for the last year and a half. About three thousand of the worst fanatics in Bosnia, Begs who had lost their rayah serfs, Mahometan villagers dispossessed by the insurgents, townspeople whose bigotry had at all times been conspicuous even in Bosnia, were crowded within its walls, and if I went my head would be added to a considerable collection already accumulated by the local Begs.

Now, as I had already learned from my Mahometan friend at Czerni Potuk that some of his relations across the border were only just waiting for the first Englishman they saw, and as I was not ignorant that the head of at least one Giaour had been kicked about the streets of Vakup a few days previously, I thought it advisable to take every reasonable precaution before trusting myself in this Bosnian hornets' nest. Accordingly I had a letter drawn up in the choicest Bosniac, and addressed to the 'Right Hand of the Sultan in Kulen Vakup,' stating that an Englishman with an English passport, duly viséd at the Ottoman Embassy in London, was desirous to pay a visit to his city, but, having heard that there might be some difficulties in the way of such a visit, wished to know if the Mudir was willing to guarantee his personal security.

This missive I despatched to Vakup by a Turkish *employé*, a Christian, who, with his brother, also in the Turkish service, are the only two outsiders who dare trust their heads in the town ; while among the Mahometan burghers only two merchants who are less bigoted than the rest continue their intercourse with Christendom. The letter despatched, as it was my intention first to

Note (right margin):

LETTER X.

Warnings against visiting Vakup.

I address a letter to the Right Hand of the Sultan in Kulen Vakup.

*My coming
impatiently
awaited by
Mahometan
Bosniacs.*

complete my investigation into the outrages at Očievo
and elsewhere, I left the Croatian frontier village of
Lapatz to return a week later and learn the result of my
negotiation.

On my return to Lapatz I found the whole place agog
with the news that the Turks were awaiting my arrival
with feverish impatience, that messages had been sent to
the Austrian authorities to know when they might hope
to see me, that the Kaimakams, or chief officials, from
Bihać and Petrovatz and elsewhere had flocked to Vakup
to meet me, and, in short, that I was looked upon there
as a kind of Saviour of Society !

It appears that the Bosnian Mahometans of Kulen
Vakup and elsewhere, cut off for nearly two years by the
insurrection and their fear of the Croatian 'grenzers' from
the outside world, impoverished by the loss of their rayahs
and the destruction of their property, hailed the appearance of the first stranger among them—and that stranger
an Englishman—as a sign of approaching deliverance,
and, interpreting my letter by the light of their extravagant
wishes, regarded my mission, and persisted to the end in
so regarding it, not (as indeed it was) as a purely personal
undertaking of my own, but as official, and of deep political import to themselves.

Accordingly I found a letter, written in antique[1]
Cyrillian characters—your Bosnian Mahometans know
nothing of Osmanlì or Arabic—awaiting me 'from the

---

[1] The characters in which this
letter was written are of a kind
peculiar to the Bosniac Mahometans, and differ so considerably
from the ordinary Cyrillian, in use
among the Orthodox Slavs as to
be quite illegible to them. It is
only merchants of the border towns
who, from their commercial con-
nection with Bosnia, are able to
read this writing; Slavonic professors even have confessed to me
their inability to read it.

Mudir of the Ottoman Czar in Kulen Vakup.' On the cover of this precious document was written—

'OFFICIAL.
> '*This letter is to be given*
> '*to*

'THE CZAR OF ENGLAND AND EVENSA ARTURA.'

And here is a translation of what I found inside.

'*THE MUDIR OF THE OTTOMAN CZAR AT VAKUP,*
> '*to*

'*THE KING OF ENGLAND AND EVENSA ARTURA.*

'I have received thy letter, conveyed to me by George Pavićić, and I have understood what thou writest to me, that thou wouldst willingly come here to Vakup as Imperial Ambassador (*kao Carski Poslanik*), but that, notwithstanding, thou hast heard that there be evil-disposed persons in this city; therefore do I say that those who speak thus speak falsely; for our wishes are friendly, and to him that cometh in the name of two Empires let there be no fear.'

So true it is that some have greatness thrust upon them! Who the *two* Emperors were whose commission I was supposed to hold I have never quite been able to determine, but I think I can set my readers' minds at rest as to the 'Emperor of England.' The Czar of England in the eyes of all true Vakupers is, as I have already intimated in a former letter, no one else than His Most Gracious Majesty the Sultan—though with infinite politeness they admit the co-existence of our '*King*.'

Under the circumstances there was nothing for it but to put a bold face on the matter and accept my new character, whatever it might be. One of the two Christian *employés* of the Turks, Mili Pavićić, who is in great favour with the Vakupers, but had not been able to set

LETTER
X.

*Necessary
precautions.*

foot in their town for the last year for fear of compromising himself on the Croatian side of the border and sharing the fate of a Turkish spy from the insurgents and their friends, readily volunteered to accompany me, and was invaluable as a guide and interpreter. His brother George, who has never broken off his communication with the Turks, and who, in fact, was in Vakup when the Bashi-bazouks brought in the head of the village elder from Očievo, I sent on to inform the Turks of my coming.

Next I took the precaution to orientalize my personal appearance as much as possible by enfolding my too Western hat in a puggaree, and arraying myself in a gorgeous mantle of marvellous make and scarlet lining, with the antecedents of which I need not trouble my readers, but which, I flatter myself, had something Beg-like in its colour and dimensions, and which certainly inspired no small amount of admiration in the bosoms of true believers. Before all things it was necessary not to appear in the garb of an ordinary Giaour !

*Dreams
and omens.*

So we started on foot, expecting to meet an escort at the frontier ; but none arrived, which was a little ominous under the circumstances. 'Do you know,' said my guide, 'that my wife tried hard to keep me from going with you to-day, for she had dreamed that a serpent stung me on the way and that I fell down dead?' We passed through a long stretch of waste lands which the Vakupers, who are in mortal fear of the insurgents, dare not work. An hour or so later we came to some fields still cultivated, and passed by some Mahometan peasants armed to the teeth, but they knew Pavičić, and allowed us to pass. In a narrow lane nearing the descent towards Vakup we had a more formidable encounter. A man in dingy Redif clothing, but with the half turban of a Bashi-ᴊazouk on his head, and with one of the most diabolical expressions of countenance that I have ever set eyes on, walked straight in our path with a gun and fixed bayonet. Though I will confess to a feeling of alarm at his appearance, I walked on, and was preparing to allow him the usual elbow-room accorded by one passer-by to another, and with as much seeming *nonchalance* as if this were my usual morning's stroll, when my guide whispered imperatively, 'Stand to the hedge!' I took his advice, but not a moment too soon. The fanatic was already raising his bayonet to stab me. 'Dog of a Giaour!' he muttered, and without looking to right or left marched on.

From the brow of a hill the first view of Kulen Vakup broke upon me, and its position is one of the most beautiful that can be imagined. The little town is huddled on an island of the Unna, with its peaked tops of dark woodwork and white soaring minarets set off by emerald streams, meadow land, and tree-covered heights, the fruit trees now in the first blossom of spring. On either side and all around are considerable mountains. On a small rock at one end of the town is the old Castle of Avala, now mostly dismantled. Towering over a precipice on the other side are the still magnificent ruins of Ostrovizza, an old castle of Bosnian kings, and later of the Venetians. From a narrow gorge a little further up the valley the Unna leaps·among the green meadow lands below in a beautiful cascade.

We now perceived that our arrival had been signalled to the Turks from Ostrovizza. The whole town was astir to welcome me, and a Turkish Kolash riding up the hill insisted on my mounting his beautiful Arab.

'Effendi,' he said, 'when first my eyes rested upon

H

LETTER
X.

*Received
with ova-
tion by offi-
cials, sol-
diers, and
Mahometan
population.*

your red mantle I doubted not who approached, for as
you stand before me now, even so had you appeared to
me in the visions of the night.'

Both he and the other officials were warm in their
protestations that, had they known of my coming, they
would have sent a guard of honour to escort me from
the frontier ; and it turned out that my letter, which
should have arrived the day before, had not been received, and in fact the messenger, who had delayed on
the other side of the border, only came up after our
arrival.

At the bridge over the Unna and the narrow portal
of the town the Redifs and townspeople were drawn up
on either side of the way to receive me, the soldiers presenting arms as I passed. Then a band of drummers
and trumpeters formed in front and blew and beat the
Bosnian devil's-tattoo before me, winding up with a
magnificent flourish as I dismounted from my coal-black
steed at the official residence. But I need not trouble
you with all the official hobnobbings, and salutes, and
blowing of trumpets with which my humble presence in
Kulen Vakup was honoured, down to the final escort of
Redifs that accompanied me to the frontier on my return
journey. Suffice it to say that had I been the Padishah
himself they could hardly have done more.

*Grant au-
diences to
the Begs.*

What is more to the purpose, the exalted ideas which
the Turks possessed of my powers and dignities enabled
me to prosecute my inquiry with complete success. I
had interviews with, or rather granted audiences to, the
Begs and the Mahometan merchants to my full content-
ment, and heard from their own lips their grievances,
their hopes and fears, and their views on things in
general. The main ingredients of society here are, first,

a very small Osmanlì element, due to the presence of about 150 Redifs and their officer in the town, an element otherwise solely represented by the Mudir, who is here a mere puppet in the hands of the Begs and native Mahometan Bosniacs, who, as my readers are aware, are of Slavonic race, and not in any sense Turks. Of the natives, who in normal circumstances form the entire population, three classes may at present be distinguished. First there are the Begs, or great landholders, the old feudal nobility of Bosnia under a Mahometan guise, these nearly all belonging to the great family of Kulenović, the most powerful and numerous of the noble families of Bosnia ; next are the merchants and lesser tradesmen ; and inferior to them a crowd of Mahometan villagers from the suburbs and surrounding country who have taken refuge in Kulen Vakup from the insurgents, who in many cases have burnt their villages, but, as far as I could learn, without any other circumstances of atrocity. Besides these there are a few rayahs who, having better masters than the average, have not fled.

LETTER X.

The population of Kulen Vakup.

I received several of the Begs, mostly of the Kulenović family, in audience in the official residence. I·said that the English people had heard that there was much misery in Bosnia, and that they wished to know whether an end could not be put to it. 'Yes,' they said, 'they had suffered much.' One had lost so many houses and villages, and another so many ; and,·worse than all, their rayah serfs had fled, and there was no one now to till their fields for them, while others had turned Haiduks (brigands) and robbed and threatened them every day. Was that not misery enough? I held up a spray of blackthorn in full bloom (one must harangue these old-world folk in Eastern fashion), and said, 'You see these

Conversation with the Begs.

blossoms. I picked them on my way here amongst your untilled fields. Spring has come. Why should not the land bloom again as this spray? You have had your winter, and cold enough it has been. Surely you must be ready for the spring of peace? You are impoverished and ruined by the flight of the rayah. Why not hold out your hand to him and welcome his return?'

'They can return to-morrow,' they replied with one accord, 'and we shall be only too glad to see them back—but on the old footing.'

'But do not think,' said old Mahomed Beg Kulenović, who was one of the chief speakers, and by no means one of the worst of the Begs—' do not think that their lot will be the same. Yes, we will receive them back; we will not harm them or their wives or their children; but their lot will never be so favourable as before.' And this he said with determined emphasis.

'Will you take more from them,' I asked, 'if they return?'

'No,' was the short reply; 'we will not take more, but their lot will be worse.'

'Property is property,' remarked another, sententiously.

I observed that we had very much the same idea in England, that with us, too, there were great landowners—Begs—and their rayahs But our rayahs did not fly or turn Haiduk; they paid more to their Begs without grumbling. And why? Because in England everything was regular. The Begs gave the rayahs a writing that said what they must pay and when they must pay it. The Beg had his right and the rayah had his. It was arbitrariness and irregularity in demands which roused the discontent of the rayah more even than the amount paid.

This produced a certain impression. I then asked them, if they really were willing to see the rayahs back, how it was that we in England had heard that returning rayahs had been maltreated. Some rayahs had returned, so we had heard, near Kulen Vakup itself, and had rebuilt their villages. And what had happened? Their villages had been reburnt, and the Christian villagers had fled once more beyond the border.

This allusion to the recent outrages at Očievo and elsewhere took the Begs visibly aback. They were silent for a while, and then one said that the whole account was false. But Halil Beg, one of the worst characters present, simply scowled.

'We know,' I said, 'that Bosnia is the lion that guards the gate of Stamboul (a favourite boast among the native Bosniacs). But the lion is surrounded by bears and mountain wolves,[1] and what can he do against such odds? You think that England can help you. But England is, as a whale, mighty in the waters; the lion is strong upon the land; but if the lion is overmatched how can the whale aid him? Let the lion therefore make peace with the mountain wolves, lest the bears devour him!'

The Bosnian Begs understood the parable, but replied—'Yes, Bosnia is the lion that guards the gate of Stamboul; you have spoken truly. But he lion shall eat up the mountain wolves. And as to Austria, our Czar will never grant permission to theirs to send troops into Bosnia. No, never!' The Begs still hold to their persuasion that all the European monarchs are obedient vassals of the Sultan!

As to putting the Bosnian Christians in any sense

[1] Mountain wolves, the name by which the Bosnian Mahometans speak of the insurgents.

LETTER
X.

*Equality of
rayahs be-
fore the law.*

*How viewed
by Bosnian
Mahome-
tans.*

on a level with true believers, the Begs would not hear of it.

On this head I cannot do better than give you the words of Ahmed Abdughić, the leading merchant of the place, and by no means so bigoted as many—'a Turk,' as he was described to me by an inhabitant of Lapatz, 'among fifty thousand.'

'Rather than submit to that,' he replied, 'if that is what is meant by the new Constitution, we will shut ourselves up in our houses, with our wives and our children, and with our own hands we will slay our wives and our children, and last of all we will cut our own throats with our own handjars.'[1]

There is something grand and terrible in this Essene-like resolution of fanaticism which must at least command respect. For these are not idle words. I do not doubt that in certain eventualities some at least of the leading Mahometans of Bosnia are prepared to carry them into effect. Yet Allah is great, and 'Kismet' greater, and children of the Prophet not less fanatical have before now bowed their heads to the irresistible decrees of Fate. Were it once conclusively demonstrated to the Begs and other Bosnian fanatics that Destiny was against them, without doubt the large majority would submit to *force majeure.*

But I think I have clearly proved to my readers from the lips of those who are the mouthpieces of the dominant caste that at the present moment the Bosnian Begs have learned nothing and have forgotten nothing. They will not, except under extreme compulsion, consent in any way to ameliorate the condition of the rayah, to grant him equality before the law, to respect his religion, or set a limit to their feudal licence. As a serf

---

[1] Sword-knives worn by Mahometan Bosnians.

and pariah he went forth, as a serf and pariah he shall return.   Before the first foundations of peace and security can be laid in Bosnia, *force majeure* is an absolute necessity.

Force majeure; but whence is it to come ?

There is at present no one element in Bosnia strong enough to obtain a mastery over the rest.   The insurrection, though gaining ground every day, is too weak in siege material and the sinews of regular war even to hope to obtain possession of the larger towns, where the armed native Mahometans and Turkish troops are at present congregated.   Serbia has retired from the contest ; but if, as is most probable, she should renew it, Austro-Hungary would never consent to a Serbian annexation of Bosnia.   Montenegro will certainly annex new cantons in the Herzegovinian Alps before she lays down her arms ; but this does not touch Bosnia.   From Russia, Bosnia is too remote, and, besides, comparative abstention from Bosnian affairs is the price paid by Russia for Austro-Hungarian neutrality.

Of course we know the official theory—the theory of statesmen who take their ideas about Bosnian affairs from our Embassy at Constantinople and our Consulate at Serajevo—the comfortable notion that the Imperial Ottoman authorities, backed by the Imperial Ottoman troops, are capable and willing to break the opposition of the Mahometan Slavs, and to introduce the new *régime* of toleration—even-handed justice and parliamentary liberty—into this pandemonium of fanaticism and tyranny.

But I am coming to another part of my evidence.

As to the part which the Osmanli is playing in Bosnia at the present moment, and as to the close

LETTER
X.

*Tyranny
of Begs con-
demned by
moderate
Mahome-
tans.*

alliance that he has struck with the worst and most
fanatical elements in the province, I obtained some
astonishing revelations in the course of my conversations
with the chief representatives of the mercantile classes
in Kulen Vakup. I visited and spoke with several of
these, and my guide and interpreter, who is on the best of
terms with them, was very useful in obtaining their confidence. Their opinions were very different from those
of the Begs, whom they hate and detest, and far more
reasonable. Méchmed Omić, the leading merchant of
the place, was particularly moderate and sensible, and I
will give you his views as a good sample of those of a
respectable part of the Mahometan *bourgeoisie.* He
said : 'We are ruined ; trade is stopped ; public security
in abeyance ; and who is to blame? First and foremost,
the Begs. It is their savagery and their oppression of
the rayah that has brought all this evil upon us.' He
instanced Tahir Beg Kulenović as the worst of the petty
tyrants of the neighbourhood. I now heard deeds that
had hitherto rested on rayah evidence corroborated from
a Mahometan source. Omić was a staunch Mahometan ;
but he held in detestation the insults which this ruffian
perpetually heaped on the religion of the rayah.

*A Mahome-
tan mer-
chant on the
misdoings
of the Begs.*

I will give one example of what Tahir was in the
habit of doing. Ermanja, the ruins and desecrations of
whose church I have already described to you, was this
Beg's property. Whenever he visited it he rode on
horseback into the church, and profaned it. After that
he was in the habit of dismounting, and, seizing the
priest's vestments, he made them into a kind of saddle,
set them on the priest's back, and then mounting on it
himself, made the wretched pope crawl along on all
fours and serve the purpose of a beast till the poor man

sank with exhaustion. Deeds like these old Méchmed Omić held in abhorrence.

' And how,' I asked, 'is it possible for the Begs to do all this if even Mahometans are against it ? '

'Because,' said he, 'they have their armed following' —(this armed following, I may explain to your readers, is in Bosnia nothing else than the Bashi-bazouks)—'men from the lowest classes, who do their bidding for pay and plunder.' But he added that they could not do all this were it not for the connivance of the Osmanlì officials. The native Slavonic lords of Bosnia hate the Osmanlì, it is true, as an alien intruder. But since Omar Pasha's days they have found it advisable to effect a compromise with the powers that be. The Begs are, or at any rate were, rich, and there is hardly a Turkish official in the province who is not in their pay. The Mudir at Kulen Vakup, though an Osmanlì by birth, is the tool of the dominant caste. But what Méchmed Omić stated of the Kaimakam of a neighbouring town,[1] also belonging to the Stamboul bureaucracy, is still more damning, and agrees but too well with the evidence I took down from the Očievo refugees. This Kaimakam, in league with the worst of the neighbouring Begs, appears to have played a leading part in the second day's arson, butchery, and rapine at that unhappy village ; and I have already told you that Ali Beg Kulenović, a fat, jolly old Bosnian, who can drink his five bottles of rum a day, but is by no means a bad specimen of a Bosnian landlord, during

---

[1] I understood at the time that this was the Kaimakam of Pétro-vatz, but Mr. Freeman, who knew him personally, vouches for his character and brings forward an instance of his humanity, which I have already cited on rayah evidence. It is, however, more probable that I was in error as to the locality, than that a man of Omić's character should have invented the story.

LETTER
X.

*Part played
by local re-
presentative
of Turkish
government
in the recent
massacres.*

the minor outrages of the first day's raid on the villagers distinguished himself by saving some girls and women from the usual fate. Well, if Omić's account be correct, he tried on the second day to exert his influence once more in favour of comparative moderation with the mingled gang of Redifs and Bashi-bazouks. But the Kaimakam, the representative of the Turkish Government, was for letting the ruffians have free vent. Words passed between the two, and as the Kaimakam was seconded by the more villanous among the Begs, he was able to seize fat Ali, who has since been languishing in a Turkish prison. Of the complicity between the Turkish Government and the worst elements among the natives its very last official act in the Herzegovina has given new and convincing proof. Two of the Begs—Redji-pašić and Rizvanbegović—who are among the most notorious oppressors of the rayahs, and whose iniquities were among the principal causes of the first outbreak of the insurrection in the Herzegovina, have just been appointed to the command of the irregulars in that province.

*Monstrous
idea that
pacification
of Bosnia
should be
looked for
from Os-
manlìs.*

From what I have already said my readers will have perceived that the pacification of Bosnia is hardly likely to be accomplished, as English diplomatists seem to imagine, by these Osmanlì officials, nor is it likely that ravishers, robbers, and assassins should be punished by their sworn accomplices. Therefore, as far as I can see, the only possible solution of the present difficulty is Austrian occupation. Many of the lesser Begs, as well as the Mahometan merchants both in Bosnia and in the Herzegovina, are, as I have the best reasons for assuring you, ready to welcome such an occupation. So far as the Bosnian insurgents are concerned, I have the authority of one of their chiefs for saying that they would loyally submit to such a measure—indeed, they would have very little choice in the matter. The Turkish Government, thoroughly occupied with the Russian war, would never attempt a serious opposition, though it is true that feints of possible resistance have been made on the frontier near Ragusa, where some new guard-houses have been constructed. Austria might well act in this matter as the executor of Europe. The aim of our own Government, the aim of all men who value the interests of humanity or the lasting peace of Europe, should be to induce the Austrian Government to fulfil this civilizing mission.

The crying necessity of the present moment, as I cannot too often repeat, is the application of *force majeure* to control the fanatic elements of the province and to expel the present Osmanlì rulers, who prolong their precarious dominion in Bosnia by pitting caste against caste and creed against creed. A probationary period of control, the enforcement of public security, let us hope education of a largely secular kind, would pave the way for ultimate reconciliation between the warring elements of Bosnia, and render home rule possible at last. Both Mahometans and Christians in Bosnia are Slavs, both hate the alien Turkish intruder, and both, even now, are beginning to weary of civil strife.

As to the probable results of such a period of European or Austrian control on the balance of political power in Bosnia and the numerical strength of the various sectaries, I have obtained here at Kulen Vakup, and along the Bosnian frontier, a variety of data which strikingly corroborate a view that I have already expressed elsewhere, namely, that such a period of control

LETTER
X.

Austrian occupation only solution of the difficulty.

Probable effects of Austrian government on Bosnia.,

LETTER
X.

*Probable
effect of
Austrian
rule in
largely in-
creasing the
Christian
element.*

and security would have the effect of largely strengthen-
ing the Christian element in the province, at present
numerically almost as two to one compared with the
Mahometan.   Public security would enable foreign capital to develop the vast mineral and other resources of
the Bosnian mountains, and capital is Christian.   All
economic laws would work in favour of the non-fatalistic,
and therefore most enterprising, part of the population.
It is not, perhaps, known beyond the Croatian frontier
that in the poor and arid tracts of the old Military Frontier, thousands of hard-working peasants are only waiting
for Austrian occupation to emigrate in a body into Bosnia, and till the rich and at present uncultivated lands
beyond the border.

At Udbina I have already given you an instance of a
Mahometan population which, coming under the Austrian
sceptre, has gradually re-adopted Christianity.   The forefathers of the native Mahometans of Bosnia renegaded
originally from a Puritan form of Christianity ; and what
was possible in times past may be possible in the future.
Even the Begs, and notably some of the Kulenović
family, have not forgotten their Christian ancestry, and
repeat perhaps even now the words of that fatalistic
chant sung by their fathers only a generation back, when
feudal and old-believing Bosnia marched against the
hosts of the ' Giaour-Sultan ' Mahmoud,

> Our fathers lost their faith of yore,
> And we, perchance, can do no more.

Kulen Vakup, as I have already said, is even in Bosnia
celebrated for the peculiar rigour of its Mahometanism.
Indeed, in a certain sense, it may be called the Delphi
of Mahometan Bosnia, since here exists what I can only

describe as a Mahometan oracle. In the last century a pious family of the town made a pilgrimage to the Caaba, and came home with such an odour of sanctity that they have ever since been regarded as soothsayers. There are two pythonesses of this family who go of nights to the mosque, when they bow themselves before certain holy stones, and become inspired of the oracles which they impart next morning to those who have sought their advice about futurity. Of these holy stones I learned that they have on them old Arabic inscriptions, and that they were brought in ancient times from near Medina. ' Once,' say the Bosniacs, 'Saint Mahomet was out hunting and climbed up on to a rock to rest,' and ever since this rock, from which the fragments in the mosque are taken, has been esteemed holy. They keep also in this same mosque certain smooth pebbles in a net which the true-believers of Vakup let down into the water in. times of drought, and by this means obtain abundant rain ; but great care is requisite, for if he that lets down the net were to let it slip and the stones were to go to the bottom, then—so I was told—the deluge would come over again, and Kulen Vakup and all the world would be drowned. I have not seen the pebbles, but even a Giaour may have that privilege by paying down a thousand ducats !

In Bosnia, in general, women are veiled and se-cluded as they are veiled and secluded nowhere else in Turkey in Europe. In Kulen Vakup their seclusion is said to be greater than anywhere else in Bosnia. It is far more rigorous than even at the neighbouring town of Bihać for example. Except their mid-day pilgrimage to the mosque, when no man may look on them, they are entirely confined to the harem, and only on St.

George's Day—mark how these fanatics still reckon by Christian festivals—are they allowed, as a great concession, to walk about in the gardens. Indeed, the greatest objection urged by Vakupers against Austrian occupation is that it would interfere with the privacy of their women. Yet even here, in this nest of fanaticism, there is a saying (to be heard in other parts of Bosnia), 'Your cross does not weigh a hundred okas;' and true believers who have never read the Essays of Elia hesitate not to repeat a suggestive little adage, which may be translated—

What's the cross?—a piece of wood !
And sucking pig, they say, is good.

LETTER XI.

FREE BOSNIA REVISITED (I).

May 12.

LTHOUGH I have already acquainted my readers with the more melancholy results of my recent journey, they may not be displeased to obtain some less painful experiences of Free Bosnia 'revisited,' and may pardon a few disquisitions on insurgent politics suggested in the course of my recent rambles. The parts of the insurgent territory through which I made my way lie almost entirely outside the districts described on my previous visit, and in some respects they surpassed what I had seen before in natural beauty and in the strength of the citadels of freedom.

There are certain pseudo-philanthropists—mostly of a diplomatic turn of mind—who from time to time ask in-

LETTER
XI.

*Historical
justification
of Bosnian
insurrec-
tion.*

dignantly how the Bosniac rayahs could have committed
the mad folly of rising against their masters, when they
must know that it is beyond their power to snatch
Bosnia from the Turkish grip.   (As if it had ever entered
the minds of the insurgents to imagine that they could
seize the whole province !) To all such the history and
present condition of the neighbouring tracts of Dalmatia
and Croatia, that one must. pass to approach the insurgent district, supply, to my thinking, a most eloquent reply.   It is really hard to know when you actually
cross the Bosnian frontier on this side.   There is no great
river to mark the boundary.   Before and behind you—
different as is the political aspect of the two countries—
Nature still wears the same. As you climb the first steep of
Bosnian soil and look back on the Dalmatian and Croatian
border-lands that you are quitting, you see spread out
behind you just the same landscape that lies before you.
There are the same ' polje ' valleys, the same limestone
rocks, the same green forest-mountains; the people
are the same—in language, in physique, to a great
extent, in dress.   How, indeed, should they be different?
Only a few generations back they too were rayah subjects of the Sultan, and the lands they tilled were under
the Vizier of Bosnia.   Do you ask how they changed
their lot and passed under the sceptre of the Hapsburghs?
The diplomatist will answer, ' by Imperialist victories.'
The natives of these frontier districts tell you a truer tale.
They tell you that their frontier was ' rectified,' because
their grandfathers and great-grandfathers took the ' recti-
fication ' into their own hands.   These frontier districts of
Dalmatia and Croatia have, in fact, been disintegrated
piecemeal from the Turkish lands behind them by just
the same process by which the little mountain tract that

I have called ' Free Bosnia ' is being carved out to-day. There is nothing new about the present insurrection ; there is nothing new about the armed peasant bands that have excited the rage of the English Consul at Serajevo. Ask any Croatian or Dalmatian peasant of the border-country, and he will tell you that the beech-forests and limestone peaks that girdle his mountain valley sheltered just such insurgent ' chétas' as lurk to-day among the opposite Bosnian ranges, and that the rude Bosnian Vojvodes are only imitating at the present moment the work of liberation which Croat and Dalmatian guerilla chiefs—such as Janković and Smilianić—a descendant of whom I have already mentioned among the Bosnian heroes of the hour,—effected in the Lika and elsewhere.

LETTER XI.

Nothing new about the Bosnian insurrection.

As to the desirableness of the work, no one can doubt it who has visited these once Bosnian districts that have been added to Christendom and Austria by this gradual process of disintegration continued through two centuries. I have just passed through the flourishing Croatian village of Lapatz, reclaimed from the Turk almost within the memory of man by these same insurgent ' chétas.' Up to that time the whole land was the property of two Begs —a Kulenović and a certain Ibrahim Bašić, whose ' cardak,' or country house, was on the site now occupied by the Pravoslav Church—you can see the landmarks of the two Mahometan lords still. There were then in the whole valley, exclusive of the residences of the two Begs, exactly nine houses ; there is now a population of nearly four thousand.

Districts reclaimed from Turks in former times by same process.

I started on foot from Serb, on the Croatian frontier, to make my way to the great insurgent stronghold of Sienitza Grad, distant about a day's journey, on the summit of a mountain of the same name. Two Bosnian

I

guides and a Croat, an ex-inspector of forests, accompanied me. Croatia was soon left behind us, and we
were making our way over an easy mountain swell
covered with stunted beech woods, overgrown with prim-
roses, blue hepaticas, yellow anemones, and violets,
which perfumed every mountain breeze. Here and there
were scattered grey boulders, from whose chinks and
crevices the ' zelembatz,' the great green lizard of these
lands, was perpetually darting into the sunlight, agleam
with gold and emerald. Presently came a steep descent
to the rivulet of Trogerla, which plunges forth, as its
name implies, from three grottoes in the rock ; then a
mysterious roaring sound filled me with wonder and
expectation, and, climbing round a rocky angle of the
gully, there broke upon my view something more like a
miracle than anything that I ever remember having seen.

*Source of
the Kerka.*

This was the source of the Kerka, a superb cascade, or
rather series of cascades, leaping forth—but from where?
The solid rock seemed to be converted into a roaring
cataract as by magic ! Here was a river darting with
millstream force from the roots of a cliff in which there
was no crevice visible, squirting forth from a myriad of
imperceptible pores—as a natural phenomenon it seemed
almost uncanny.

*Signs of
Turkish
havoc.*

Alas ! one cannot wander far in this country without
having other sights forced on one's notice besides the
marvels of Nature. The mountain path we followed led
presently between the blackened ruins of two burnt
villages—Veliki and Mali Svietnić—burnt by the Turks
September 20, 1876. The inhabitants had all fled in time,
but I passed the spot on the hillside where two herdsmen
were surprised and butchered.

Our way now led through mysterious labyrinths of

beech and pine, and then up a tremendous mountain steep to the insurgent stronghold, Sienitza Grad. So admirable is the position that up to the very last moment of our ascent no sign of human habitation was perceptible, much less of a camp where a hundred and fifty armed men were congregated. Only on reaching the very spit of the mountain a crater-like hollow broke upon my view, scooped out of the mountain summit by the elements, and in which were clustered the huts of the insurgent 'chéta.' It was indeed a very eagle's nest, commanding far and wide, range upon range, the mountains of Free and Turkish Bosnia, cleft asunder far below by the stupendous rock chasm of the Unnatz; while halfway down the mountain steep it overlooked another spectacle, which might well keep alive in those rude bosoms the spirit of resistance—the charred chaotic remnants of the Christian village of Boboljuša. For a while drifting folds of fleecy cloud floated beneath our gaze, obscuring the Alpine panorama in a sea of sunset gold; and then through a rift in the misty veil, set as in an aureole of consecrated light, there opened out far below a last evening glimpse of this small free land. It would have been hard, as one stood amidst that rugged garrison and looked down from that solemn cloudland citadel, not to have caught some inspiration from the mountain air of liberty.

The local Vojvoda, Paulo Vukanović, seeing a stranger arrive, stepped forward and, without further ado, welcomed me into his hut, after the usual hospitable fashion of Free Bosnia; and, during the two days that in the prosecution of my researches I remained his guest, never ceased to treat me with all the good cheer that insurgent resources could supply. Though it happened to be a

LETTER XI.

Insurgent Chéta of Sienitza Grad.

Entertained by Vojvode.

1 2

Greek Church fast, which both he and his followers observed with a rigour that surprised me, he killed a lamb for his guest, and despatched one of his men to catch most excellent trout for me in the Unnatz. Paulo was quite a young fellow, a native Bosniac (as were all his followers to a man), born at Petrovatz, but who had spent most of his life at Mostar. I found him extremely amiable, not a bit fanatical, and by no means illiterate. Wherever he went he carried about with him a well-worn volume of Serbian heroic lays, whole pages of which he would repeat to me by rote with a kind of simple delight that did one's heart good.

We had many talks about the prospects of Free Bosnia, and I found that he shared to the full my opinion that the true policy of the insurgents was to aim at little, not to beat themselves against the bars in a vain attempt to conquer the whole province, but rather to form a small mountain State—a little Montenegro, which might gradually become the nucleus of something larger. I asked him what course the Bosnian insurgents would adopt in view of the probable occupation of the province by Austria, for I have no doubt that these mountaineers are in a position to make a very obstinate resistance even against regular troops ignorant of the intricacies of their strongholds. 'We would submit at once,' he replied, 'and willingly, too ; for we have never fought for anything else than guarantees of good government, which the Austrians would give us, but which the Turks neither will nor can.' But supposing this desirable solution was not forthcoming, and the struggle had to be continued, Vukanović, like all the other insurgent leaders with whom I have spoken, admitted that it was most necessary, if possible, to come to terms with the native

Mahometans and obtain their co-operation against the Osmanlì and the worst of the Begs.

LETTER
XI.

*Attitude of
insurgents
towards
native Ma-
hometans.*

For the Bosnian insurrection to attain success on a large scale such an understanding is indispensable, for it must be remembered that there is a very important distinction to be drawn between Bosnia and Herzegovina.

The Herzegovinian insurgents have achieved more striking successes against the Turks than their Bosnian brothers, not only because of their proximity to Montenegro, but because in the rural districts there are hardly any Mahometans.

But in Bosnia it is far otherwise. Here there is a very large rural Mahometan population, which to a great extent has neutralised the efforts of the rayah. And where, as in Southern Bosnia, the insurgents have achieved so much success as to carve out a little free district of their own, this success has been due to the fact that in this district there were no Mahometan peasants, and that the conditions of the struggle thus approached those of the Herzegovina. Nothing, for example, would seem more feasible than for the insurgents by concentrating their forces to have cleared the Kraina, or Turkish Croatia, of the enemy, and held this mountainous angle of country, which juts out into the friendly territory of Croatia, against all comers. But here are a number of small country towns and larger villages inhabited by Mahometans, and all the efforts of the insurgents have ended in the occupation of a few isolated mountain ranges.

But why, it may be asked, did not the insurgents effect a compromise here with the true-believers?

There is, as I have already intimated to my readers,

a party among the native Mahometans not by any means averse to joining hands with the rayah against the hated aliens, the Osmanli bureaucracy, as well as against the more tyrannous of the native Begs. And the insurgents on their side have not been by any means blind as to the advisability of such an agreement.

To what, then, is their failure due?

*Negotia-
tions
between in-
surgents
and native
Mahome-
tans.*

I have obtained most interesting evidence on this subject from the insurgent chief Hubmeier, a Slovene by birth, who has been the principal insurgent leader in that part of Bosnia. He said that he had entered into several promising negotiations with the native Mahometans, and even the landlords, but all had been frustrated by the want of unity amongst the insurgents. Thus he succeeded in putting himself in communication with a certain Suli Aga, a most influential Mahometan chief, of the important town of Novi. By means of an Austrian merchant who was a friend of both parties a meeting between the insurgent leader and the Aga was arranged and actually took place at Costainitza, across the Croatian border. Good-will was not wanting on either side, but the agreement shattered, like every other attempt at pacification in Bosnia, on the question of guarantees.

Speaking in the name of the Mahometan Slavs of his district, or at any rate of the more moderate among them, Suli Aga said, as nearly as Hubmeier could give me his words, ' If we submit to you or take your part, we want two things—not only that you should give us security that this agreement and every one of our privileges should be respected by all your bands, but also that you should show yourselves strong enough to protect us against the Osmanli. You are chief here, and I believe what you say ; but there are other Vojvodas who do not own your authority—what security can you give us against your own free-lances, and are you united enough to protect us from the Nizam? We would rather see you at our side than the Osmanlì, but at the same time we do not wish to share the fate of renegades.'

I could give you the particulars of another such negotiation entered into by another insurgent chief with some of the more moderate Mahometan Begs and Agas near Stari Maidan. The affair was taking a favourable turn when the Stamboul officials got wind of it.

Up to this point the Turkish Government had taken very little heed of the revolt in this district, but the instant this intelligence reached them they saw the necessity for energetic action. There is nothing that the Osmanlì so much fears in Bosnia as an *entente cordiale* between the native Slavs, Christian and Mahometan. The whole—the only—basis of Ottoman rule in Bosnia is the perpetual alienation of the rival sectaries among the natives. There is no more damning impeachment of Turkish rule in Bosnia than the fact that it is the direct interest of the governors to foment and render eternal the brutal fanaticism of the governed. Aliens as they are— with alien interests, an alien language, alien morals—they know that if Slavonic Christians and Slavonic Mahometans in Bosnia were once to patch up their mutual rivalries such a reconciliation would seal the fate of their alien *régime.* These parasites from Stamboul have battened, and batten every day, on the internecine feuds of unhappy Bosnia. The mutual hatred of Christian and Mahometan is their daily bread. It is not too much to say that there is not a murder of a rayah serf, a violation of a Christian

LETTER
XI.

*Attempts at
reconcilia-
tion between
rayah in-
surgents
and native
Mahome-
tans
thwarted by
Ottoman
employés.*

girl, a raid on a rayah village, but has its market value to the Ottoman *employé*.

Thus this negotiation between the insurgent and Mahometan chieftains was looked on by the Turkish officials—and looked on justly—as more dangerous to their interests than a dozen insurgent victories. The Stamboul authorities had hitherto contented themselves with looking on at the struggle in that district, not, perhaps, without some cynical complacency,—for why should not the Bosnian Slavs of either profession bleed each other if they chose? And if the horrors of this inter-necine war intensified the animosities of the opposing castes and creeds, might not the insurrection after all be playing into their own bureaucratic hands?

But affairs wore a very different complexion now that Christian and true-believer began to seek a reconciliation. The officials at Serajevo, who had hitherto left the armed native Mahometans to hold their own as best they might against the insurgent rayahs, on getting wind of this negotiation at once hurried 5,000 Nizams (or Turkish regulars) to the neighbourhood of Stari Maidan. The insurgents at the approach of this overwhelming force withdrew to their mountain fastnesses, and the native Ma ometans got up most loyal demonstrations of affec-tion for their Osmanli protectors.

'*Post*' and
'*telegraphs*'
*in insur-
gent dis-
trict.*

In the camp at Sienitza Grad every one took a most cheerful view of the situation, and I may mention as an example of the precaution they exercise against any sur-prise from the side of the Turks that a watch is kept day and night, and a telegraphic system of signals from mountain to mountain keeps the whole insurgent territory well informed as to every motion of the enemy. Every day, too, a post goes from end to end of Free Bosnia, calling at the various 'chétas'; and I may add that my hospitable chieftain resorted to a most irrefragable argument of coming victory, taking the shoulder-blade from the lamb of my repast and drawing therefrom most certain omens of the confusion of the Turks and the triumph of the Serbian cause.

LETTER
XII.

May 17.

AKING leave of my hospitable friends at Sienitza Grad, another beautiful day's walk brought me to the insurgent 'chéta' of Caménia, where the Pope Ilija Bilbija at present commands. It was a lovely spring evening when I arrived, and I found the whole troop assembled on a grassy mountain lawn engaged in athletic sports. Of course, what could an Englishman do but join them? And really, but for the outlandish costume of these 'muscular Christians,' one might just as well have been in the Vale of the White Horse. First we had 'metati'—nothing else, I can assure you, than the good old English game of ' putting the stone.' The insurgents showed great strength but little skill—

> Bosnian born and Bosnian bred,
> Strong i' the arm and weak i' the head,

as certain also of our own poets hath said. At any rate,

Athletic sports among the insurgents.

though I am by no means an athlete, I found that by a little judicious knack I could throw as far as the best, and felt rather like little Jack when he did the giant! Then we had football—a primitive football, with a ball compounded of insurgent caps, and with no goal in particular—but still football. Then there was another game of ' chevy,' the details of which are too long to describe here ; but all these sports have a real significance. I believe that there is no other people in Europe endowed so largely with the English love of field sports as these much-maligned Southern Slavs ; and surely it is a most hopeful sign. The traveller in the Black Mountain meets with just the same experience ; the same in the Herzegovina ; the same among even the grave Mahometans of Bosnia, who have inherited this along with many of their old Slavonic customs. The true believers of Kulen Vakup, for example, may be seen of an evening 'putting the stone' with a will. In the Croat villages just across the Bosnian border (and doubtless the same may be seen in Bosnia too) I found the lads gathered on the village green playing a game called ' lopta,' or ' crivat,' which is nothing else than a rudimentary form of cricket, with primitive bats, stumps, bowlers, wicket-keepers, fielders, all complete. May one perhaps look forward to the day when Bashi-bazouk and Rayah shall join their teams in less warlike contest, or even with prophetic eye decipher a challenge from the 'All-Bosnian Eleven' to the M.C.C.!

The night I passed in this camp was miserable enough, and made one realize the hardships these poor people must undergo. The pope's shed, where I slept, or tried to sleep, was a typhus hospital without doctors. But I had finished my investigations, and was glad to be off at a very early hour next morning.

Our way now led over the steeps of Mount Korita, through beautiful forest paths, there growing here and there among the trees one of the most delicious shrubs I have ever seen, covered with bunches of pink flowers that had all the scent of garden hyacinths.   Then we followed an ancient road—now a mere mule-track and impassable for vehicles, but showing here and there, eaten into the rock pavement, ancient wheel tracks—such as may be seen in the exhumed streets of Roman cities.   Further on was another trace of bygone industry and civilization—a well, or rather stone cistern, beside what once had been the highway, and (removed to a churchyard below) a square column that within the memory of man had stood beside the well.   My Bosniac guide said that there were five such columns along the road, and that he had followed it to the ruins of King Bela's castle, on a mountain

far in the interior of Bosnia.   Everybody knew, he said, that this was once the King's highway ; that King Bela had made the road, and when the Turks came he fled out of the country by it.   The only difficulty about the flight was, it seems, suggested by the King's daughter, who asked the pertinent question, ' What shall we do with the golden treasure, father ? '   ' Thou shalt become a dragon, my daughter,' grimly replied the Monarch, 'and keep it to the end of the world.'   So to this day in a cavern above the ruins of King Bela's castle of Germetz the royal serpent keeps watch and ward over her father's hoards.   But if any one who has been baptized shall discover the dragon and make the sign of the cross, the scales will fall from the beautiful princess, and he may obtain bride and dowry together.   So, at least, the Bosnian assured me, and I am convinced that he was a truthful man.

LETTER
XII.

*Monuments
of perished
civilization
in Bosnia.*

Yes—my Bosnian was right. These legends of dragon
guards and buried treasures and transformed princesses
have a truth and application in Bosnia as it exists
at this moment which even the most unskilled in
allegories may read and inwardly digest! Making one's
way along ruined highways, gazing on the monuments of
perished civilization, one has ample leisure to realize that
it is no fancied spell that locks up the treasures of this
rich land in the bowels of the earth. The myrmidons of
this dead weight of Oriental barbarism have blasted each
progressive effort of Bosnian industry more effectually
than all the fire-spitting phantoms of Oriental magic.
Arts and learning—what little there ever was in this unhappy land—have long since vanished, or left their traces
only in the vaults of some retired monastery or amid the
crumbling ruins of some feudal castle. In Serajevo, the
capital of the country, with a population of 60,000 souls,
there is not a single book shop, and books are seized
upon the frontier like so much contraband of war. The
rich frescoes of Bosnian kings and Serbian emperors are
mutilated with Turkish bullet-holes. History, geography,
everything that can expand the mind is hunted from the
schools ; science is unborn ; and the small fanatic training that the children do receive is worse than none at all.
This ruined highway through the wilderness is but a
sample of the industrial prostration of the whole land.
Wander where you will in Bosnia, it is still the same—
roads fallen to rack and ruin, bridges broken down, or
where some mightier work of engineering still withstands
the hand of time, like the massive stone bridges of Koinitza
or Mostar, the curious traveller discovers that they are
the handiwork of Serbian kings or Roman emperors.
The gold veins of the Bosnian mountains, which brought

LETTER
XII.

*Material
ruin of
Bosnia
under the
Turk.*

such wealth to Roman and Ragusan in former ages, the copious salt mines of Tuzla, the vast coal measures of the Bosna Valley, the neighbouring iron mines of Foinica, the quicksilver veins of Kreševo, known to be as rich as any in Europe—all alike are deserted, unworked, hermetically sealed.   Timber which might supply a hundred dockyards rots away year by year in the stately Bosnian forests because rivers which might be rendered navigable whirl their useless waters over rapids and shallows.   The one Bosnian railway that was to be has foundered, and every enterprise of foreign capital has foundered like it. English and German companies, tempted by these vast resources to risk the cost and labour of exploiting them, have seen their industry paralysed by want of roads, want of bridges, want of public security and public faith, and their money sucked away in the unfathomable sink of Imperial Ottoman corruption.   Look where one will in Bosnia, the melancholy conclusion is forced on one that the mediæval civilization of the Christian kingdom was distinctly on a higher level than the nineteenth century standard of the provincial Turk.

Is it Islâm, then, that is to blame? Is the Puritan service of the mosques so far below the *quasi* idolatry of Greek and Roman churches? Is Mahometanism *per se* more opposed to human science than the rival creeds? Most certainly not; and those who try to make the question of the future of these lands a religious question confuse and conceal the issues.   It is not Mahometanism itself that is so pernicious here ; but it is Mahometanism as impressed and perverted by the characteristics of the Ottoman race.   It is the race that determines the character of the religion, and not the religion the character of the race.   It is because the associations of the

Osmanlì lie with Asiatic stagnation—because as a race they are intolerant, unprogressive, and apparently incapable of taking a high culture—that their form of Mahometanism, the form which they have imposed upon the Bosnian Slavs, is prohibitive of progress.   So, too, on the other side, the question is not whether certain low forms of Christianity are peculiarly favourable to culture, but whether the races which profess these creeds are by their historical antecedents associated with the cause of civilization.   And undoubtedly they are bound up in every possible way with that civilization which, of all the civilizations that have ever existed in the world, has shown itself most capable of progress—the Greco-Roman. While the Christian creeds under notice are borne along in a great current which they can neither fathom nor control, the Mahometanism of the Ottoman lies rotting in the slough of Oriental stagnation.   These Christian creeds move with the times, and may be trusted to effect their own 'euthanasia'—that happy despatch which Slavonic Romanism has already effected on itself at Ragusa and elsewhere, and which Slavonic orthodoxy is accomplishing more slowly but not less surely in the schools of Neusatz and Belgrade.   But Islâm under the Turks is a mere dead weight of helpless inertia.   The question is not, and never was, one between Christianity as such and Mahometanism as such, but one between Western progress and Asiatic stagnation.   Turn out the Osmanlì bureaucracy from Bosnia, establish Western control, cut off the native Mahometan from his Oriental associations, and it may yet be found that Islâm in Bosnia is no more opposed to liberal ideas than it was amongst the Moors of Spain.

But I am recalled from such more general reflections

on the creeds which to-day contend for mastery in Bosnia, to the relics of something older than either Mahometanism or Christianity, without the mention of which these little sketches of Free Bosnia would be incomplete.

Our way led us to a retired gorge where are clustered one or two huts belonging to the village of Resanovce that had escaped the Turkish destroyer when he burnt the rest of this straggling hamlet. Here we stopped to ask for water, which was brought us fresh and cool from a cavern in the rocky steep above. They said it came from 'the Vila's basin.' Now as the Vila is nothing else than the nymph of Slavonic heathendom, my curiosity was naturally aroused, and by the exercise of a little judicious diplomacy I succeeded in obtaining from a native of the village a full and particular account of the personal appearance and attributes of the guardian nymph of the grot. At first the good man was a little shy, but when he saw that I took a sympathetic interest in the Vila and her doings, he unbosomed to me all he knew about her with an air of profound faith, which showed that the Vila is believed in as sincerely at Resanovce as was any nymph of pagan days.

The Vila or Slavonic nymph: her grot at Resanovce.

Her personal appearance.

The Vila who lives in Resanovce Cave has long fair hair and blueish eyes, and is clad in a light white smock. My informant could not swear that any one he knew had seen her, but it was a matter of public notoriety that many had seen her footprints, which are very like a goose's. Besides, once upon a time a certain villager of the name of Vukotić had actually caught and wedded her. The Vila had two children by her mortal husband—a boy and a girl,—but she never took to the little boy, and gave all the new clothes to the little girl. So the two children grew up, and very strange wayward children they were;

with restless wandering eyes, and with two little red caps, which, however, their mother kept locked up in a box. But the children were always sullen, and would not join in the games or the 'kolo' dance, till one night, when they had been unusually naughty and had kept crying for their little red caps, their mother said, 'Well, then, you *shall* have them!' and, unlocking the box, she gave them to her brats, saying,—

> Dance and play
> While you may.[1]

Thereupon the children ran off to the 'kolo' dance, but hardly had they lifted a foot from the ground when they disappeared, and were never seen again. But the Vila lives still in Resanovce Cavern, which goes so deep into the earth that though men have been along it a day's journey with torches, they have never found the end. And there are her basins in the rock whence the Resanovce folk fetch their water to drink, and when there is sickness in the village the sick are carried up to the Vila's basins and bathed in her holy water, and thus are healed of their diseases. And on great feast days sometimes you may hear the Vila singing in the dark recesses of the cavern, and on such days when folk go to fetch water they are often well splashed for their pains.

By a strange irony of fate it has come to this, that these still surviving relics of old Slavonic heathendom are to-day the one religious link between Greek, Latin, and Mahometan in Bosnia. The children of the Prophet in Kulen Vakup have their Vila too, and turn the eye of faith not only to Mecca but to Mount Klek, across the

---

[1] In the original Bosnian, Skoći nogo Nećeš mnogo.

K

St. Alias.

*Still exist-
ing bonds
of union
among
Bosniacs,
Christian
and Ma-
hometan.*

Croatian frontier—the Brocken of the Southern Slavs, where all the unhallowed sprites from Bohemia to the Black Mountain gather together on St. George's Day, lighting up the whole mountain-top with a weird galaxy of sparks. And were I writing a treatise on Bosnian folk-lore I could tell you more of the heathen worship which these Vakup true-believers pay on the 1st of August to St. Elias; for it is certain that in all these lands the mantle of the Slavonic Thunder-god has fallen on the Prophet of the fiery chariot. In Croatia, as we have already seen, the Angels have tripped into the footsteps of the Vila.

To-day, in this unhappy land, look where we will, we see nothing but divisions—barriers political, social, and religious. But whenever we go back a step, whether we look at the relics of the primitive family organization of the Slavs as they still exist in the country districts among rayah and Mahometan alike, or whether, overlooking creed and caste, we examine that common national character to which a common origin gives currency, a stamp of race, with cruel traits perhaps, but in the main good-humoured, conciliatory, deliberate, and sober; or whether we look on at children's games and village sports; or whether even we go back to these still surviving superstitions of heathen antiquity,—wherever we turn our gaze, our search reveals the still existing bonds of union, of which the strongest and most binding is a common mother tongue, spoken alike by Bosnian Christian and Bosnian Mahometan, and spoken, too, beyond the frontier by Serb and Montenegrin, Slavonian, Croat, and Dalmatian; intelligible, besides, to Bulgarian, Bohemian, and Slovene.

LETTER XIII.

ALBANIA AND THE EASTERN KEY OF THE ADRIATIC.

Ragusa: *May* 27.

 HAVE just returned from a short trip to Albania, and more especially to that city which from the traveller's point of view anciently stood to the eastern shores of the Adriatic in the same relation as Brindisi still stands to the Italian Durazzo—Durs, as the Albanians call her, better known, perhaps, to English readers as the classic Dyrrhachium— owed its former importance not only to the fact of its being the most convenient port at the point where the Adriatic *cul de sac* begins to narrow and the Italian shore draws near to that of the Balkan peninsula—not only to its being opposite to the great Italian harbour of Brindisi, but to its standing at the *embouchure* of the main pass

K 2

that conducted the land traffic from Thessalonica, Constantinople, and the furthest East to meet the Adriatic seaways to West and North. Durazzo was the western terminus of the great commercial highway to the East, the Via Egnatia, which was barred from debouching in a more northerly direction by the mighty parallel ranges of what is now Bosnia and the mountain knot-work of Montenegro and North Albania. Thus Durazzo stood to Brindisi in much the same relation with regard to the Greek and Latin worlds as Calais stands to Dover; commercially she stood to Venice as at the present day New York stands to Liverpool. Thus in all past ages, whether as a Greek republic (known also as Epidamnos), a Roman colony, a Byzantine municipality, or dependency of Venice, Durazzo ranked among the most important commercial cities in the whole of Eastern Europe. Whenever the West moved its aggressive force against the East, from the time of the Roman civil wars—for the conflict between Pompey and Cæsar was in some sense a conflict between East and West—to the day when the Norman invaders of the Byzantine Empire threatened to make Durazzo the Hastings of the Eastern world (and, by some strange fatality, it was beneath these walls that the English exiles who fought as mercenaries in the service of the Greek Emperor tried to avenge the shame of Senlac on the kinsmen of the Conqueror)—in every age, classical and mediæval, Durazzo has been regarded by the ambition of Latin Europe as the most important stepping-stone to Greek and Oriental conquest—the first and richest prize of successful valour

*Battle of
Durazzo,
A.D. 1081 :
Robert
Guiscard
defeats the
Emperor
Alexius
and his
Varan-
gians.*

What, then, is the Durazzo of the Turk? It was with no ordinary feelings of curiosity—my mind filled with the memories of her mighty past—that I took my

stand on the deck of the little Austrian Lloyds' steamer
that now forms almost the only link between Durazzo
and the outside world to catch the first glimpse of the
modern Albanian town. The bare limestone ranges of
Dalmatia and the Black Mountain had been long left in
our wake, and, as the steamer sped along the Albanian
coast, gave place to hills of a more fertile formation, overgrown with luxuriant verdure, infinitely refreshing to the
eye wearied with the wilderness of the Dinaric Alps, but
with fields and houses how few and far between ! Then
we passed the promontory of Cape Pali, which, jutting
out into the Adriatic, offers a welcome bulwark against
the force of the boreal gales, and is the northern arm
of the bay which forms the harbour of Durazzo. In this
bay the steamer anchored, but some way from the shore,
as the harbour has to a great extent been allowed to silt
up, and no attempt to improve or in any way secure it
has been made by the Turkish authorities. From the
sea opens the best view of Durazzo as it still exists,
extending up the hillside, enclosed in a triangle of
mediæval walls. The walls in their present state, as I
discovered from an almost effaced inscription on the
northern tower, date from the year 1474—from the period
of Venetian dominion, when, in the universal anarchy of
the Balkan peninsula, the overthrow of the commercial
empire of Byzantium, and the ravages of the Turks, the
fortunes of the city were at a very low ebb. There can
be little doubt—and the remains of old walls on the hills
and plain about bear out the assertion—that Durazzo in
her palmier days occupied a much larger area than that
enclosed by the fifteenth century walls. But the few
hundred houses that compose the modern townlet do
not nearly occupy even this more limited area, and the

LETTER
XIII.

*Squalor
and degra-
dation of
Turkish
Durazzo.*

whole of the upper town is now an aching void, set apart
at the present moment for Turkish soldiers.   As one
lands on the cranky wooden pier and makes one's way
into the narrow streets through a gloomy sea-gate which
seems the portal of a dungeon, the melancholy impressions suggested by the first sight of modern Durazzo from
the sea are increased by the signs of squalor and stagnation around.   From the Lloyds' agent here I learned that
the whole population, including that of the dirty little
suburbs outside the east gate, amounts to no more than
4,000 souls.   He told me that trade was almost extinct.
In ordinary years there was a small export of corn and
oil from Durazzo and the neighbourhood to Trieste; but
the commercial intercourse with Italy, the overland
traffic with Stamboul, have long since vanished, and now
even the export of corn has been prohibited by reason of
the war.   Nay, the very channels of Durazzo's former
affluence have by a strange irony of fate been perverted
to add misery to her present degradation, and the
splendid maritime canal, which once cut across the peninsula on which she stands and gave two havens to the
city, has partly silted up and partly spread itself in a
great stagnant pool which makes Durazzo a perpetual
fever haunt.

*Relics of
antiquity.*

But what a field for the antiquary!   I do not mean
that classic temples and palaces still rear themselves
amid the ruins of Dyrrhachium.   There is nothing here
to compare with the hoary piles of Treves or Nismes, of
Spalato, or Pola, or Verona.   Time and the Turk have
done their work too well for that!   But in the smaller
fragments, the flotsam and jetsam of ancient magnificence,
Durazzo exceeds any old-world city I have ever seen.
In the courtyard of the Turkish Konak, whither I pro-

ceeded, to be informed that without a special order from
the Sublime Porte no one could view the antiquities of
Durazzo (by which he meant the mediæval walls) amidst
filth and rubble lay two beautiful monuments of Hellenic
art, the torsos of a hero and a goddess, both of super-
human mould ; and near lay a slab in the very act
of being broken up by the barbarian, but the pieces of
which I collected and put together. On this slab was a
Greek inscription in iambic verse, recording how a
Byzantine prince built one of the towers of the ancient
city.[1] The tower in which it was originally fixed was still
existing only the other day, but the Turks had pulled it
down to hunt, I believe, for treasure ! Despite my appeal
for mercy, I can hardly hope that the inscription will long
survive it ; but one half of it may endure a little longer,
as it has been made use of to support the wooden pillar
of a cranky Turkish verandah !

In the streets people follow you with handfuls of silver
coins, most of them from the Dyrrhachian mint, coined
in the days of the old Greek Republic ; and it is note-
worthy, as attesting her ancient commercial importance
and the consequent activity of the mint, that the cow and
calf, or gardens—if so they be—of Alcinous, displayed
upon her coins, are familiar to every numismatist. Stuck
anyhow into the pavement, the gateways, the walls of the
modern houses, are the waifs of Durazzo's shipwrecked fortunes—a Corinthian capital, a Roman inscription, the fragments of a temple cornice ; the turbaned pillars that mark
the last resting-place of true-believers are economically
wrought from the shafts of pagan columns, and Roman
gravestones mingle with the Turkish. The city walls,

LETTER XIII.

Monuments of Hellenic art and Turkish Vandalism

Relics of Dyrrha-chium.

[1] I notice that this inscription has been given by Hahn (*Albanesische Studien*).

LETTER
XIII.

*Durazzo at
the moment
of Turkish
conquest.*

*Turkish
rule more
odious for
what it does
not do than
even for
what it
does.*

the exterior of which I succeeded in exploring—taking
French leave, as I could not get Turkish—are a vast
museum of ancient monuments.

But where are those mightier relics of antiquity mentioned as existing here by Barlettius, the contemporary of
Skanderbeg? I looked in vain for the ' consecrated
buildings, the temples august and sumptuous, the statues
of kings and emperors, the mighty colossus of Hadrian
standing aloft at the Cavalla Gate ; the amphitheatre
lying to the west of the city, constructed with wondrous
art and beauty, and with walls strengthened and adorned
with towers and works of splendour.' At the moment
of Turkish conquest all these existed at Durazzo ; it was
reserved for the Asiatic barbarian to level with the dust
what Goth and Avar, Serb, Bulgarian, and Norman had
respected. Yet, after all, it is less the actual ruin of
what has existed that rouses the indignation of the
observer than the absence of anything to worthily supply
its place. To me the sight of the squalid rows and
beggarly hovels of modern Durazzo is more eloquent as
to the evils of Turkish rule than the blackened ruins of
rayah villages and all the monuments of Bashi-bazouk
ferocity. To me Turkish rule is infinitely more pernicious for what it does not do than for what it does.
Great cities in other parts of Europe have passed away
even more completely than Durazzo, but others have
sprung up to fulfil their functions in the world's economy.
To go no further than the Adriatic shores, Salona lives
again in the modern Spalato, and Aquileja has found her
commercial representatives in Venice and Trieste. But
Durazzo in her decrepit age has left no children. The
commercial highway between Europe and Asia has sunk
into a mule track ; but no railroad supplies its place.

The merchant navy has vanished from her waters, but it frequents no rival port ; it has simply ceased to be. Really, the Sick Man's passion-fits of savagery are quite a vivifying break to this normal paralysis of all the most necessary functions of government—to this brutal torpor and squalid negligence, that have converted what was once Dyrrhachium into a fever-stricken hamlet—to this reign of Chaos,

> At whose felt approach and secret might
> Art after art goes out, and all is night.

However, the narcotic fumes of Ottoman administration do not seem to have affected the character of the race that peoples Durazzo and its neighbourhood. The brisk, lively tread, the haughty bearing, the keen, flashing eyes, the powerful yet finely-chiselled features, less, as it seemed to me, in contradiction with pure Hellenic types than those of any other race, the modern Greeks included ; the white, flowing fustanella, calling up at once reminiscences of Roman warriors ; the carnation vest—a male costume out-and-out the most magnificent in Europe —everything reminds me that I am among people neither Turk nor Slav. These are the meet compatriots of Skanderbeg and Ali of Jannina—Albanians, Skipetars, ' children of the rock,'—the Highlanders of Turkey— the most warlike and indomitable race that owns allegiance to the Sultan.

Albanian characteristics : the Highlanders of Turkey.

The Albanians about Durazzo, and indeed the whole group of clans, Mahometan and Christian, that lie to the north of the Shkumbi river and the ancient Egnatian Way, belong to the Ghegga division of the race ; those to the south of this line, including the non-Greek population of Epirus, being known by the general appellation

Two main divisions of Albanian race: Tosks and Gheggas.·

of Tosks.   The Gheggas, though to myself, coming from the Slavonic regions beyond them, they appeared very unslavonic in their characteristics—more lively, more masterful, and haughty—are described by travellers who are well acquainted with Tosks as less energetic and keen-witted than their southern relatives, and as more approaching the Slavs in temperament and manners. Certainly the Gheggas have in the course of their history had a large intermixture of Slavic blood, both Serb and Bulgarian, and I found that the Serbian language was intelligible to many at Durazzo, while at Antivari and elsewhere it is spoken by a large part of the population. The Tosks, on the other hand, have had at different times a large Greek intermixture, and it is a significant fact that in certain localities in their area the ancient Hellenic type of beauty (some approaches to which I noticed among the Gheggas), which has vanished elsewhere, survives in its full perfection.   To this Hellenic intermixture is probably due the superior keenness of the Tosk intellect.

*Greek and
Montene-
grin
leanings of
rival
Albanian
clans.*

Thus it is that by their special characteristics and antecedents the two great divisions of the Albanian race, each jealous of the other, turn their eyes in different directions.   The independent spirits among the Gheggas seek allies among the Slavs, the Tosk and Epirote malcontents turn to the Greek kingdom.   The Christian hill tribes of North Albania, the Clementi, Miridites, and others who have never conceded more than a vague suzerainty to the Porte, are at the present moment in the closest relation with Montenegro ; indeed, if the report current among the Albanians is to be relied on, the Miridite Prince (or ' Prink,' as he styles himself; most words for civilized ideas having been borrowed from their Roman conquerors by the Illyrian forefathers of the Albanians)—Prink Bibedoda, a young man of about twenty-three, has recently concluded a negotiation of eventual marriage with one of the little daughters of Nicholas of Montenegro. So, while the clans both in North and South Albania bide their time, the Miridites and Clementi wait for a signal from the Montenegrin camp; the Epirotes are at the beck of the Greek committees.

And Italy? What is the meaning of an Italian transport taking soundings in the harbour of Durazzo, flitting from Durazzo to Antivari, from Antivari to Valona, scattering rumours of the approach of the Italian fleet? What is the meaning of solemn warnings addressed to little Montenegro against a too adventurous policy on the Albanian side? It is true that in the towns of the Albanian littoral Italian is the language of civilized intercommunication; it is true that Albanian colonies exist in Southern Italy and Sicily, and that particularly close relations have always subsisted between the Catholic Albanians and their co-religionists on the other side of the Adriatic. Yet until some further development takes place there is no real need to assume that the Roman Cabinet has any other object than the protection of co-religionists and what small commercial interests Italy still possesses on this coast. It must, however, always be borne in mind that for this reason alone anarchy in Albania may render at least a temporary Italian protectorate indispensable; nor can it be denied that the recent ' observations ' of their neighbours have created a belief among Adriatic populations beyond the borders of Albania that Italy, being notoriously weak in harbours on her Eastern coasts, and possessing none, indeed, between Ancona and Brindisi, covets the

Recent Italian observations on Albanian coast.

Possibilities of an Italian Protectorate.

LETTER
XIII.

*Durazzo a
bone of
contention
between
Italy and
Austria.*

*Durazzo a
natural
outlet of
Macedonia
on the West.*

*Pessimist
views of
Turkish
employés as
to situation
in Albania.*

Eastern key of the Adriatic, and would make use of any
favourable opportunity to seize Durazzo. Perhaps the
best security against such a step is to be found in the
determined opposition of Austria, which, even in the
event of Bosnian annexation, would hardly be inclined to
grant Italy compensations on the side of Albania, much
less to place such an important naval station as Durazzo
in the hands of her Adriatic rival. Nor, on the whole, is
an Italian occupation of Durazzo to be desired in the
general interests of the Balkan peninsula. Durazzo belongs by nature to whoever rules in Macedonia—it is the
natural western outlet for the commerce of those midland
regions. If this generation lives to see the revival of the
industrious Bulgarian nationality on both sides of the
Balkan, there can be little doubt that it will also see
Durazzo and Salonica dependencies of the Crowned
Lion.

Meanwhile the Turkish *employés*, with whom I conversed here and at Antivari, took a most pessimist view
of the situation from the Ottoman point of view, and
their apprehensions were borne out by the opinions of
European residents. They did not conceal their belief
that the fate of Albania was being decided on the
Danube, that a great Russian victory might kindle the
flames of revolt from end to end of the province. They
admitted that the reported subjugation of the Miridites,
in spite of the influence which the Romish propaganda
exercised on behalf of the Turk, was a mere sham; that
the Miridites had but retired to the more inaccessible
peaks of their own mountains to choose their own moment
for taking action; that 20,000 armed Clementi were
biding their time; that in Epirus, or South Albania,
especially the districts of Suli and Zagori, the Greeks and

allied Albanian clans were expected to rise any day. Sixteen thousand men are said to have been already well supplied with arms on that side by the Greek committees, and the inhabitants pay besides a war tax of from four to ten piastres a house to a secret government of their own.

But the greatest anxiety of the Osmanlì officials in Albania is the uncertain reliance to be placed on the native Mahometans.

Albania is like Bosnia in this respect, that the Mahometan population is Turkish neither in race, language, nor sympathies. Here, too, there exists still a half-feudal aristocracy, and each of the Albanian Begs has his clannish following of true-believers, and resembles a Highland chieftain of a century or so back. The clan organization is far more developed than in Bosnia, and the Begs are proportionately more powerful. But what chiefly distinguishes Albania from other provinces lies in the peculiar characteristics of the race. By nature quick, energetic, intolerant of control, sceptical, and fickle, the Skipetar, unlike the Slav, has ever made freedom all in all, and religion a question of secondary importance. 'Religion goes with the sword' is an Albanian proverb ; and whenever his profession of faith stands in the way of his interests your true Arnaout does not hesitate, at least outwardly, to conform to a more convenient creed. Thus about Prisrend and elsewhere there are thousands of Roman Catholics (Crypto-Catholics they are called) who made a public profession of Islamism to avoid the vexations to which as rayahs they were subjected. An Albanian will attend a mosque at noon and a church at night with the greatest *sang froid*. The memory of Skanderbeg —the last and mightiest champion of Christian Albania against the Turks—is treasured by the Mahometans of

LETTER XIII.

Preparations of Greek committees for revolt in Epirus.

Anxiety of Turks as to attitude of native Mahometans.

*Revolt of
Maho-
metan
Albanians
against the
conscrip-
tion.*

the province with a fanatical devotion which strangely
contrasts with the cold respect they vouchsafe to the
founder of their faith.   The subtle genius of the Albanian
knows how to put forward religion as a pretext, but his
own interest has ever been the mainspring of his action.

The Turks have reason not to place reliance on the
fidelity of such a race, and grave fears are excited at
Durazzo by the result of an attempt of the Turkish
authorities to call out the Mustafiz, the militia or 'Land-
sturm,' an *alias* for the Bashi-bazouks.   I saw a few
gangs of them defiling through the streets to receive new
breechloaders in place of antiquated flintlocks ; but in
some of the neighbouring hill districts the Mahometan
villagers have taken to the mountains to avoid the con-
scription, and are burning and plundering the villages of
their neighbours, chiefly Mahometans, with great zest.
What will be the effect on the Albanian ' true-believers '
of a complete triumph of the Russian arms, of a Greek
declaration of war, a general revolt of the Christian hill
tribes from the Black Mountain to those mysterious pre-
cincts of Dodona where the Zeus of once-free Hellas is
preparing even now to speak in tones of thunder ?   The
Turks may rely that Kismet is inscrutable ; but meantime this much is certain, that in Albania 'nothing
succeeds like success.'

LETTER XIV.

THE REIGN OF TERROR IN BOSNIA.

Spalato, Dalmatia: *July* 9.

FRESH colony of Bosnian refugees having sought shelter in a lonely mountain glen just on the other side of the Bosnian frontier, to the east of Knin, I have made an expedition to the spot. My object was partly to aid in the distribution of relief for Miss Irby and Miss Johnston's fund, partly to gain particulars of recent Turkish barbarities that had been continually swelling the number of Christian fugitives at this and other points.

Leaving Knin and its fertile valley, after a terrible journey under an almost tropical sun across a desert waste of naked limestone ranges—a journey the effects of

which have considerably delayed this letter—I arrived at
the Bosnian border, in company with an intelligent and
kind-hearted gendarme of the Austrian frontier service,
who has been invaluable to Miss Irby in the distribution
of relief in the more remote districts.

*The glen of
refuge.*

Certainly in their choice of a place of refuge the fugitives had left nothing to be desired.   The prospect that
opened before me on surmounting the last rocky summit
that concealed the glen of Kamen (so this spot is called)
could hardly be surpassed in picturesque and romantic
beauty.   Imagine, after spending hour after hour in toil-
ing over the monotonous steeps of a wilderness of white
disintegrated rock that seemed to redouble the pitiless
glare of the sun above, coming upon a fresh green oasis,
a beautiful gorge overgrown with fine beech trees, from
amidst whose verdure, and partly clothed by it, started
up endless peaks and towers and pinnacles of what from
a remote point of vision might have been mistaken for
the ruins of some quaint Düreresque stronghold of the
Middle Ages, but which was, indeed, nothing but a rock
citadel of Nature.

*A misera-
ble scene.*

In the shade of the trees in the green glen below, the
refugees had put together the wretched little wood shan-
ties that served them for shelter against the elements ;
and here in miserable groups, as we approached each
homestead, the various households clustered around us to
receive our alms.   English help has been reaching them
now for some weeks, but their sufferings have been fright-
ful.   Here and there beneath the trees, with no doctors
to attend them, with no bed to lie on but the kindly
bosom of mother earth, lay victims of hunger, typhus,
and small-pox, from which latter disease there had been
one death that day.

Since the end of winter the mortality in this wood has been terrible. In this little colony over 100 have died in the last six months; about 40 per cent. of the whole number.

Remember that there are or were in all about a quarter of a million Bosnian refugees, and the full significance of these figures can be faintly realised. Doubtless the mortality has not been everywhere so great as here; but it seems to me that Christian Europe has accumulated a terrible responsibility by turning the cold shoulder to these helpless suppliants. The Austrian Government has given some relief, but fitfully and partially, by the hands, in many cases, of corrupt agents, and not enough to keep the bulk of the refugees even above ground. Once it gave them about twopence a day; now it gives them on an average about a halfpenny, bidding the able-bodied find employment. Employment in the Dinaric Alps, where the natives themselves scarce glean subsistence! Employment in the Illyrian Desert! When the whole doleful statistics come to be known—and known they will be, in spite of the efforts of the Austrian and Magyar authorities to suppress publicity—it will be found that Austro-Hungary has accumulated a weight of moral responsibility which I suppose no other Government in Europe could support. But Austro-Hungary, happily or unhappily for herself, is at present but a 'geographical expression,' unencumbered either with a national heart or a national conscience. It would, indeed, be unjust to deny that to provide for the multitude of the refugees must have caused a severe strain on the slender finances of the Empire; but what would be thought of an English Minister who should allow some 30,000 destitute fugitives

L

to starve to death on English soil rather than face a deficit in the Budget?

It was sad to see the children here; it was sad to contrast these jaundiced hollow cheeks, from which the roses had faded in the very April of their years—these slender lean-ribbed frames, frail as little cockle-shells—with the chubby-faced lads and lasses to be seen among the more fortunate Herzegovinian refugees who have sought refuge at Ragusa, and have hardly known what it is to want. But death has been very busy among the children here at Kamen. Among those that survive, the misery of weeks has imprinted on too many of their wizened little faces the furrows of long years. Bread has come to them at last, the icy Bora has ceased to blow, and the cold cf an Alpine winter has given place to summer heats; but it was not hard to see that no return-ing sunshine could ever open those withered buds—they await the pitiful hand of Death to pluck them off.

For them relief has come too late—but not for all. There are many stubborn little constitutions even here that are doing credit to the relief sent by the English ladies. On the whole it is surprising that there are so many of the small folk still flourishing, and it is curious what fine children there are among the refugees generally. In them lies the only hope of this down-trodden race. They alone are not as yet degraded by the brand of op-pression. This fact must be thoroughly realised: the present generation of Bosnian rayahs is past reclaiming; the children alone are still plastic, and by them alone can one hope to elevate the race. There is nothing, indeed, that Miss Irby has more consistently aimed at in her system of relief than to educate as well as feed the children. She has now established no less than twenty-one schools, and the Ragusa Committee has an additional seven. Nor can anything be more remarkable than the ability and real thirst for acquiring knowledge which these refugee children display. Their aptitude is continually startling teachers accustomed to instruct Dalmatian and other children, and, indeed, any one who is present at their lessons or examinations. I may mention that not long ago, being anxious to counteract the too clerical instruction in vogue in the Ragusan refugee schools, I procured as reading books some hundred popular histories of the Serbs, and now there is scarcely a small Herzegovinian there who cannot pass a creditable examination in the history of the national heroes and of the ancient Serbian Czardom.

And for what ages has the mental soil of these downtrodden Bosnians lain fallow ! These long-neglected Slavs come fresh to their books after centuries of rayless ignorance ; and, as to one first emerging on the light of day from one of their own Illyrian caverns, all objects are more brilliant to their mental vision.

'The Germans,' according to the Bohemian poet, 'have reached their day, the English their midday, the French their afternoon, the Italians their evening, the Spaniards their night—but the Slavs stand on the threshold of the morning.' Yet an Englishman may retort that a new dawn is perpetually breaking on his race in the backwoods of the world.

But I am straying from this Bosnian forest.

Further on in the wood I came upon some still more lamentable groups. These were the fresh arrivals, the latest victims of the Turk. Women and children lay about or leant against the trees, quite worn out by their recent flight. They had now nothing, absolutely nothing,

LETTER
XIV.

*Some effects
of Mr.
Holmes'
' urging the
Vali.'*
but the rags upon their backs, and for food were thrown
upon the charity of their miserable fellow-exiles.   I wish
Mr. Consul Holmes had been at my side to learn the
cause of their flight.   The world is perhaps by this time
aware, for Mr. Holmes has published the fact in his
despatches, how the English representative in Bosnia
pressed the Turkish governor of the province to drive out
the Christian bands who still presumed to protect their
hearths and homes in Southern Bosnia.   The Vali, it
appears, yielded to the pressing solicitations of a consul
more actively Turkish than the Turks themselves, and
let loose his dogs of war in this direction.

On the approach of large numbers of Turkish troops,
Despotović, as I have already informed you, withdrew
his bands from the more outlying districts of what I have
described as ' Free Bosnia,' and concentrated his forces
at Czerni Potuk.

The valiant forces of the Vali, however, have not
attempted to storm these positions.   The withdrawal of
the insurgent garrisons left a considerable number of
Christian villages, hitherto protected from the destroyer,
at the mercy of the Turks ; and the brave men despatched at Mr. Holmes's request (and now, as we know
from Mr. Bourke, with the full approval of the present
Government) to restore Mahometan ' order' and to stamp
out this Christian ' brigandage,' as our consul perpetually
called it, till forced to eat his words by his own vice-consul,
have diverted their energies from attacking armed men in
their mountain strongholds to the more easy and congenial
task of burning defenceless villages, trampling under
foot or carrying off the seed corn with which the humane
zeal of the English ladies had supplied the starving
peasantry, cutting down unarmed villagers, and outraging

the girls and women. I have already informed you by
telegraph of the fate of the villages of the Unnatz Valley ;
I have already touched on the worst of the outrages ;
and the terrible evidence collected by Miss Irby on the
harrying of this part of 'Free Bosnia' lies before the
English public.[1] I have now to record that these Turkish
hordes have changed their venue to the South and West
of this first desolated region.

I examined the freshly arrived refugees that I met
with in different parts of the wood of Kamen as to the
cause of their flight, and the accounts I received tallied
even to the names of the victims. About eight days
before, the Turks had first appeared in the district indicated by the villages of Stekerovatz, Otkovatz, Czerni-
verch, and Ćerdić. This region, according to information
of my own received before any of the outrages took
place, had been evacuated, weeks before, by the troops
of Colonel Despotović, and the refugees were unanimous
in stating that there was no insurgent in the neighbourhood when the Turks came.

But the fact that the villagers were rayahs—that they
had once held allegiance to the insurgent commanders—
was quite sufficient to provoke the Turkish hordes who
appeared among them only ten days ago to a savage
revenge. Cottages were burnt, the usual outrages took
place, cattle were driven off, and after murdering five
individuals, including a village elder, the Turks collected
twenty-six villagers, 'house-fathers' and others, threw

---

[1] The outrages here referred to
were subsequent to those already
described at Očievo, &c., and took
place soon after Mr. Vice-Consul
Freeman had completed his investigation as to these earlier barbarities. On p. 90 will be found an
account, from Miss Irby's pen, of
the fate of some of the girls and
women.

*Rayahs
driven off by
the Turks
and mur-
dered in
prison.*

them into irons, and drove them off like a herd of cattle
in the direction of Travnik. Nothing has since been
heard of them.

This driving off of captives is perhaps the most
terrible feature in the present Reign of Terror in Bosnia.
Rarely indeed do men so driven off return to their
homes. Many sink under the fatigues of the march
alone, and the cruelties perpetrated on them by their
armed captors surpass belief. Those who arrive at their
destination are thrown into Turkish prisons, and are
there subjected to the visits of Mahometan fanatics,
who mutilate them with their sword-knives. Many are
starved to death, and others, as the unfortunate refugee
captives who were recently driven to the dungeons of

*Massacre
at Derbend.*

Derbend, are assassinated outright. I have already telegraphed that I am in a position to give the names of
thirteen rayahs so assassinated at Derbend, and the total
number of the returning refugees who on that occasion
met a similar fate is estimated by a correspondent of the
Vienna 'Tagespresse' at not less than sixty. Nor is the
account I have given of the treatment to which the human
herds driven off by the Bashi-bazouks are subjected at
all imaginary. A terrible and circumstantial relation has
lately appeared in the 'Politik' of Prag, communicated
by an Austrian who had joined the insurgent ranks in
Bosnia and had been captured by the Turks, which
shows that there is nothing in the horrors of mediæval
dungeons that is not reproduced at the present day in
the Turkish prisons of Bosnia.

*Massacre
at Stekero-
vatz.*

Glutted for the moment with vengeance and plunder,
the Turkish troops left this district for a while ; but two
days before my visit to Kamen they had returned, and a
ferocious act of savagery which they perpetrated on their

arrival at the village of Stekerovatz had driven the Christian inhabitants who still remained in the district to seek
refuge by flight.

The Turks on their arrival in the village collected
thirteen of the villagers—peasants, perfectly unarmed,
who had never joined the insurrection,—and, falling on
them then and there (driving them off to a more lingering
fate was, it seems, this time too much trouble), shot some
and butchered the rest with their 'handjars.'

About this atrocious massacre there is no room for
doubt. I have the details from a variety of witnesses—
from men who escaped from the scene of the outrages,
and from two witnesses who after the departure of the
Turks buried some of the mutilated remains.

The Turks, after plundering the village, carried off the
heads of the victims with their loot in the direction of
Glamoš. Of the murdered I have the names of Marko
Serdić, Vaso Berberović, Mili Čegora, three brothers of
the name of Peskegović, Mihail and Nikolo Bošniak,
Marko Travas, Simo Diurman, and Jovo Bošniak.

I cannot close this ghastly chronicle without the   *Relics of tyranny.*
mention of two relics of the normal state of things in
Bosnia in the period immediately preceding the present
uprising. One of them is an implement, the other a
victim of the feudal tyranny of the Mahometan Begs.

I have lately held in my hand an instrument the use   *The 'nadjak and its uses.*
of which might well excite the curiosity of a spectator.
It is like a heavy hammer, but the pointed extremity is
shaped like a beak or claw of iron. With one end you
might fell an ox; with the other you might dig three
inches into the trunk of an oak tree. This mysterious
and deadly weapon is called a 'nadjak'; and its use is
only too well known to the Bosnian rayah. The 'nadjak'

is the inseparable companion of the worst of the Bosnian Begs when he goes among his Christian serfs, and woe to the man who on such occasions shall fail to satisfy his worst behests. With a blow from this terrible instrument he can brain his victim or tear his flesh ; he can murder outright, or maim for life, or simply inflict severe bodily pain. I am happy to be able to record that this ' nadjak ' is at present only used by the worst of the Mahometan landlords. Used, however, it still is. That under notice was taken by the insurgents from the country-house of a neighbouring Beg—if I mistake not, a member of the Kulenović family. The iron of its material is most artistically inlaid with silver ; among the ruling caste in Bosnia refined taste can coexist with refined cruelty.

The other relic that I spoke of is a living monument of the ferocious tyranny which provoked the present outbreak. A short time since I saw among the Bosnian refugees at Ploča, in Croatia, an aged cripple, and heard the story of his wrongs. A few years ago there was no more hale old man near Stari Maidan than Lazar Czerni-marković. He was then the house-father of a family community which, owing to its superior industry, was better off than the other rayah households of the neighbourhood. But the mere fact that he was comparatively well-to-do marked him out for the special extortion of his Mahometan landlord, who, suspecting that his serf might have some hidden hoard, made an exorbitant demand for a hundred ducats. The poor man was at his wits' end ; he brought out all the little savings of his lifetime, which did not, I believe, amount to a fifth of the sum demanded. But the Beg would not be satisfied. As old Lazar persisted in his assertion that he had nothing more, the Beg had recourse to the bastinado. The aged house-

father received a hundred strokes, but this did not add
to his ability to pay. He was beaten again more horribly
than before, and left almost inanimate. He was then
buried up to his neck in dung and left three days, the
Beg giving orders to his apparitors to strangle the wretched
man if at the end of that period he should be found alive
and still refused to pay. Meanwhile the friends and
relatives of the victim collected among them a sum
sufficient to buy off the Beg. Lazar Czernimarković was
dug out, and lives still, a wreck of his former self. Even
when I saw him he could scarcely hobble with a staff,
and his toeless stumps bore witness to the pitiless rigour
of his torturers.

Sketch Map
of
MONTENEGRO
and Adjacent Austrian
and Turkish Territory

NOTE.

A SHORT REVIEW OF THE WAR IN MONTENEGRO

*From the expiration of the armistice and the triple invasion of the
Principality to the final evacuation of the Montenegrin soil by
the Turkish armies.*

JUST after the expiration of the armistice, Prince Nikola of Montenegro was walking with a Russian officer in the high street of
the small capital, when a convoy of stores that had been landed as
usual from a Russian vessel in the Austrian port of Cattaro happened to pass by. 'Voilà!' exclaimed the Prince, 'nous avons
de la poudre et des grains, c'est tout ce qu'il nous faut. Vous
verrez maintenant comment nous les rosserons! Nous les laisserons
entrer dans notre pays; mais c'est alors là que nous les batterons.'

This remark quite truly foreshadowed the defensive strategy
adhered to by the Montenegrins throughout the earlier part of the
present campaign. The Montenegrins contented themselves by

assuming a defensive attitude on their own frontiers and the parts
of Herzegovina in their possession, and with endeavouring to
blockade Nikšić and the Duga forts—the islands of Turkish
territory within their limits. Thus the armistice was practically
prolonged till the beginning of June.

After a strange amount of hesitation, marching, and counter-
marching, the details of which I need not repeat here, the simultaneous attack of the Turkish forces in Albania, Rascia, and
Herzegovina on Montenegro and her insurgent allies was planned
for June 4.

Suleiman Pasha, breaking up his camp at Blagai, near the
Herzegovinian capital, had marched *viâ* Nevešinje and Stolatz, to
Gatzko, where the 16,000 or 18,000 men he had with him effected
a junction with twenty-eight battalions—some 14,000 and more—
from the side of Sienitza and Priepolje.

On the other hand, Ali Saib Pasha, in Albania, had pushed
forward the forces still about Skutari to the neighbourhood of
Podgoritza and Spuž. It appears that the number of regulars and
irregulars under his command had seriously diminished during the
last few weeks, owing to the general demoralization and the
unwillingness of the Albanian Bashi-bazouks, originally estimated
at not less than 32,000, to fight. Thus, regulars and irregulars
together, the Montenegrins do not estimate their enemies on the
Albanian side at over 30,000. From the side of Rascia or the
Pashalic of Novipazar Mehemet Ali, using Kolašine as his base,
directed a third attack of his forces, inclusive of a large number of
Albanian Bashi-bazouks, amounting certainly to over 20,000 men.

Thus, no less than 82,000 men were hurled simultaneously
against a small Principality, whose total population, men, women,
and children included, does not number 200,000 souls. The
motive of the Turks, in diverting such large forces at the critical
moment on the Danube, to what must seem to all observers to
have been a comparatively trifling issue, is partly explained by the
fact that in striking what they hoped would prove a death-blow at
Montenegro, they were also aiming at the heart of disaffection and
revolt in Bosnia, Albania, Macedonia, and, in fact, their whole
Western provinces, by which they might also paralyse the possible
action of Greece.

The two points against which the Turks directed their main

attack were, on the side of Albania, the valley of the Zeta—the object of the Turks being, as was stated very openly in the camp at Skutari, to capture Danilovgrad, the late-erected Montenegrin town, which the Principality looks on as its future capital—while on the Herzegovinian side the purpose was to force the passage of the Duga Pass and relieve Nikšić, which the Montenegrins held in strict blockade.

The offensive movement against these several points was carried out as planned—simultaneously, the attack on the Albanian side being slightly the earliest. On this side the Montenegrin southern army, numbering perhaps 8,000, was very strongly posted on the heights of Majlat and Martinići, under the command of Bozidar Petrović. The Montenegrins, true to the defensive strategy resolved on from the beginning, awaited the Turks in their intrenchments, and simply mowed down their ranks when they attempted to advance. The positions were indeed so strong that the whole attack was little better than a useless waste of life on the part of the Turkish commander, as can be gathered from the immense disparity of the losses, the Montenegrin dead being no more than 18, while the Turks lost at least 500, and the triumphant mountaineers took over 1,000 rifles from their fallen and retreating foes. The Turks were hurled back in confusion on Spuž, and did not for the present attempt to renew their attack from this side.

Defeat of Turks on Albanian side.

On the side of Herzegovina the Turkish attack was more serious in its extent and its results. On Monday, while Ali Saib was making his vain and ill-judged attack on the valley of the Zeta, Suleiman Pasha from Gatzko pushed forward his vanguard to assail the heights of Kristatz and Golia, which commanded the northern entrance to the Duga Pass—his necessary avenue of approach in undertaking the relief of Nikšić. Although Kristatz was the key to the whole mountain avenue, the commander of the Montenegrin northern army, Vojvoda Vukotić, had only posted four battalions at this critical point, and had so scattered the rest of his forces, amounting collectively to less than half the attacking Turkish army, that it was impossible that any support could be given to the devoted four battalions at Kristatz.

Battle of Kristatz.

These battalions, however, amounting to all accounts to no more than 2,100 men, hurled back the advancing columns down the side of the hill, and while one half kept their positions to avoid a flank attack, the other pursued the Turks till the retreat became a rout, and the rout an indiscriminate slaughter. No quarter appears to have been given on either side. A Montenegrin who had taken part in this fight told me that the pursuers were excited to fury by finding three of their comrades who at an early period of the day had fallen into the enemy's hands impaled, and with fires lighted beneath their bodies. In some cases it appears that the old barbarous practice of cutting off the noses of the fallen slain was revived, but this seems rather to have been perpetrated by the ruder Herzegovinian bands, who fought under Socica. about Goransko.

The slaughter of the Turks on the rocky steeps between Kristatz and Golia was described to me by eye-witnesses as something awful. The pursuing battalions claim to have taken as many as 1,900 rifles from the fallen; the loss of the Turks amounted to over 2,000 in this quarter. The headlong pursuit of the Montenegrins was, however, stopped by the advance of the Turkish reserves, and seeing themselves in danger of being sur rounded, the pursuers in their turn were obliged to give ground and fight their way back to their brothers on the height. The Turks now made another attempt to storm the heights of Kristatz, but were still continually repulsed, till, attacked in front and flank, the brave defenders found it necessary to evacuate the contested position, and retired, fighting, to more inaccessible localities in the mountains. It was then found that they had lost in killed and wounded a third of their number.

Meanwhile another Turkish division had been despatched to re-provision the fort of Goransko, about five hours to the east of Kristatz, which was held blockaded by Lazar Socica with two Herzegovinian battalions and two battalions representing the clan of Drobnieki. It is certain that the relief of Goransko was partially accomplished; but Socica next day effectually interrupted any further provisionment by seizing in a gallant attack 700 horses laden with stores, besides large quantities of arms.

Meanwhile in Cettinje it was known that Kristatz had been taken and Goransko relieved, and that the Kristatz battalions had lost from 600 to 700 in killed and wounded. But the next day, and the day after, and the day after that passed, and still the Turks made no attempt to advance on the Duga Pass; the great losses

inflicted on them beeame known, and tidings began to pour in from
the towns of Herzegovina that the Bashi-bazouk auxiliaries of
Suleiman Pasha were so disheartened by the slaughter of Kristatz
that they were deserting his camp by hundreds at a time—500 as I
know appeared in a body in Trebinje alone on Thursday morning.
Then came news of successful skirmishes, of Lazar Socica's feat
near Goransko, of the repulse of a Turkish attack on the side of
Kolašine and another on the side of Kutchi, and the capture of
large quantities of guns and horses. Finally it appeared that the
main body of the Turks had fallen back on the camp of Gatzko.

*Turkish
advance up
the Duga
Pass.*

Meantime Vukotić employed the comparative lull in withdrawing
what battalions he had about the northern extremity of the Duga
Pass and uniting them with the bulk of the northern army about
Presieka, which position blocks the southern exit of the Duga and
the road by which the Turks must advance on Nikšić. The total
Montenegrin forces, the Herzegovinian allies included, collected at
this point and at the neighbouring mountains, amounted, it is said,
to twenty-six battalions, or about 15,000 men. After a long delay
the Turkish advance through the Duga Pass commenced on Tuesday, and on Thursday at daybreak the two armies found themselves
face to face, that of the Turks being at least two and a half times
greater than that of the Montenegrins under Vukotić. Every one
at Cettinje was awaiting the news of a battle on a far larger scale
than any of the previous engagements.

*Relief of
Nikšić.*

On Saturday (June 15) the ominous news arrived in the little
capital of Montenegro that the Turks had, in fact, succeeded in
relieving Nikšić on Thursday. The result was partly due to the
incapacity of Vukotić to combine his forces for a simultaneous
movement, but largely to the determination expressed by the
Prince, who was much moved at the losses suffered by the Kristatz
battalions, and is economical of nothing more than of the lives of
his warriors, not to fight a battle except at such great advantage
as would secure small losses to the Montenegrins. Thus, after a
short engagement in which the Montenegrin loss was about fifty,
the clans withdrew to the mountains and left the passage to Nikšić
open to the Turks.

It was now open to Suleiman Pasha, using Nikšić as a base, to
advance across the plain of the city, which runs at this point like
a wedge into Montenegrin territory, and attempt to storm the

breach in the mountain walls of the Principality, which at this
point forms a convenient avenue of approach to the Zeta valley.
The heights of Slivie here rise only 600 feet above the plain, and
these, to a great extent, owing to the want of united action among
the Montenegrin battalions, Suleiman Pasha succeeded in carrying
after a desperate struggle, and subsequently the old monastery of
Ostrog, which the Turks reduced to ashes. On Sunday (June 17)
the Turks had forced an entrance into Montenegro. The Montenegrin
battalions were divided, and the Montenegrin commander Vukotić
completely lost his head ; yet the resistance had only begun. The
Turks were repulsed in an attempt to force the upper ford of the
Zeta, their retreat in the direction of Nikšić was cut off, and
Suleiman Pasha, after nine days' combat, during which he advanced
a short day's march, barely succeeded in cutting his way out of the
Principality on the Albanian side. Weeks afterwards, on passing
over the same ground that the Turks had to contest inch by inch
with the stubborn mountaineers, I observed the relics of this
disastrous march—skeletons of horses lying about in every direction amidst the tangled brushwood, and bones choking the hollows
of the rocks.

The plan of the Turkish commanders had been for the two
armies of Suleiman Pasha and Ali Saib to penetrate simultaneously
into the Principality from the Herzegovinian and Albanian sides,
and, effecting a junction at Danilovgrad, to march on Cettinje and
annihilate Montenegro. And, difficult as was the advance of Suleiman Pasha, and serious the losses that he suffered, the plan might
yet have been carried into execution had it not been for the crushing
defeat inflicted on the Albanian army by the brave Božo Petrović.
On Saturday, June 16, simultaneously with the advance of Suleiman
from Nikšić, Ali Saib moved forward a division of his forces
amounting to about 10,000 men from Spuž and Podgoritza, and
attempted to storm the Montenegrin intrenchments held by Božo
Petrović with no more than 2,500 men, a little to the south of
Danilovgrad. Four unsuccessful assaults were made, and at the
fourth repulse the Montenegrins leapt from their intrenchments, and,
falling 'handjar' in hand on the retreating Turks, inflicted great
slaughter. The Turkish rout was increased by two fresh battalions
under Vojvoda Plamenatz dashing down upon their flank, and the
pursuit stopped only under the guns of Spuž. The Turkish loss in

THE WAR
IN MONTE-
NEGRO.

*Storming
of the
heights of
Slivie by
Suleiman
Pasha.*

*Disastrous
march of
Suleiman
Pasha
down Zeta
Valley.*

*The nine
days' fight.*

*Repulse of
Ali Saib by
Božo
Petrović.*

killed and wounded in this engagement was over 1,000. Ali Saib, however, on learning the successful issue of Suleiman's attempt to force an entrance into the Zeta valley from the north, resolved on a final effort to push his way up the valley from the south, and join hands with Suleiman's army at Danilovgrad. He accordingly collected his whole forces, amounting, with irregulars, to about 28,000 men ; and carrying with him tents, arms, and provisions, as for a prolonged occupation of Montenegro, commenced his march up the Zeta valley.

Prince Nikola appeals to Austria.

It must be admitted that at this juncture a very gloomy view of affairs was taken by the authorities in Montenegro, and I am in a position to state that a confidential appeal was made by the Prince Nikola to the Austrian Government to save the Principality from such a catastrophe as a Turkish occupation of Cettinje. The Austrian Government at once expressed its readiness to exercise its good offices to save the Principality from annihilation, but the event proved that diplomatic intervention was not needed.

Brilliant victory of Božo Petrović over Albanian army.

On Wednesday, June 20, the attack of Ali Saib was met by the Montenegrin battalions under Božo Petrović and Plamenatz about Martinići : the Turks were taken in a trap by a flank and rear attack, and after a sanguinary engagement were utterly routed ; the tents and stores of provisions and ammunition which they had brought with them with a view to the occupation of the Principality fell into the hands of the Montenegrins, and witnesses described to me the rout as a massacre. All the positions that the Turks had held just within the Montenegrin border were evacuated, and the Turkish camp abandoned to the mountaineers. The main loss was suffered by the Nizam, the Albanian Bashi-bazouks escaping for the most part over Mount Berdo. This brilliant victory prevented the junction of the two Turkish armies at Danilovgrad. Ali Saib's troops were completely demoralized, and henceforth ceased to form a serious factor in the issue. It was only after Suleiman, harassed on both flanks and the rear by the Prince's artillery on the right bank of the Zeta, and the scattered battalions of the Montenegrin northern army, had succeeded in passing Danilovgrad on the opposite shore of the river, and had actually approached the Albanian frontier, that Ali Saib was able to hold out a feeble hand to aid his retreat on to Turkish soil. After nine days' prolonged combat, during which he is stated to have lost no less than

6,000 men in killed alone,—though, considering the difficulty of arriving at an exact estimate of losses in mountain warfare, the statement must be received with reserve—Suleiman Pasha succeeded in entering the Albanian town of Podgoritza with the remains of the finest army that the Turks had in the field. To this must be added the losses of Ali Saib's army, which can hardly be set down at less than four thousand killed and wounded.

THE WAR IN MONTE-NEGRO.

First period of the war concluded.

Meanwhile, Mehemet Ali, who with the third Turkish invading army had been devastating the mountain cantons of north-eastern Montenegro, finding his army reduced by the disappearance of the Albanian Bashi bazouks who had returned home with their plunder, and having suffered a check from the brave inhabitants of the Morača, retired to Kolašine.

Thus by Thursday, June 28, the first chapter of the Montenegrin war of this year, including the Turkish invasion of the Principality, ended with the entire evacuation of Montenegrin territory; and on the 15th of July, Suleiman Pasha embarked from Antivari with forty battalions to transfer his operations to the Balkan.

The second period in the Montenegrin war is marked by the siege of Nikšić, prolonged in a desultory way from the end of July to September 8, when the capitulation took place; of which and the short but decisive campaign in the Herzegovina, I shall speak more at length.

The following letter which I wrote from Cettinje on the 3rd of September, a few days before the fall of Nikšić, may throw some light on the policy of the Montenegrin Government during this period of the war, marked by the protracted siege of Nikšić. The complete triumph of the Russians afterwards gave a more active turn to the military operations of Montenegro, both on the side of Old Serbia and of Albania :—

'The Montenegrins are a "canny" people. No one can understand the policy of the Principality without first grasping this prominent trait in the national character. Brave even to temerity in action, they are shrewd even to over-cautiousness in the council chamber. Four hundred years' incessant struggle with a mighty empire has taught them to economise their national resources in the same remarkable manner in which the ceaseless struggle for bare existence in their mountain wilderness has taught them to husband their domestic. For centuries Nature and the Turk have been

Policy of the Montenegrins during the siege of Nikšić.

M

THE WAR
IN MONTE-
NEGRO.

*A letter on
Montene-
grin policy
during the
siege of
Nikšić.*

drumming into them the same stern lesson. Nor is it any secret
that their present ruler carries these national tendencies to a fault.
It was, as I have already intimated, the natural but excessive desire
of Prince Nikola to spare the lives of his people which prevented
the Montenegrins from offering the resistance they might have done
to the Turkish army in the Duga Pass, and that resulted not only in
Suleiman Pasha's relieving Nikšić, but in forcing a passage into the
heart of Czernagora itself. It is precisely the same cause that is
now retarding the capture of Nikšić, which might have been taken
over and over again if the Prince would only have given his consent
to an assault. But though the fighting force of the garrison cannot
number more than two thousand men, of whom only one half are
regulars and the other half but armed citizens, the assault has been
countermanded and delayed even when all the forts environing the
town were in the hands of the Montenegrins, and although the
recent capture of Fort Chadelitza puts them in actual possession of
part of the suburbs.

' The humane and quite intelligible desire of the Prince, with
the hospitals of his little Principality already overflowing with
wounded, to spare the lives of his brave retainers, has doubtless very
largely contributed to this procrastinating generalship ; but I may
state that this is by no means the only reason that has weighed with
him in preferring the slow and uncertain reduction by blockade to a
speedier and more sanguinary method. To put it briefly, the siege
of Nikšić has been useful to Montenegro. The political caution of
the Prince makes him averse to attempting too great things with his
small means. He perceives, or thinks he perceives, that little that
Montenegro can at present do, will have any great influence in
making the ultimate re-adjustment of her frontiers more favourable.

' The great service has been performed. Sixty thousand Turkish
regulars, who might have turned the scale against Russia at Simnitza,
were drawn off from taking part in the Danubian operations at the
critical moment. Russia has already contracted her debt of honour
to the Principality. Whether the present war be terminated in one
or more campaigns, few military critics doubt that Russia will issue
victorious from the contest, and Montenegrin statesmen may have
the best reasons for knowing that when the day of reckoning comes
neither the brave men who died at Kristatz nor the Turkish ravages
in the Zeta valley and the Morača will be forgotten by the Czar.

'This being the case, the Prince and his advisers might well ask themselves what need there was for a too adventurous strategy beyond the borders of the Principality. The withdrawal of the greater part of the Turkish troops seemed, indeed, to offer a splendid field for Montenegrin ambition. Both at Mostar and Skutari, the Turks—Herzegovinian as well as Albanian—expected to see a Montenegrin army at their gates. But the discreet ruler of Montenegro perceived Italian susceptibilities in Albania and Austrian in Herzegovina, and forbore to threaten either Mostar or Skutari. It is true that neither of these objections applied to an invasion of "Old" Serbia. On that side, indeed, the temptation to advance seemed irresistible. On that side these indomitable highlanders, who alone of all their race have preserved the continuity of Serbian independence, look down from their mountain fastnesses upon Ipek, the ancient seat of their national metropolitans, and far away at the other extremity of the rich valley of the Drin may catch a glimpse of the minarets of Prisrend, the cradle of the national dynasty, the Czarigrad of Serbian Emperors. There is no Montenegrin—there is hardly a Croat or Dalmatian— who has lost the hope of liberating this sacred land from the infidel yoke. It was only to be expected that great influence should be brought to bear to induce the Prince to order an advance in this direction.

'But no advance has been made on the side of Stara Serbia. The Prince and his advisers know too well that the broad plains of the Drin are no place in which to hazard his heroic mountaineers. Brave as they are among their native rocks, their tactics are little fitted for the open. Even were they possessed of bayonets (which they are not), they would disdain to form a square. They would be trampled down like a field of standing corn by the first charge of cavalry. And even were it not for these obvious military considerations, it may be taken for granted that so far as Prisrend is concerned the susceptibilities of the Serbian Government, which looks on that city as a birthright of the Danubian principality, will be respected at Cettinje. I believe that the most perfect understanding exists between Serbia and Montenegro on the subject of "Old" Serbia in case of the eventualities of annexation, and that Belgrade would see with equal equanimity the Montenegrin lion set its paw on Ipek and Diakova.

Montene- grin policy.

M 2

THE WAR
IN MONTE-
NEGRO.

*Letter on
the policy of
the Prince's
Govern-
ment.*

*Montenegro
and Stara
Serbia.*

'Meanwhile there is a general and well-founded conviction that in any re-settlement of the Balkan Peninsula consequent on a Russian triumph, this small historic strip of country, Stara or " Old" Serbia, will not be neglected. My readers will look for it in vain in their maps, where it lurks divided and concealed by portions of the Bosnian and Albanian pashaliks of Novi Pazar and Prisrend. Probably its very existence is hardly known to English statesmen. But Englishmen may rest assured that neither the fate of Bulgaria nor Bosnia nor Herzegovina is so dear to the Slavs—and to the Russians as well as those of the South—as that of this ancient cradle of the Serbian Empire, this desecrated shrine of the Serbian Church. At the present moment it acts at once as a wall of division between the two free Serbian principalities, and at the same time as the wasp's waist of Turkish Bosnia. This district taken from the Turks, Montenegro and Danubian Serbia join hands, and Bosnia is cut adrift. The Turks, therefore, may be trusted to cling to it to the last—nay, even at the present moment, valuable as every man is at Kezanlik and Plevna, 10,000 men are left to garrison Stara Serbia. The Prince of Montenegro shows his sagacity in perceiving that the liberation of this sacred land must be fought for for the present on Bulgarian soil. Should the Russians cross the Balkans, a military parade may be open to him in this direction ; and so much it is safe to say, that any peace which leaves Old Serbia in Turkish hands will be a hollow truce.'

'For the present, therefore, the policy chalked out for the Montenegrin Government may be described as masterly inactivity. But a vent must be found at the same time for the martial ardour of the race, roused almost to Berserker fury by the recent raid of Suleiman Pasha and the sight of devastated Zeta. Now it is precisely this vent that the siege of Nikšić has supplied. The Prince has discovered a pleasing little " Iliad" wherewith to entertain his warriors, and though they grumble a little at the slowness of operations and shout now and again in vain for an assault, still they have had the satisfaction of feeling that they are not absolutely idle. Sometimes they were treated to the capture of a fort, just to stop their mouths ; and then there was the desultory pounding away of some very harmless artillery,—to add fireworks to the entertainment. However, the longest siege must come to an end.'

LETTER XV.

PEACEFUL SKETCHES OF MONTENEGRO IN WAR TIME.
(I.) FROM CATTARO TO CETTINJE.

From Cattaro to Cettinje. Contrast between the Bocche and the Black Mountain. Montenegrin 'transport service.' A death-wail for the heroes of Kristatz. Montenegrin wounded. The burden of war in Montenegro. Ninety thousand refugees. Nieguš, the cradle of the dynasty. Reminiscences of Lapland. Montenegro cut off from the sea. Cattaro taken from our then allies, the Montenegrins, by English diplomacy.

Cettinje : *June* 11.[1]

HE mountain ascent that the traveller must accomplish who would penetrate to the eyrie fastnesses of Montenegro opens in a rare conjunction visions of all that is most soft and terrible in landscape. As you zig-zag up the precipitous steeps of the Sella Gora, the old Venetian walls of Cattaro lie immediately below you, and beyond expands a bird's-eye view of her beautiful Bocche, connected, indeed, with the open Adriatic by a narrow channel, but enfolded by mountain arms, shrouded and sheltered by those vague and mighty sinuosities of rock and forest, till the still blue-emerald

---

[1] The letter, as will be seen from the date, was written at the beginning of the events recorded in the preceding Note on the war in Montenegro.

expanse of winding waters at your feet seems the bosom
of some Alpine lake.   And round about its margin
blooms a vegetation as rich but more tropical in its
luxuriance than that of Como or of Garda.   Here are
groves of lemon and orange and myrtle, thickets of rosy
oleander, trailing passion flowers, aloes, and majestic
palms that cannot be matched nearer than the shores of
Africa.   Approaching Castelnuovo—they call it 'the
Serbian Nice'—from the Suttorina yesterday, I made my
way between hedges, any bush of which would be an
ornament to an English garden, where giant clematis of
wondrous purple entwines its tendrils with white convol-
vulus whose flowers might serve for vases, and snowy
eglantine weighed down with the profusion of its own
roses is overhung with the fiery scarlet bells of myrtle-
leaved pomegranates.

With visions like this 'haunting him like a passion,'
the traveller turns his gaze from the lake-like sea below
to the heights above, which form the mountain portal of
Montenegro on the Adriatic side.   No contrast could be
more overwhelming.   Nothing above you but bare rock
steeps, stupendous crags up which the path is hewn in
zig-zags, ever ascending, till you look down from it 4,000
feet on the sea below.   The fresh mountain breeze tells
you that you already tread the free soil of Czernagora.
Soil !—but there is not pasture for the mountain goat in
this wilderness of naked rock !   As we cross the mountain frontier into the little Principality the path itself
becomes more rugged, and, indeed, it has been said to
be a principle of Montenegrin statecraft that the avenue
of approach should not be made too easy for the military Monarchy that stretches its greedy arm along the
Adriatic coastland below.

Now and then there passed me trains of Montenegrin peasants chiefly non-combatants, lads and women, driving mules below to buy stores of corn and other necessaries in the bazaar outside the gate of Cattaro— the 'transport' service of the Principality is performed by women and children! They were a rough but sturdy set, the prevailing colours of their costume black and dingy white—sackcloth and ashes compared with the more brilliant peasant throng of Bocchese and Ragusan market-places, and with little of the Venetian aptitudes and Italian blood-infusion of the lowlanders. But the faces of all, and notably the lads, wore that bold and frank expression which freedom alone can give. There was nothing here of that sullen, hang-dog look which in all his provinces distinguishes the rayah subject of the Turk—that brand of degradation which seems as indelible on those who once have suffered from its impress as the 'three letters' on the felon's brow.

Presently I heard a low monotonous chant dying and re-echoing among the peaks above, and on looking up saw that it proceeded from a fresh caravan of Montenegrin mule-drivers, women, singing as they slowly wended their way down the mountains a song that sounded strangely like a dirge. And a dirge indeed it was; I was told that they were singing a death-wail for the 700 slain three days before in the fight at Kristatz,[1] when four Montenegrin battalions withstood for a day the whole army of Suleiman Pasha—just fifteen times their number, and only yielded their position to overwhelming odds, when a third of their devoted band lay dead and wounded among the rocks, and five Turks had fallen for every Montenegrin. The Turkish losses about Kristatz

[1] See p. 156.

were at least 2,000.　But such a feat by no means stands alone in the annals of this Black Mountain, whose poet can sing,—

> Not whiter is with foam the shore
> Than red our rock with Turkish gore.

*Montene-
grin losses.*

　It was an inspiring thought, as one climbed the last rock rampart of this land of heroes, that even now the sea of Turkish barbarism was lashing its impotent waves against the rocks around, to be hurled back in blood. But the losses of the Montenegrins are severely felt by this little population, and by none more keenly than the Prince himself, who looks on his subjects as his own children in a way which more civilized communities can hardly realize.　Seven hundred may not seem a very large tale of killed and wounded, but it is large in proportion to the total population, serious in respect to the value of the blood spilled.　Great Britain has a population more than a hundred times as large as that of this little Principality, but it is likely that a loss of 70,000 men in a battle would affect the British Government very considerably.　In relation to the size of the contending forces, the loss of the Montenegrins is far greater than that of the Turks.　I realized keenly the count the Montenegrins make of their losses as I arrived at the first Montenegrin village, Nieguš, the cradle of the present dynasty, where two wounded warriors were just being carried in.　The personal sympathy, the visible emotion, among these rude mountaineers, —and they were nurtured in too severe a school to be apt to waste their sentiment !—the tender care with which fresh branches were placed above their faces to protect them from the sun, were touching in the extreme.　These were being conveyed to the hospital at Cettinje, to be tended by Russian sisters of charity.　Only yesterday, 40 Montenegrin wounded were carried into Cattaro ; the Principality is LETTER XV. already too small and poor to meet so large a call for hospital accommodation.   What if another batch of 500 are borne off the field to-morrow ?   Add to this, that this penniless people has at the present moment to house and feed 90,000 Christian refugees from Herzegovina.

Nieguš stands in a little oasis amidst a wilderness of *Nieguš.* limestone peaks in a lake-like bed of cultivable soil, a ' polje ' such as I have described in Free Bosnia, supporting crops of cereals and potatoes, with every square inch of reclaimable soil around its margin walled up in terraces along the hillside, and husbanded as so much precious ore.   Though till lately the largest place in the whole Principality, the capital included, it is quite a little village, the first and most conspicuous building being, as generally in Montenegro, the school-house, now converted into a hospital.   Miserably poor as this little State is, every one of its children receives a good rudimentary education. At Nieguš begins what is intended to be a carriage-way, leading to Cettinje, but at present one soon has to quit this for the arduous mule-track over the mountains, which at present is the only route.   Near Nieguš the mountain plateau of the Black Mountain attains its greatest elevation, and at one point a magnificent *A Monte-* prospect opened out, embracing the Bocche di Cattaro *negrin* *landscape.* and the Adriatic on one side, and on the other discovering a dim vision of the lake of Skutari and its rich and ample plain.   Immediately around, however, was the usual wilderness of rock, scattered here and there with a few stunted and overgrown beeches.   Pour lakes into the Polje oases, square off the too conical mountain tops with a little ice action, transform the beeches into birch, and you find yourself in Lapland.   No traveller

LETTER
XV.

*The wisdom
and grati-
tude of
English
diplomacy.*

turning his gaze from the desolation around him to the distant sea and lake and the semi-tropical exuberance of vegetation that clothes their margin, can fail to protest against the lot which shuts off this deserving little people from all the avenues of wealth and industrial development. Montenegro represents the continuity of Serbian independence ; but Skodra, the legendary foundation of Serbian princes, and Cattaro, the haven of the greatest of the Serbian Czars, both lying at her feet, are to-day the very strongholds which debar her from the sea. Yet it was not always so. At the beginning of this century the Montenegrins, then the faithful allies of England, aided us in capturing Cattaro from the hands of the French ; but English 'diplomacy' showed its gratitude by adding Cattaro to the nearest despot at hand (the Austrian), thus cutting off the little free State once more from its natural emporium.

At last, from a rugged summit beyond Nieguš, I caught a first glimpse of the grassy 'polje' of Cettinje ; and seven hours of difficult progress after my start from Cattaro brought me to Cettinje itself, the capital of Montenegro— a little one-streeted village, with a cottage at one end a little larger than the rest, which is the Prince's palace, and an inn, between which and the princely residence there is not much to choose. But I must reserve for more peaceful times a description of what is undoubtedly 'the smallest capital in Europe.'

LETTER XVI.

PEACEFUL SKETCHES OF MONTENEGRO IN WAR TIME.
(II.) IN THE VILLAGE CAPITAL.

Immense tax of war on male population of the Principality. Marvellous carrying power of the women. Their queenliness. The Princess and Princely Family of Montenegro. The Elders of the People. A Capitan of a Montenegrin Nahia. Dislike of the Russians in Montenegro. Conversations with wounded heroes.

Cettinje : *September 6.*

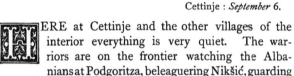ERE at Cettinje and the other villages of the interior everything is very quiet. The warriors are on the frontier watching the Albanians at Podgoritza, beleaguering Nikšić, guarding the northern mouth of the Duga Pass against the Mahometan irregulars of Bosnia and Herzegovina collected to relieve the straitened garrison.

All is quiet ; but one has plenty of evidence as to the hardships which this gallant little people is cheerfully enduring. One meets few men except on crutches. Women and children are doing men's work—mules' work, I should rather say !—you pass women on the mountain paths carrying cannon balls to the troops. A single village will give a very good idea of what Montenegro is at the present moment. At Nieguš, the other day, I found the school turned into a hospital, and a church converted into a magazine for cartridges.

LETTER
XVI.

*A Monte-
negrin
village in
war-time.*
I asked how many men there were belonging to the
village, and was told there were 500.

'And how many of these are now away in the war?'

'Three hundred and fifty.'

But what women and children they are! It is not
only their strength, incredible as it is ; the usual regula-
tion burden for a woman making the day's mountain
ascent from Cattaro to Cettinje is 60 lb., supported by
many day after day, weather permitting, the year round.
It is not only this marvellous carrying power, but, what
one would not have expected side by side with it—and
what it must be allowed is more perceptible in the girls
and younger women—they are possessed of a straightness
of limb, and, when without their heavier burdens, of a
dignity of carriage which, so far as I am aware, cannot be
rivalled anywhere else in Europe. Tall and majestic,
like the male portion of their race, every Montenegrin
woman that progresses along the high street of Cettinje
—to say she walked would be to travesty that stately gait!
—is a queen by birthright ; every girl a born princess.

The Princess of Montenegro herself, who is much
beloved here, and who, blending as she does the characteristic charms of Italian and Slavonic beauty, is one of
the few princesses of Europe who scarcely yields the
golden apple to our own future Queen, stays at home in
her little palace as a good wife should whose husband is
on the battle-field, receiving no one but official personages. There are seven little daughters, two of whom are
now being educated in St. Petersburg, and one son, who
bears the name of the greatest of his dynasty, Danilo.
The little boy is only six and a half years old, but he is
being trained in the way he should go. With a small
retinue of Montenegrin guards—Perianiks they are called

—he goes out hunting among the brushwood-covered rocks that environ Cettinje, armed with a gun adapted to his small hands, and very rarely does he return without some small deer to show as a trophy of his sport. Only yesterday I saw the little Prince, surrounded by his tall guards, coming back from such an excursion, and holding up a small bird in triumph. The Princess and his sisters hurried down to the garden gate to meet their sportsman, who did not seem to think their kisses beneath his dignity.

Of the men still here the most striking are a few grave senators—Capitans of Nahias (as the chiefs of the Montenegrin cantons are called), whose days of active service have passed, and who stay at home to judge the people in the absence of the host. Nothing can exceed the severe dignity of these men; they sit apart, clothed in their patriarchal state, and exercise a kind of sovereign sway over all around. To find their like one must go back two thousand years to that ' Senate of Kings.' While at Nieguš I made the acquaintance of the Capitan of the Nahia, who was sitting in state outside the roadside hovel that calls itself an inn. Probably he has no more worldly wealth than an English farm labourer, but he has the air of royalty itself; indeed, he happens to be uncle of the reigning Prince. While I was there some women, who, it appears, had assaulted the husband of one of them (they can be viragos as well as queens when they like!), were brought up for judgment before the capitan, and, the evidence being conclusive, he exercised his judicial function by committing them to 'prison,' the prison being a ruined hovel, where the three women were shut up with a pig, the usual tenant of the premises.

Picture now to yourself the stately capitan sitting a

LETTER
XVI.

*The little
Prince.*

*A Montenegrin
Capitan.*

little apart on his rustic curule chair, and now and again
indulging his English guests with a leisurely question
between the whiffs of a chibouk full four feet long.

All of a sudden our patriarchal serenity is broken
into by an excited figure in European costume bustling
into our midst and demanding in a most peremptory
tone, 'Where is the Capitan? You, sir—do you hear me,
sir? What do you mean by shutting up those women in
the sty instead of sending them to fetch wood for the
hospital?' [The schoolhouse converted into a hospital
was just opposite, and there was a goodly pile of wood
ready stacked before it, so that it was hard to see any just
ground of complaint.]

The Capitan starts from his curule chair, fairly taken
aback, and the Russian doctor—for the Russian doctor
it was—pours in a fresh volley. But our Capitan has
got his broadside fairly round by this time, and after a
short but animated engagement the Russian had to sheer
off. The Montenegrin informed him flatly that he was
judge there, and that the women should stay in prison
just as long as he chose, and not a moment less.

How could one wonder after this that the Russians
are unpopular in Montenegro? Unpopular they certainly are, even among those who owe most to their
charitable exertions. The fact is that they cannot understand the *égalitaire* spirit of the Montenegrins. They
come here (of course I except Russian gentlemen like the
Superintendent of Hospitals at Cettinje) with a general
air of patronage, thinking that the mountaineers will fawn
upon their benefactors, and are unpleasantly undeceived.
Then they resent this sturdy independence, and try to
swagger it down, but with as little success.

Montenegro is willing enough to accept Russian help,

but she certainly has given a *quid pro quo,* and does not choose to be treated as a pensioner. Nor can the Montenegrins forget how often Russia in her Turkish wars has made the little Principality a cat's-paw, and left it in the lurch when the day of settling came. People here are very suspicious of England, and there is hardly a Montenegrin who does not believe that our Government has given great pecuniary aid to the Porte; but against Englishmen as individuals no such feeling exists, and an Englishman is much more likely to meet with a favourable reception here than a Russian. At bottom there is a great respect for us and our free institutions, and a corresponding dread of Russian autocracy. A singularly intelligent Montenegrin slowly recovering from his wounds—under the care, be it remarked, of Russian doctors—spoke of the Russians here in a very hostile spirit. 'When you have dealings with an Englishman,' he said, 'you know what you are about; but you must keep your eye on the Russian!'

'Would you like to visit England?' I asked him.

'No,' he answered gravely, 'I could never leave our rock—a day on the sea and out of sight of our high mountains would kill me.'

These wounded Montenegrins are fine fellows and endowed with a wonderful power of recovery. Only about five per cent. of the wounded carried to the Hospital die, and none but grave cases are admitted; the slightly injured being carried to their huts.

'I only pray to God,' said one with whom I conversed the other day, 'that I may meet five Turks alone!'

LETTER XVII.

THE FALL OF NIKŠIĆ.[1]

Sept. 8.

IVI KNJAŽE NIKOLA!—Long live Prince Nicholas. Our little Iliad is ended, and after four hundred years of Ottoman captivity and just forty days' siege, Nikšić, the old Serbian Onogost of epic fame, is again in Christian hands.

The siege had been much delayed by the weakness of the Montenegrins in artillery, but a few days since a Greek vessel appeared off the Austrian port of Castelastua and then and there proceeded to land four cannon, —two of them twelve-and-a-half pounder Krupps—a Russian gift to the Principality. Thereupon the Austrian authorities of Castelastua telegraphed to Cattaro for in-

---

[1] This letter never reached its destination. I have thus been able to add some details to what I had originally written. The military actions described were related to me by friends who had actually taken part in them.

structions, and appear to have waited some time, for in the interval two battalions of Montenegrins, about 1,000 in all, descended from the mountains into the Austrian town and carried off the cannon in triumph to their rocks, aided by the native Pastrovichians. It is pretty generally understood at Cettinje that the whole thing was executed with Austrian collusion.

The Krupp guns despatched from Russia once in position, events advanced apace.

On Tuesday, September 4, the impression produced by the new arrivals led the Turkish commandant, Skanderbeg (a Hungarian by birth), to ask a truce, which the Prince granted on condition that the garrison would employ the interval in considering the necessity of surrender.[1] On Thursday, however, the Turks, who still hoped for relief from Hafiz Pasha, renewed hostilities, having, during the night re-occupied the rocky knoll of Petrova Glavitza, which had been taken at an earlier period by a Montenegrin battalion, but evacuated by the Prince's command, 'because they had acted without orders.' So now Petrova Glavitza had to be retaken,

LETTER XVII.

Cannon carried off by Montenegrins from Austrian territory.

Truce granted to garrison of Nikšić.

Hostilities renewed.

---

[1] It may amuse my readers if I recall a Turkish telegram with reference to this day's occurrence, that went the round of the English papers. This telegraphic gem is dated Podgoritza, Wednesday, September 5—the day of the truce between the Montenegrins and the garrison of Nikšić. Here it is :—

'Podgoritza, Wednesday.—Two columns of Montenegrin troops who were advancing to make an assault on Nikšić came into collision with one another, in consequence of the obscurity caused by the smoke from the burning crops in the neighbourhood. They attacked each other; and the garrison of Nikšić, profiting by the confusion which ensued, made a sortie, and inflicted on the Montenegrins a loss of 1,300 killed.'

While the Turkish telegraphist was composing this, the Turks of Nikšić and the Montenegrins were mixing freely with one another in the fields about the town, discussing the incidents of the siege and even taking coffee together !

not without loss. Two bodies of 150 men, with a third of the same strength, as a reserve, were detached to accomplish this difficult task. The actual assault was entrusted to the band under Captain Simonić, the other 150 making a feint on the opposite side of the hill.

It was about half an hour after midnight when Simonić's storm party advanced to the attack, while, as a surprise was intended, a lively fire was kept up from the Montenegrin positions over their heads. The attacking party had now to cross a large maize field, their friends' bullets whistling in a continual shower close above their heads, but the Turks, who seem to have scented danger, not answering a shot. The Montenegrins were now within fifty paces of the Turkish position, when they were observed by the enemy. A shout of 'Allah! Allah!' rang from the rocks above, and a murderous fire, such as no Montenegrin present had ever experienced, was poured on the attacking party. The Montenegrins answered with a hearty 'Czernogorska!' but advanced still some twenty paces through a storm of shot which cost them several men—they lost here ten dead and seventeen wounded—before replying with a well-directed volley. Another ringing 'Czernogorska!' told their friends that they had gained the rocks; another moment and they were bounding up the Turkish position like mountain goats.

It was now all over with the Turks, who were no match for the Montenegrins in a hand-to-hand struggle among their native rocks, and the defenders fled pell-mell towards the city, leaving eighteen dead on the Glavitza.

The Montenegrins might have profited by the confusion to take Nikšić by assault, but the Turkish

commandant seeing the danger, and fearing some further
surprise in the darkness, resorted to the expedient of
setting fire to two large magazines, which soon lit up the
Glavitza rocks and the other fell strongholds of the
besiegers, almost with the light of day. The Montenegrins, therefore, contented themselves with employing
the rest of the night in rearing stone breastworks along
the flanks of the captured ridge looking towards Nikšić,
the Turks, meanwhile, making some excellent artillery
practice, striking two Montenegrin batteries, in one of
which they killed, or disabled, seven gunners ; in the
other, only one.

LETTER XVII.

Desperate expedient of commandant.

Thus ended the last serious fighting of the siege.
When day broke, the Turks and Montenegrins found
themselves within speaking distance, and then occurred
one of those strange old-world episodes—so little in
harmony with modern scientific warfare—of which the
siege of Nikšić has been so prolific. The warriors on
either side might be heard singing ballads of their own
composing, in which they vaunted the ' gestes' of their
own heroes or ' Junaks,' and jeered at the discomfiture
of their foes. These ' gestes,' indeed, of Paynim and
Giaour alike take us back to Acre or Ascalon !

Jeering ballads.

Only a few days since a mighty Montenegrin man of
valour, priest and warrior at once, in the good old style,
one Pope Milo, rode towards the Turkish lines and
challenged any infidel who dared meet him to single
combat. A Turk of Nikšić (one has to call them Turks,
though they are as pure-blooded Slavs as their opponents)
forthwith accepted the challenge. The opposing ranks
sheathed their handjars, and the mortal combat took place
in the presence of Turks and Montenegrins. Both sides
awaited the issue with bated breath. Suddenly the Mon-

A single combat.

tenegrin falls. The Moslem with a few dexterous strokes with his handjar severs his head from his body. He was proceeding to complete his spoil by stripping his adversary's body, but the mountaineers, already infuriated by the fall of their champion, could contain themselves no longer; they rushed forward, and in the mêlée the Turkish 'Junak' met the fate of his rival.

*Final
assault on
outworks.*

Except a prolonged cannonade and this interchange of 'winged words' little was attempted on Friday; but during the night the Turkish rock strongholds of Stude-natz, on the side of the town remote from Glavitza, were taken by a rear surprise. The Montenegrins leaped into the entrenchment almost before the Turks were aware of their proximity. Two small forts were captured in this manner; the Turks were stricken with panic and hardly offered any resistance, though they were well provided with the means, two hundred unused hand-grenades falling into the hands of the Montenegrins. The assailants only lost 1 killed and 2 wounded; the Turks left 9 dead and 18 wounded in the captured positions.

The Montenegrins were now practically masters of the suburbs of Nikšić, and the possession of Mt. Chade-litza gave them a dominating position from which to pound the citadel. During the night a happily directed shell struck, scattered, and destroyed some valuable stores of ammunition:—the Turks had only twenty-four rounds of shot left at the moment of surrender.

*Turkish
command-
ant
resolves to
surrender.*

The Turkish commandant, despairing of relief from without, conscious that he had done all that a brave man could do, and further encouraged by some previous inti-mations that the garrison might expect generous treatment at the Prince's hands, determined to surrender. On Sa-turday morning, September 8th, a Turkish Parlementaire with a deputation of forty Turks of Nikšić made their way to the Montenegrin head-quarters, and were conducted to the Prince. The Prince received them reclining on a 'struka' or Montenegrin plaid spread upon a rock, and, having first taken coffee with them in true Oriental fashion and paid a well-deserved tribute to their heroism, expressed his willingness to grant them the honours of war.

The Terms of Capitulation finally ratified were as follows:

Article 1.—The garrison of Nikšić surrenders itself unconditionally and without reserve into the hands of Prince Nikola of Montenegro.

Article 2.—In consideration of the great valour displayed by the garrison during the siege, his Highness is willing to concede that the garrison, after first defiling before the Montenegrin army and lowering their flags, shall retire to Gatzko, retaining their arms.

Article 3.—That all cannon, stores, and munitions of war at present in Nikšić shall be handed over to the Prince's officers.

Article 4.—That all inhabitants of Nikšić who elect to remain under the Prince's government shall be left in secure possession of their lands, houses, goods, and chattels; that they shall enjoy free toleration for their religion, and all the privileges and immunities of natives of the Principality: that those on the other hand who elect to withdraw from Nikšić shall be allowed to depart unmolested, carrying with them all their moveable possessions, and that up to a certain date a guard of Montenegrin soldiers shall escort them to those points of the Turkish frontier whither they may wish to emigrate.

*The garri-
son march
out.*

The garrison defiled past in excellent order. But the Montenegrins opened their eyes when they saw the small force of the defenders—only two-and-a-half battalions, of which only one consisted entirely of regulars. No one was more astonished than the Prince himself, who had on one occasion expressed his belief that the garrison consisted of at least 4,000 men. It seemed almost incredible that with the Montenegrins in possession of the surrounding hills this small force should have successfully defended their ramshackle citadel, the scattered city, and seven detached forts, for nearly six weeks, against 10,000 of the most intrepid warriors to be found in Europe.

*Remarks
of the
Turkish
command-
ant.*

'Look at the citadel! look at the fortifications!' remarked the Turkish commandant to a friend of mine. 'Again, and again, I reported their deplorable condition at Stamboul. I urged that in their present state they were quite untenable. The War Office made plans, but nothing came of them. Had my requisitions been attended to, with a few more regulars from Suleiman's army, I could have held Nikšić for years !'

*Testimony
to his
efficiency.*

No blame certainly attaches to the commandant himself. All that was possible to do he did ; and a Prussian officer, who visited the citadel immediately after the surrender, spoke to me with admiration of the scientific order in which he found everything, and the construction of the supplementary defences rendered necessary by the breaching. 'One might,' he said, 'have been in a Prussian fortress.'

The acquisition of twenty-one cannon and an almost inexhaustible store of war material, including two powder magazines and about 10,000 horse-loads of provisions, is really the least important aspect of the capture of Nikšić by the Montenegrins. It is not too much to say that with its possession begins a new era for the Principality. The acquisition of the rich plain alone which surrounds the city doubles the wealth of Montenegro at a stroke. The security of the country is indefinitely increased. Nikšić has been a perpetual thorn in the side of Montenegro. Holding Nikšić on one side and Podgoritza on the other, the Turks have contrived (of course with the aid of English diplomatists and others !) to run two wedges of hostile territory, of which these two strongholds were the steel points, into the very centre of the Principality, well-nigh splitting it in two. On the side of Nikšić a gap opens in the mountain walls of our little Slavonic Switzerland ; they sink at this point to the inconsiderable altitude of only 600 feet above the plain, and a way is thus opened into the heart of the country. This is a gate of the mountain citadel, and the Turk has held its key. Time and again, from that ill-omened September day, 1714, when Numan Pasha deluged the whole country with a Turkish horde, raised by the Montenegrin chronicler to 120,000 men, down to the invasion of Suleiman Pasha in June last, the Turks have shown that they knew how to make use of the key in their possession. The obstinate and repeated attempts made by the Montenegrins throughout their history to take Nikšić, show that they have never underrated the vital importance of its possession, though hitherto they have been prevented from effecting their object by their deficiency in siege material.

It is interesting, however, to notice that the occasion on which the Montenegrins most nearly achieved the capture of Nikšić was in 1807, when they were acting with the Russians as our allies, against the French in Dalmatia. At that time a division of about 1,000 Russians were detached to aid the Vladika in his siege operations, and

LETTER
XVII.

*Value of
Nikšić to
Monte-
negro.*

*Repeated
attempts to
capture it.*

*Siege of
Nikšić
during
alliance
between
English
and Monte-
negrins.*

Nikšić was on the point of falling, when a quarrel between
the Russian commanders deprived the mountaineers of
their siege train and foreign auxiliaries.

If one goes back even to a time when Montenegro
was not yet Montenegro, to the days of the Serbian
Empire, one finds Nikšić, then known as 'Onogost,'
playing not less an important part as an imperial city.
The stately tombs, dating from those Old Serbian days,
which still exist in Nikšić are alone sufficient to tell us that
the city was then far more important than it is to-day.
It is instructive to recall that in the last days of the Serbian Czardom, when the Empire of Czar Dūshan was
crumbling to pieces through internal dissensions—in days
of anarchy and disruption—Nikšić, or Onogost, was the
scene of perhaps the last Imperial effort towards peace
and union.   It was here, in 1392, five years before his
death, that Uroš the Young, the last Serbian Czar, ratified
in council the terms of a pacification between the lord of
what is now Herzegovina, the citizens of Cattaro, and the
Republic of Ragusa.

LETTER XVIII.

A WAR-DANCE AT CETTINJE.

*Prince Nikola announces the fall of Nikšić in a poetic telegram to the
Princess. Announcement of the tidings by the Princess to the people.
Ecstatic rejoicings. War-dance before the Palace at night. Monte-
negrin Court ladies dancing with the warriors. Epic minstrelsy.
The ' Green Apple-tree' song, ' Out there, out there—beyond the moun-
tains.*

Cettinje : *September* 8.

RINCE NIKOLA, who is a poet and a Montenegrin, telegraphed the news of the fall of
Nikšić to his consort at Cettinje in a poetic
quatrain.

Vojvode Plamenatz told me that his Highness
'knocked off' this little effusion in a gay mood while
sitting with him and the Turkish commandant shortly.
after the surrender. It has quite a Homeric ring, and
the translator must, evidently, make use of an archaic
metre[1] :—

Mine is the standard that floats to-day above Onogost's
    Castle ;
Plamenatz, leader in war, quaffs the red wine cup below ;

[1] The original lines of Prince
Nikola are as follows—it will be
seen that my translation is nearly
verbatim :—
'Na bielu Onogoštu zastava se
    moja bije,

A Plamenac Voievoda pod njim
    ruino vino pije ;
Oko njega barjaktari zagraktaše
    ka' Orlovi ;
A Nikšići sjetni. Tužni sad su meni
    sve robovi.'

> Shrieking, like mountain eagles, the standard bearers
>   around him
> Gather; but Nikšić mourns, captive to-day of my arms.

Could one ask for a more appropriate despatch where-with to wind up our little Montenegrin 'Iliad'?

It was half-past two when the glad tidings reached the small palace at Cettinje. Heralds were sent to tell the citizens that the Princess had something important to communicate to them. In five minutes the whole place was astir, and the people thronging before the palace gate.

The Princess announces the news to the people at Cettinje.

The Princess now stepped forth on to the balcony and informed the crowd, amidst a breathless silence, that Nikšić was taken. She had intended to read her husband's poetic telegram, but was cut short by a tremendous 'Živio!' (Evviva!) and a simultaneous volley from the guns and pistols of her loyal subjects, and retired kissing her hand.

Ecstatic rejoicings.

The scene that followed almost baffles description. The people surged along the street, firing, shouting, singing, leaping with joy. It is an enthusiasm, an ecstasy, unintelligible, impossible in a civilized country —hardly to be expressed in civilized terms. You, from your work-a-day island, look on as belonging to an adult world apart, conscious of a something taken from you by centuries of 'progress,'—with the half sympathies of a pedagogue watching children at their play! Yes, these are children!—children in their primitive simplicity, in the whole poetry of their being; children in their speech, their politics, their warfare; and this is the wild, self-abandoned delight of children

Ancient veterans, grim, rugged mountain giants, fall about each other's necks and kiss each other for very joy.

The wounded themselves are helped forth from the hospitals, and hobble along on crutches to take part in the rejoicings ; men, in the ambulances, dying of their wounds, lit up, I was told, when they heard these tidings, and seemed to gain a new respite of life. Crowds are continually bursting into national songs, and hymns, broken at intervals with a wild ' Živio ! Živio !' and ringing hurrahs which Czernogortzi, as well as Englishmen, know how to utter. The big ancient bells of the monastery, and the watch-tower on the rocks above, peal forth. The bronze cannon—a gift from the sister Principality—is dragged out, and salvoes of artillery tell every upland village that Nikšić has fallen ; the thunder-tones of triumph boom on from peak to peak ; they are redoubled in a thousand detonations across the rock-wilderness of Chevo ; they rumble with cavern-tones through the vine-clad dells of Cermnitzka and Rieka; they are caught far away in fainter echoes by the pine woods of the Morača—dying and re-awaking, till with a last victorious effort they burst the bounds of the Black Mountain, and roll on to the lake of Skutari, the lowlands of Albania, the bazaars of Turkish Podgoritza.

The Metropolitan of Montenegro, most unsacerdotal of prelates—have I not seen him any summer evening, undeterred by his long robes, ' putting the stone' with athletic members of his flock? have not tuns of ale been flowing at his expense for the last half-hour? is it not written in his face? and shall I hesitate about the epithet?— the *jolly* Metropolitan of Montenegro proceeds to form a ring on the greensward outside the village capital, and there—between the knoll that marks the ruins of a church destroyed centuries ago by the Turks, and the Elm of Judgment, where of old the Vladikas sat

LETTER
XVIII.

*A war-
dance before
the Palace
at night.*

and judged the people—the warriors dance in pairs a strange barbaric war-dance.

In the evening the dance is renewed before the palace. Little Cettinje illuminates itself, and the palace walls and entrance are brilliant with long rows of stearine candles. It is here, before the palace gate, that the people form a large circle, the front rank of the spectators holding lighted tapers to illumine the arena. On the palace steps sits the Princess amidst her ladies, and little Danilo, the 'Hope of Montenegro,' stands in the gateway, almost among the other bystanders.

Two old senators, whose dancing days were over, one would have thought, a generation since, step forth into the ring, and open the ball amidst a storm of cheers. Younger warriors take up the dance—the 'dance!' but how describe it? Of this I am sure, that a traveller might cross Central Africa without meeting with anything more wild, more genuinely primitive.

The warriors dance in pairs, but several pairs at a time. In turns they are warriors, wild beasts, clowns, jack-o'-lanterns, morris dancers, teetotums, madmen! They dance to one another and with one another, now on one leg, then on the other. They bounce into the air, they stamp upon the ground, they pirouette, they snatch lighted tapers from the bystanders and whirl them hither and thither in the air, like so many Will-o'-the-Wisps. In a Berserker fury they draw from their sashes their silver-mounted pistols, and take flying shots at the stars; their motions slacken; they follow each other; they are on the war-path now—they step stealthily as a panther before it springs—they have leaped! but are they bears or wild cats? They are hugging one another now; they

are kissing one another with effusion. Other pairs of
warriors enter the arena, and this bout is concluded.

At every turn in the dance they give vent to strange
guttural cries ; they yelp like dogs, or utter the short
shrieks of a bird of prey. Was there a time—one is
tempted to ask—when the dancers consciously imper-
sonated the birds and beasts whose cries they imitated?
Did they, too, once, as the American Indians do still,
disguise themselves in the skins of wolves and bears, or
the plumes of a mountain eagle?

Perhaps, after all, this was originally a hunting dance,
and has been transferred later on to the god of war.
Perhaps,—but the most fascinating of interludes cuts
short our speculations! The rank and beauty of Montenegro must pay its tribute to manly valour.

One at a time, in light white Montenegrin dress—in
delicate raiment for Cettinje—step forth from the palace
gate a bevy of fair damsels. These are the relations of
the Prince himself, among them his sister, the wife of
Vojvode Plamenatz, the new governor of Nikšić ; and
the beautiful young wife of his cousin Božo Petrović, the
hero and saviour of Montenegro, come to honour the
people's representatives by dancing with them.

Nothing can exceed the tender majesty of these
Princesses among Princesses ; their dainty tripping forms
a pleasing contrast to the more uncouth performance of
the men. Nothing is lost in this light natural attire ;
their every motion is instinct with grace ; they have flung
aside their sombre kerchiefs, and the long black tresses
of their hair are caught in wavelets by the breeze. The
scene is of Homeric times, and these are the pure, true
forms of Antiquity! 'Horo,' their dance is called, and

it might have been a 'choros' of some Hellenic festival divine.

These old-world revels have their epic minstrelsy too. The people pressing round the dancers' ring pour forth a measured flow of song, antique in tones and cadence as the dances it accompanies; vigorous only in its persistence, spirit-stirring only to the initiated; to the outsider monotonous, almost doleful; as if even the music were so intensely national as of set purpose to repel the stranger. Yet what frenzy seizes on the dancing warriors as these songs proceed! What 'joys of battle' do they not re-live! How their eyes flash, and how they brandish their weapons against imaginary foes! These ballads are the poetic chronicles of four hundred years of incessant fight for freedom against the Turk, and those who hear them seem to clothe themselves in the flesh and blood of generations of heroic forefathers. It is the infancy of music lisping of the infancy of history, and that dull measured cadence is the heart-throb of a people still in the sturdiness of youth.

Each 'fyt' begins with a short song of a more lyric character, known as 'The Green Apple-tree Song,' which gives its name to the whole, but has no connexion apparently with what follows. Like the rest, however, it is very old, and has its origin far away amid the mists of Slavonic heathendom. We have here a mystic tree, a bird of omen, a hero warned of impending danger, a reference to bygone Czars. It has the true old Slavonic ring, and one feels as if one might hear it repeated by Russian peasants on the banks of the Volga or some ice-girt island of Lake Onega. Here is an English version :—

O green apple tree !
And green fruit given thee ;
Two branches there are,
And two apples they bear,
But on the third
Sits the falcon bird,
And he looks to the plain
Where Koshūt Capitain
Sits, drinking all day,
And to him doth say :
' Hie away ! Hie away !
Poor Koshūt ! much I fear
The hunters are near—
Czernogortzi are they,
They will bear thee away ;
They will bear thee afar
To the home of the Czar.'

LETTER
XVIII.

*The Green
Apple-tree
song.*

But the night grows old. The Princess has already retired. The Metropolitan gives the signal to conclude the festivities by moving towards the monastery. The crowd follows his footsteps, and bursts as by a spontaneous instinct into that most thrilling of Montenegrin songs—a song which touches on the most hallowed memories and the dearest aspirations of a people three quarters still enslaved ; a song inspiring at any time, but tenfold inspiring now that the hopes it breathes seem nearer their realization than at any time in the past four centuries. ' Onamo, onamo, za b'rda ' (Out there, out there, beyond the mountains), where the greatest of the Serbian Czars is sleeping, like Charlemagne, and Arthur, and Barbarossa, in his legendary cavern till his Vila guardian shall awake him.

Has the day of liberation come indeed ? But the

*The
national
hymn of
Monte-
negro.*

refrain of every stanza returns with a melancholy
echo :—

> Out there, out there, beyond the mountains :
> My Czar has ceased to speak, they say ;
> Of heroes was his speech that day.

> Out there, out there, beyond the mountains ;
> In some dark cave beneath the hill,
> They say my Czar is sleeping still.
> He wakes ! and rising in our wrath
> We'll hurl the proud usurper forth :
> From Déchan church to Prisrend towers
> That olden heritage is ours !

> Out there, out there, beyond the mountains :
> They say a verdant forest quakes,
> Where Déchan's sainted race awakes ;
> A single prayer within that shrine,
> And Paradise is surely mine !

> Out there, out there, beyond the mountains :
> Where the blue sky to heavenlier light
> Is breaking—brothers, to the fight !

> Out there, out there, beyond the mountains :
> Where tramps the foaming steed of war,
> Old Jugo calls his sons afar
> ' To aid ! to aid !—in my old age
> Defend me from the foeman's rage ! '

> Out there, out there, beyond the mountains :
> My children, follow one and all,
> Where Nikola, your Prince, doth call,
> And steeps anew in Turkish gore
> The sword Czar Dūshan flashed of yore,
> Out there, out there, beyond the mountains.

LETTER XIX.

NIKŠIĆ IN MONTENEGRIN HANDS. (I.)
EXODUS OF MAHOMETAN POPULATION.

*Exodus of Mahometan population in spite of Prince Nikola's assurances.
Refusal of Turks to accept equality before the law. Obvious advan-
tages to Montenegro of Mahometan emigration. The Montenegrin
'Vespers.' Transformation of Asia into Europe. Artistic regrets.
Nikšić and its Plain indispensable to the Principality. Good conduct
of Montenegrins since the capture. Turks and Christians frater-
nizing. Calumnious tales of Montenegrin atrocity circulated in
European papers. Frank confession of a fanatic.*

Nikšić : *September* 21.

FOR the last few days I have been the witness of a
melancholy spectacle—the wholesale emigration
of the Mahometan population of Nikšić. But
do not imagine that this is due to any harshness
on the part of the conquerors. Immediately on entering
the town Prince Nikola convoked the leading Mussulman
townspeople, and informed them in the most reassuring
terms that he guaranteed for all who chose to remain
complete personal security, the possession of their houses,
lands, and all property, perfect religious freedom, and,
in fact, all the rights of Montenegrin citizenship, including
the right to carry arms. On the other hand, if any chose
to depart, they would be allowed to carry all their

*Mahome-
tan exodus
from
Nikšić.*

o

LETTER
XIX.

*Refusal of
Maho-
metan popu-
lation to
accept
equality
before the
law.*

moveables with them, and would be supplied with horses and guards by the Montenegrin Government.

The Mahometans, it might have been expected, would have accepted the generous terms offered them and remained; but it has not been so. The greater bulk of the Mahometans of Nikšić—and the fact has great importance as evidence of what in similar circumstances may be expected to take place in other parts of Turkey— have preferred poverty and exile, the loss of house and land, to remaining in a place where they could no longer feel themselves the dominant caste.

Equality before the law has been offered them; but equality before the law is precisely the thing which the Turks will not accept.

Some of them no doubt expect that at no distant date the Sultan's troops will recapture Nikšić, and that they may then return and claim their own. But such hopes are vain; there are few more certain things as to the future of these lands than that Nikšić will remain in Montenegrin hands.

*Advan-
tages of Ma-
hometan
exodus to
Monte-
negro.*

By emigrating wholesale the Mahometan inhabitants have but been playing into the hands of their conquerors. Had they elected to remain, the danger of an *émeute* within the walls would have much hampered the defensive strength of a garrison; and to keep in check an armed population of some 4,000 fanatics a large body of Montenegrin troops must continually have been drawn off from other services. Long since, the little Principality has learned the danger of possessing a large Moslem population within its borders; the renegades were always ready to conspire with their co-religionists beyond the border, and the darkest chapter in Montenegrin history tells how they opened a way for the Turk into the heart of the country. Montenegro would, indeed, long ere this have become a Turkish pashalic but for the terrible remedy devised by the greatest of her Vladikas.

Montenegro, too, has her 'Vespers.' On Christmas eve, 1702, the whole Mahometan population was massacred from one end of the country to the other.

But, with such experiences in the past, it may be imagined that the incorporation of 4,000 Turks in the body politic at one fell swoop was regarded by many Montenegrins with great misgivings, insomuch that the most respected man and the bravest general in the country, the Vojvoda Božo Petrović, told me only the other day that had he had the management of affairs he would never have given the Turks the option of remaining.

As it is, Turkish fanaticism is sparing the Montenegrin Government a great deal of trouble, and the Prince has lost nothing by his generosity. Day by day up to the present, the last day on which the Prince accords them horses and escort, these haughty Moslems have been turning their backs on their native city, carrying with them their wives and children and household goods. Some bands of emigrants have taken their way through the Zeta Valley and the very centre of Montenegro, to Podgoritza and Albania; others to Gatzko and the parts of Herzegovina still in Turkish hands—all alike secure of Montenegrin protection and good faith.

It has been a striking sight to watch the long cavalcades of Turkish fugitives, sometimes as many as sixty at a time, streaming out of the town. Now and then one of the little ones would look disconsolate enough, but the women were muffled in their long white sheets, so that you could hardly see so much as a nose, and the men were too

proud to betray any symptom of regret, and were even
dressed out in their brightest holiday costume.

How dull and dingy look the Montenegrins who
escort them beside these brilliant Orientals! How strange
and characteristic is this transformation of which I am
at this moment a witness!

There is plenty in the town still to remind us that we
were yesterday in Asia. Grave turbaned Turks still
squat, chibouk in hand, on the vermin-ridden divans of
the *cafés*. The most picturesque of children tricked out
in all the colours of the rainbow still play about the
filthy streets. You may pick up, if you have a mind to,
the elaborately-carved trunks of Turkish families remov-
ing; you may invest in gorgeous Herzegovinian rugs,
with their rich pervading orange—most creditable me-
morials of the taste and industry of Nikšić as she was;
you may purchase, from their Bashi-bazouk owners desirous of realizing, ancient Albanian flintlocks, their stocks
inlaid with mother-of-pearl, their barrels exquisitely
wrought with silverwork by the artists of Prizrend. I
have said that the Mahometans of Nikšić refuse to betray
any emotion. I was wrong. Even the stoicism of the
Moslem can break down at parting with his arms. An
ancient Turk who had covenanted with a friend of mine
to sell his flintlock for thirty florins—it had a date upon
it of three centuries back, and is destined to adorn a
museum at Berlin—fairly burst into tears as he concluded
the bargain, exclaiming 'My great-grandfather will rise
from his grave to rebuke me!'

To-day, as I have said, something of this Oriental
atmosphere still lingers around us. There are still some
fifty Mahometan families who have not yet migrated;
but it is probable that the Turks will leave Nikšić almost

to a man. Montenegrins are already settling here. Some
who resided here before the war are coming back; and
I may mention, as an example of honesty on the part of a
'true-believer,' that a Montenegrin merchant, who at the
beginning of the troubles, two years back, left his wares
to the safe keeping of a Mahometan friend, found them
intact on his return here the other day.

Yes, that old tyrannous dominant caste had its fine
side too ! Those turbaned greybeards sitting in their
fur-bordered mantles outside the city gate, awaiting the
signal for their departure, are not wanting at least in
nobleness of expression. In the time it takes me to write
this, their escort has arrived, and they are quitting their
homes for ever under the protection of the Serbian tricolor.
The black-bordered fez, that always seems to mean business,
the dull white *dolama* or tunic, the dingy brown *struka*,
the plaid of these Slavonic highlanders, may seem but a
poor exchange for the majestic turban, the brilliant flowing
tasselled fez, the rich brocaded vest, and all those fantasies of
gold and emerald. One is filled with overpowering artistic
regret ! One follows the retreating groups as their silver-
studded arms flash in the sunlight far across the plain ;
but regret ceases as the eye wanders across that rich
champaign so bare of cultivation, or lights, here and there
in the suburbs of the town, on some small garden patch,
where the growth of tobacco, tall stalks of Indian corn,
golden figs, and clustering vines attest how rich this land
might become, when no longer trodden down with Turkish
hoof-prints. You feel then that the land has need of these
gaunt, horny-handed highlanders. You turn your eyes
beyond the plain to the naked mountains that enclose it
on every side in their hungry arms, and you realize what
need Montenegro has of the rich plain of Nikšić. The

LETTER
XIX.

*Value of
Nikšić to
Monte-
negro.*
Montenegrins reckon that the amount of arable and pasture
land in this fertile 'polje,' which exceeds in size any plain
that I can recall in the whole of Dalmatia, and is watered
by two streams, equals that at present to be found in the
whole Principality. Considering the wealth that lies at her
gates, Nikšić, with her 6,000 inhabitants, ought to increase
her population tenfold in the course of a generation.
The foundations of a new order of things are already
being laid.   Thé first step taken by the Montenegrin
Government has been to extend the telegraph system of
the Principality here ; and a telegraph station is already
open in Nikšić for the first time in her history.   Perhaps
one may look forward to the time when a Zeta Valley line
will connect her with the lowlands of Albania, Skutari,
and the Adriatic, and Nikšić carpets and Nikšić tobacco
find a place in the English markets.

The conduct of the Montenegrins here since the capture has been beyond all praise.   Except that on the first
day of occupation a few houses of departed owners were
pointed out to the newcomers by the Turks themselves,
and the effects shared impartially by Turks and Montenegrins alike, there has been no plunder, no robbery of
any kind, and no single instance of violence offered to a
true-believer.   The Mahometans go and come as freely
as if they were still masters here.   They are allowed to
stalk about, carrying whole armouries of swords, knives,
and pistols, and—such, I suppose, is the force of habit –
they are still the only people here who swagger.   The
kindly feeling that apparently exists between the conquerors and conquered is such, that no one would imagine
he was in a captured city.   Montenegrins and Nikšićians
take wine and raki together, and chat about the events
of the siege in the most friendly manner ; the Turkish

townspeople, however, considering it a point of honour to conceal the number of the fallen on their side.

The Turks of Nikšić, in fact, like those of all this part of the world, are of the same Slavonic race as their enemies ; they speak the same mother tongue as the Montenegrin warriors with whom they exchange experiences ; many, in fact, are actually Montenegrins by birth, Nikšić having served as a kind of city of refuge for outlaws from the Principality. There was not an Osmanlì inhabitant in the town, a few Nizams of the garrison alone representing the Turk *pur sang.*

Though the Mahometans of Nikšić have refused to remain under the Prince's government, the consideration with which they have been treated has produced a most favourable impression on them, and will have an important influence in facilitating Montenegrin conquests in Herzegovina. It appears that their officers, taking the cue from the profligate romancers of Stamboul, had spread abroad the most atrocious stories as to the doom the inhabitants might expect if they fell into the hands of the Montenegrins. It was only the other day that a Turkish official in this part reported (to order) at Constantinople that the Montenegrins had been butchering young Turkish girls, and roasting two children alive. This abominable calumny was telegraphed over Europe, and has already been gloated over by the English organs of Turkish mendacity.

Tales of horror as well founded as the above, naturally made the Nikšićians expect small mercy at the hands of their conquerors. They were therefore not a little surprised to find their lives and property distinctly more secure than under their own Government, and to see their sick and wounded carried at once to the Monte-

LETTER XIX.

No Osmanlìs at Nikšić.

The forbearance of the Prince politic.

Calumnies about the Montenegrins circulated by Turks.

negrin ambulance tents, where they are being treated at the present moment by Russian doctors, as carefully as are the Montenegrins themselves.

'Why,' exclaimed a Turkish bravo, on hearing the terms granted by Prince Nikola to the citizens, ' if we had been conquerors and you had been in Nikšić, we should have burnt you out and then chopped you in pieces.' This was frank at any rate, and I commend the remark to those impartial persons, whose verdict on all ' comparative atrocities' is ' six of one and half a dozen of the other.'

LETTER XX.

NIKŠIĆ IN MONTENEGRIN HANDS. (II.)
THE TOWN AFTER THE SIEGE.

The effects of the bombardment. Roman aspects of the town. Proba-
bility that a Roman city existed on Nikšić Plain. Old Serbian
survivals in Nikšić architecture. Tombs of old Serbian heroes. In
the Turkish citadel. The 'black hole' of Nikšić. Use of bullets by
garrison productive of fearful lacerated wounds. Reflections on the
Montenegrin Conquest.

Nikšić : *September* 23.

HE town of Nikšić has suffered terribly from the
bombardment ; there is hardly a house that has
not been struck by a shell, and it is not by any
means safe to knock too hard at a friend's door
when paying a visit. We have had some tremendous
storms during the last few days, and of nights you might
hear the crash of falling walls and beams. Indeed, the
room of the dirty little place in which I slept was hardly
the safest place in which to find oneself. At the best of
times it has three shell-holes in the wooden ceiling and
the same number of breaches in the walls, and a goodly
portion of the remainder of one of these came down
about my pillow during the night. So, on the whole, it
is better for the present to seek tent life in the outskirts
of the town, as I am now doing (my tent being a trophy

*Effects of
the bom-
bardment.*

from Suleiman Pasha's army), though this too must have
been a warm corner during the last few weeks. In the
side wall of a magazine opposite my tent door are some
dozen holes and fractures caused by shot and shell.
Houses absolutely burnt and destroyed are numerous
enough, especially beneath the citadel ; but the city walls
and towers, the chief mosque, and the larger magazines
and buildings generally are very little injured, owing to
the small calibre of the artillery at the disposition of the
Montenegrins during most of the siege.

The town is divided into three parts—the citadel, the
inner town within the walls, and the town without the
walls, which is wide-spread and includes the bazaar and
chief streets.

*The inner
city of
Nikšić.*

The old inner city is very interesting. It is in general
plan and appearance completely Roman. It is square in
form, except that the higher side, which lies along the
citadel hill, has a more irregular outline, owing to the
rock. At every corner and in the centre of each wall
are towers, square in all cases but one, which, like some
of the Roman towers of Diocletian's palace-city, is
octagonal. The centre tower of each wall has a round
archway beneath which the street runs, and it seems as if
in the original town two main streets intersected each
other at right angles, as they should in a Roman 'Chester.'

*Roman
aspect.*

A town in general aspect and arrangement more completely Roman it is impossible to imagine. Not that I
found anything new that I could swear to as actually
dating from Roman times. Although I have enjoyed
the rare privilege of exploring minutely every nook and
cranny of a town till yesterday in Turkish hands, and
consequently almost as inaccessible to antiquarian curiosity as if it were in Central Asia instead of a fortnight's

distance from London, I found no inscription, no un-
doubted Roman moulding, and satisfied myself that much
of the walls was of comparatively recent date. But
whether the foundations of Nikšić are actually Roman or
not, whether the present walls follow the exact lines of a
city of the Cæsars, in one sense or another Nikšić may
with strict accuracy be described as a Roman city—
Roman, even if only as a most striking representative of
the continuity of Roman art in the Illyria of Slavonic
days. It has indeed been supposed from the 'Itineraries' that a Roman city actually existed on or near the
site of Nikšić,[1] and that a Roman way along the Zeta
Valley connected it with Diocletian's birthplace on the
banks of the Moratcha, while another led over the
mountains to Terbulium, Narona, and so to that more
famous spot where the world-weary Emperor fixed
his retirement and his tomb. Indeed, it is hard to
believe that the rich plain of Nikšić was without a considerable city in the palmiest days of Illyrian history—
the days of the Roman Empire, the days when these now
neglected lands gave emperor after emperor to the
world.

The main city gate, leading into the bazaar street of
the outer town—a broad and spacious street, it is to be
noted, in the Slavonic village style, very unlike the narrow antique alleys of the inner city—is of peculiar interest, and may give a date for most of the walls and
towers as they exist in their present state. It has, indeed,
a Turkish inscription above it ; but this means nothing,

---

[1] There still seems to be a trace of the Slanum of the Itineraries in the Slansko polje' near Nikšić. There are traces of habitation there, some of which may be Roman. If so, the Roman city did not occupy the present site of Nikšić.

LETTER
XX.

Old Serb-
ian carving
above city
gate.

as it was a usual practice of the Ottoman conquerors to insert inscriptions claiming for their own Sultans and Beglerbegs the works of earlier Giaour architects. I saw one such the other day above the gate of Castelnuovo, but the Turkish stonemason who described in the comfortable language of the Ottoman the rearing of the gate by Sultan Mahomet had forgotten to erase all traces of the inscription of the earlier Serbian builders ! The Turkish inscription, therefore, proves nothing whatever. But the fantastic beasts carved on the archway below— these at least do not lie. They are never the work, let us be allowed to hope, of those whose duty it was to obey the precepts of the Koran as touching the portrayal of living animals. Their peculiar and unmistakable style proclaims them at once of the same date and by the same workmen as the similar animals to be seen carved on old Serbian tombs. They date from before the Turkish conquest, or, if they do not, they are at least no more Turkish than St. Michael's Tower at Oxford is Norman, even though it date from Norman days.

I should like to linger over the other antiquities of Nikšić—the old Greek church and ancient Serbian cemetery, with its really stately tombs [1] of bygone Vojvodas and Junaks, dating from the days of the Serbian Empire, and exhibiting a continuous series of Christian monuments down to the present day, for in Turkish Nikšić there were about forty Christian families. Those tombstones are a mute but eloquent testimony to the degradation of the rayah under Turkish rule. As they advance in date towards modern times the Christian art here

---

[1] A representation of one of these old Serbian tombs will be seen on the cover of this book.

becomes more and more debased ; inscriptions vanish; the tombs grow smaller and meaner ; they dwindle finally into unsightly heaps of turf and unhewn stones.

But it is war-time, and my readers may prefer a glimpse of the citadel as the Montenegrins found it. I went over the whole place with Martinović, the present commandant, an intelligent Montenegrin artillery officer, who has studied in Austria, speaks German well, understands his business, and personally superintended the whole bombardment.

The fortress is a long, straggling building, stretching along the rocky ridge that overlooks the older part of the town, with two octagonal towers at either end, which, so far as their general aspect goes, may date from the Middle Ages ; and a central block of more pretentious construction, but which could not stand a day against good modern artillery. From the numerous breaches in the walls and the supplementary earthworks one got a good view of the various positions successively occupied by the Montenegrins ; to the east, the dominating limestone mass of Mount Trebjesa, carried at the beginning of the siege ; below, the small rocky knoll of Petrova Glavitza, taken and retaken, and the scene of the last serious fighting ; to the west, a rocky ridge within pistol-shot of the fortress and completely commanding both citadel and city, taken by the Montenegrins on the last day of the bombardment. In the middle of the citadel were the traces of an explosion occasioned by the Montenegrin artillery from this position, which destroyed most of the remaining ammunition and hastened the surrender. The Turks had only twenty-four rounds left when they gave in ; but it was shot, not powder, of which they stood in want. Two out of the five powder magazines were found completely full by the Montenegrins on entering, and this, with the twenty-one cannon, eight of them Krupp's and one 25-pounder, in addition to 4,000 sacks of corn and provisions found in the chief magazine, afforded most timely supplies to the conquerors.

I did not, however, pass through the citadel without observing some most disagreeable traces of the former occupants.

One was a hollow in front of one of the towers where the Turks, to save the trouble of decent interment, had buried their men in hay.

In the same tower, used as a barrack by the former garrison, the present commandant said he would show me the Turkish prison. Ascending some filthy stairs and entering a dark and even a filthier chamber, I was considering this abominable enough as a place of detention, when Martinović told two of his men to take up part of the floor. This, I now perceived, was arranged so as to open, and, the beams being removed, there was disclosed a dark and loathsome pit, in which those who offended against the late beneficent masters of Nikšić were, according to ancient usage, immured ! It was hardly to be expected that the owners of dungeons like this should be squeamish as to the obligations of international law.

Scattered about in the citadel magazines you may pick up scores of bullets, the use of which sets those who employ them on a level with the South Sea savages who still make use of poisoned arrows in their warfare. These bullets have a small plug of wood imbedded in their cones, which on striking a human body splits up the middle and produces a fearful lacerated wound, which in nearly all cases results in gangrene.

Who, after sights like these, can wish to see the tattered cross of Montenegro that floats to-day over Nikšić citadel again replaced by a Turkish crescent?

The capture and occupation of Nikšić may seem to some a small matter compared with the mighty events that are working out their course beneath the shadows of the Balkans ; but the transformation that I have seen perfected here before my eyes is a microcosm of that greater Revolution whose tocsin is already sounding to the Black Sea and the Ægean. *Magnus ab integro sæclorum nascitur ordo.* Centuries hence half Europe will look back to that Revolution as the greatest since the fall of the Eastern Empire.

NOTE.

THE MONTENEGRIN CAMPAIGN IN HERZEGOVINA.

As a sequel to the fall of Nikšić—although, as I have already stated,
it was never my intention in this work to touch largely on events of
a purely military character—I venture to subjoin a short summary
of the subsequent operations of the Montenegrins on the side of
Herzegovina, which I wrote at Nikšić on September 30th, from
materials supplied me by officers who actually took part in it.

'On the fall of Nikšić it was generally believed at head-quarters,
even amongst those most conversant with the intentions of Prince
Nikola, that the Montenegrin forces, amounting to 8,500 men, till
then engaged in the siege operations, would be marched in the
direction of Jezero, where Hafiz Pasha was held in check by the
battalions under Vojvodas Lazar Socića and Peiović; and that,
having given a good account of the 10,000 Bosnian Turks there
encamped, the Prince's army would wind up the campaign by
the capture of Kolašine, and retire to winter quarters in time to avoid
the autumn rains.

'On the evening of the 11th general orders were issued to prepare
to march on the following morning. Every one in camp believed
that a movement to the east, in the direction of Jezero and Kolašine, had been decided on, and it was not till the tents were struck
that the actual destination was divulged. Then, to the surprise of
all, the order was given to turn westwards, and take the road to Bilekia.

Whether this expedition was based on real strategical considerations (Bilekia, it must be remembered, commands the road from
the important city of Trebinje to the Duga Pass), or whether it had
an object of a more political character, or whether, again, it was
a mere freak of the Prince's, who prides himself on his sudden

resolves, and is altogether of too Oriental a cast not to be influenced at times by personal caprices,—the precise object is difficult to determine, being only known to the Prince himself. So much, however, I have sufficient authority for saying, that the move was at least partially due to a desire on the Prince's part to elicit more definite declarations on the part of the Austrian Government, and to fix within more precise limits the sphere of probably impending Austrian action. In a word, the Prince wanted to know for certain whether he might acquire the ancient city of Trebinje, or whether that city, distant only three hours from the Dalmatian frontier and five from Ragusa, came within the scope of the annexationist views of the military party at Vienna.

The course ultimately pursued by the Prince Nikola demonstrates pretty clearly the character of the representations made to him by the Austrian military *attaché*, who, in conjunction with the Russian, was during this time in constant conference with him. Nikola took Bilekia, but though a good road lay open to him to Trebinje, lying completely at his mercy five hours to the east, he turned due north to take the comparatively unimportant Turkish fortresses of Gatzko and Goransko.

A two days' march from Nikšić brought the Montenegrins before Bilekia, which is a small town of about 150 houses, commanded and defended by a 'kula' and a large fortress, enclosing various magazines. The large artillery which the Montenegrins have recently obtained from Russia sufficed the Vojvoda in command, Verbitza, to capture the 'kula' on the second day, and the two large cannon that the Montenegrins had taken with them being advanced to the captured position, and earthworks being thrown up there during the night, the citadel itself capitulated on the third day. This speedy capture of a fortress which, according to competent military critics, could have held out for six months against any forces the Principality could have brought to bear against it, was the first fruits of the wise and conciliatory terms granted by Prince Nikola to Nikšić.

In the old days, when Montenegrins and Turks gave no quarter on either side, when the capture of a town was followed by the massacre of its inhabitants, the besieged on either side fought with desperation, as for dear life. But the garrison of Bilekia, among

CAMPAIGN IN HERZE-GOVINA.

The objective of the Prince's movement.

Austrian susceptibilities.

Capture of Bilekia.

P

whom were Turkish soldiers who had been allowed to march out of Nikšić arms in hand, had no such motives to prolong resistance. They only demanded and accepted honourable terms, and were allowed to march off, to the number of 420 regulars and 6 officers, retaining their arms like the garrison of Nikšić. The same generous policy has now borne even more conspicuous fruit in the easy capture, one after the other, of the almost impregnable Turkish fortresses in the Duga Pass.

The inhabitants of Bilekia, however, met with a very different treatment from that which the Nikšićians had received. They had incurred the implacable vengeance of the Montenegrins for having profited by the defeat at Kristatz to cut off stray divisions of the retreating Czernogortzi, to whom they showed no quarter, and having further carried off a convoy of provisions.

Severe penalty inflicted on the inhabitants.

The penalty now inflicted by the Prince's orders was severe. All the Turkish houses in Bilekia were burnt to the ground, and the fortress and magazines shared the same fate ; three captured cannon, 2,000 sacks of wheat, and relatively enormous stores of other provisions being first removed. The destruction of private property was, however, tempered with mercy. The Mahometan inhabitants of Bilekia were allowed before the destruction of their houses to remove all their moveable property. All plundering was so absolutely prohibited that in the case of a single detected culprit the Prince inflicted personal chastisement with his own hands. One of the

Paternal government in Montenegro!

Vojvodas had, it seems, purchased some stolen articles from one of his troop ; the Prince, getting wind of it, taxed his officer with the offence, and the Montenegrin answering in the free and easy manner of his race, His Highness flew into a passion, and drubbed him then and there with his stick in the presence of his troops. Such is paternal government in Montenegro !

From Bilekia, as I have already said, the army turned north a two days' march to the plateau of Gatzko, there being little to record on the way except that at Plana, at seven on the evening of

Shock of earthquake.

the 17th, a shock of earthquake travelling in a south-eastern direction was felt by all in camp, and was immediately succeeded by a tremendous storm. On the 18th head-quarters were fixed at Kristatz, which commands the Gatzko plain. On the evening of the 19th a small division detached for that purpose captured the fort of Zlostup, the northernmost key of the Duga Pass. A detachment of two battalions had been already operating on this important pass from the side of Nikšić, and had captured in succession the Turkish strongholds of Presieka, Hodjina Poljana, Nosren, and Smenderov, including in all about 400 prisoners and immense quantities of stores. By the capture of Zlostup, the Duga Pass, which is the tactical key of the whole of North-eastern Herzegovina, was completely cleared of Turks, and the advantage gained for the Montenegrins for any future operations in Central Herzegovina can hardly be over-estimated. The Duga Pass is, of its kind, unique in Europe. It is not, indeed, a smooth path between overhanging precipices, but a fairly broad succession of rocky undulations, hemmed on either side by mountain walls from 1,000 ft. to 1,800 ft. above the pass, and culminating in still loftier mountain citadels, on which the Turks have reared forts almost inaccessible to artillery.

On the 21st, the way to Nikšić through the Duga Pass being now in Montenegrin hands, and the autumn rains having begun with more than usual violence, the Prince resolved to transfer his head-quarters to Nikšić, whither he arrived from Presieka the same day, for the first time in his life enjoying the prospect of the magnificent Duga defile. The Prince took with him only a single battalion, leaving six-and-a-half battalions to besiege the important Turkish town and stronghold of Metokia (sometimes known, from the surrounding plain, as the town of Gatzko), and despatching another four battalions under Vojvoda Vukotić to capture the Turkish fortress and magazines of Goransko. This was successfully accomplished on the 26th, and a garrison of 300, three cannon, and very large quantities of stores have thus fallen into the Montenegrin hands.

While the above operations were being carried out by the Prince's main army to the north and west of Nikšić, a most brilliant success was being won by the eastern division, under Vojvodas Lazar Socića and Peiović. Having been reinforced by two battalions from before Nikšić, the forces at the disposal of Vojvoda Socića amounted in all to eight battalions, or about 5,000 men, with which he had to hold in check Hafiz Pasha, who with about 10,000 troops, largely irregulars drawn from Bosnia and Herzegovina, had crossed the Tara river, and having entered the district of

P 2

*Battle of
Jezero.*

Jezero, had already ravaged parts of Herzegovina in Montenegrin possession, and was threatening an invasion of the north-eastern cantons of the Principality.

It was by Jezero that the two armies came into conflict with one another. The Turks, with their back to the Tara river, were posted on the edge of a rocky plateau which juts forward in three promontories overlooking a small plain, if so can be called a depression broken by a hundred rocky knolls and strewn with blocks of limestone, which made advance over such ground almost an impossibility to any but mountaineers.

The three divisions of the Turkish forces, the centre and two wings, were posted respectively on the three promontories indicated, and faced beyond the narrow plain nothing but a wall of mountain so steep that even the Montenegrins could not attack on this side.

*Blunders
of Hafiz
Pasha.*

This was the main blunder committed by the Turkish commander—his army was posted facing nothing. But the blundering of Hafiz Pasha did not end here. The rocky knoll on which he had stationed his centre was at least an hour in the rear of any possible line of battle; the position held by his right wing was good in itself, but cut off by an intervening ravine from all co-operation with the centre. The point at which the Montenegrins must debouch, if desirous of attacking, lay on the left of Hafiz Pasha's position. It was therefore certain that his left wing must bear the brunt of the action, and at least half his forces should have been concentrated on this side, but instead of this the left Turkish wing was the weaker.

*Turkish
left routed.*

At 9.30 a.m. on September 12 the Montenegrins advanced to the attack along a mountain saddle-path that conducted them to Hafiz's left, and which, indeed, was the only avenue of attack open to them. The commander, Socíca, at once perceived the errors of his adversary, and concentrated his whole attack on the Turkish left, which was quickly turned, almost surrounded, and hurled back in confusion.

This Turkish division was already routed when Hafiz perceived his blunder and ordered the centre to advance to the relief of his left.

But it was already too late. The centre, struggling forward among the rocks, got inextricably entangled with the division which was now hurled back upon them. Fighting among the limestone boulders in confused order, the mingled left and centre of Hafiz became an easy prey to the sure-footed mountaineers who now swept down upon them. By midday the whole Turkish force was in full retreat, and the Montenegrins found 480 dead and wounded on the field of battle, to which must be added the number of bodies undetected amidst the rocks and gullies, what wounded the Turks carried with them, 32 prisoners, two flags, and large convoys of horses, cattle, and provisions. The Montenegrin loss was not more than 13 killed and 23 wounded.

Very little pains, however, seem to have been taken to follow up this success. Hafiz Pasha, though his rearguard and three cannon were threatened for some days, finally succeeded in withdrawing his forces beyond the Tara.

The battle of Jezero was signalized on the part of the Montenegrins by a splendid instance of individual valour which certainly deserves chronicling. A Montenegrin of the tribe of Piperi, Luka Philipov by name, had distinguished himself at the battle of Vucidol by taking Osman Pasha alive and carrying him bodily to Prince Nikola, who presented the gallant fellow with 500 ducats for his prize, and jestingly bade him bear him another Turk in the same fashion. Now for a Montenegrin to be told by 'the Master'—the 'Gospodar,' as the Prince is generally called here—to do a thing is for him to do it or die. Accordingly, our hero of Piperi being present at the battle of Jezero, and mindful of 'the Master's' order, seized the moment of attack to rush into the Turkish lines, hug a true-believer round the waist in a bear-like embrace, and lug him off bodily through flashing arms and leaden storm, disarming him by the way.

To carry his prize safely to the rear the Montenegrin made a slight *détour*, but he had not got half way to the Montenegrin position to which he was making when a bullet struck him, passing through both thigh-bones, and letting go his captive he fell heavily to the ground.

The Turk, with a shout of triumph, sprang upon his fallen captor, but despite the agony in which he lay the Black Mountaineer retained strength of body and firmness of mind sufficient for the occasion. He laid one heavy hand upon the Turk, who had sprung at his throat, and with the other pointed his revolver at his adversary's head, quietly remarking, 'Now then, Turk, if you don't want to be blown into another world, just lift me on to your back. And now, my fine horse,' as the cowed and astonished Turk complied, 'just trot me over to my friends out there !' Kismet being obviously against him, our Moslem obeyed his driver, and stumbled on over the rocks groaning under the weight of the burly Montenegrin, to where the men of Piperi stood marvelling at the approach of what they believed to be a Turkish Goliath, ten feet tall ! But the warriors burst into a roar of laughter when, on the apparition approaching nearer, they perceived a Turk bearing, as it appeared, in the most humane manner, their wounded Luka to the lines. My readers will be glad to learn that Luka Philipov is recovering from his wound. He was almost senseless when his captive delivered him to his friends.

*Results of
the cam-
paign
summed up.*

In the battle of Jezero and the ensuing operations, which ended in the withdrawal of Hafiz Pasha beyond the Tara, the Turkish losses have been not less than 1,000 men. From every point of view the recent operations of the Montenegrins in Herzegovina have been most successful, and the aggregate gains to the Principality very considerable. To sum up the results of the last three weeks' campaign, including the capture of Nikšić, the Montenegrins have gained one pitched battle against forces double their own ; they have taken two important towns, eight fortresses, twenty-seven cannon, supplies of food and military stores sufficient to support the whole Principality for say half a year ; in Nikšić alone 10,000 horse-loads of provisions were captured ; they have put about 1,500 Turks *hors de combat* and taken 3,000 prisoners ; they hold in their own occupation one third of Herzegovina, and possess the keys of half that province ; and all this with infinitesimal losses to themselves. The road to Mostar, the capital of the Herzegovina, lies open.

*Would the
Prince
march on
Mostar ?*

Would the Prince march there ? This has been the question of the last few days. His Highness himself, elated by his recent conquests, was desirous of doing so, but his great political tact rendered him averse to acting without the consent of the Austrian Government. Very animated negotiations have been carried on on this subject, but the Prince's desire has met with a most resolute veto on the part of the Austrian Government. Add to this that the strenuous efforts made by the Turks to collect troops in Bosnia

sufficient to check the Montenegrin advance made it possible that
by the time the Prince's troops arrived before Mostar the coast
might not be so clear, that the autumn rains are already down upon
us with a vengeance, and that winter is already closing in among
the Herzegovinian Alps, and it will be seen that all prudential
considerations conspired with the recommendations of diplomatists.

In a council of war held September 28 it was decided to close
the campaign in the Herzegovina, and, maintaining a strictly defensive attitude on this side, to transfer active hostilities to the milder
region of the Morača Valley and the Albanian littoral, where even a
winter campaign is possible. The three chief fortresses to be reduced in the Morača Valley are Spuž and the towns of Podgoritza
and Zabljak. The territory to be acquired is at least as valuable to
Montenegro as the plain of Nikšić; it is not only fertile and well
watered, but it commands access to a large part of the coast of the
lake of Skutari, with its prolific fisheries; while its potential importance is best shown by the fact that in ancient days this district
supported the great city of Dioclea, according to one account the
birthplace and name-giver of Diocletian. In early Serbian days this
favoured champaign between lake and mountains had not lost its
importance. It was the very kernel of the renowned Principality
of Zenta, of which Montenegro is the modern representative, and
gave Emperors to the Serbs, as it had done before to the Romans.

The importance of the narrow strip of sea-coast lying between
the lake of Skutari and the Adriatic, and extending from the Austrian
frontier to the river Bojana, is of equal importance to the Principality, as giving it access to the sea, from which it has hitherto been
cut off by European diplomacy. The possession of the town and
port of Antivari and the free navigation of the river Bojana are vital
questions for Montenegro.

CAMPAIGN
IN HERZE-
GOVINA.

*Operations
transferred
to the
Albanian
side.*

LETTER XXI.

THE HOPE OF BOSNIA : MISS IRBY AND MISS JOHNSTON'S CHILDREN.

Pakratz, Slavonia : *November* 15.

O star of hope rises above the political horizon of unhappy Bosnia. The insurrection still drags on; there are camps still on Mounts Kossaratz and Germetz, and in the district which I once described as 'Free Bosnia.' But the rigour of an Alpine winter is closing on us, and the bulk of the Christian population of Bosnia are still hopeless refugees beyond the borders of the province. I have been visiting these wretched colonies lately at various spots along the Croatian and Slavonian frontiers, and I find the destitution almost as great as I have already described it to be among the limestone peaks of Dalmatia.

My readers must weary of the monotonous tale.

Indeed, how can it be adequately told? After all, it is only by individual cases of wretchedness that our hearts are really touched. A man may pity the misfortunes of a single family and yet be almost callous to a tale of national disaster. That is, perhaps, partly why, looking back at those wan, haggard crowds, one's mind's eye does not dwell upon the many, but rather here and there on some group or image standing forth in egregious pathos.

I can still see an aged Bosnian hag, shivering in the mud of a Slavonian village as she stands clutching with her skeleton fingers, two—how can one name them?—it would be mockery to call *them* children!—two deformed and half-clad punies, who are clinging to her rags and huddling piteously to her side—as if for warmth! 'Their mother is dead,' the old woman answered me, 'their father went away with the *Ustashi* (the insurgents), and no one knows where he is. Most likely the Turks have killed him.' I turned to the little creatures themselves—What were their names? How old were they? Could they remember where their homes were in Bosnia? But they only gaped vacantly at the stranger, and it hardly needed to look into their lack-lustre eyes to know why they did not speak.—It was blank, hopeless idiotcy that alone stared forth! Everything that had ever raised them above the level of a brute had been scared and starved and frozen out of them!

'They don't speak,' was all she said, and *that*, perhaps, was a disadvantage—but her old eyes spared her from knowing more—she did not even seem to realize that there was anything hideous to recoil from. After all, they were her property; she had found the waifs, and taken to them—and what else had she in the world to care

for? So she fondled the two diminutive monstrosities
that knew her not from a mother, and pushed back the
tangled mat of hair from their dull brows.

Repulsive certainly the group to artistic eyes !—yet
worthier the pitying contemplation of that Christendom
on whose soil they stood than many and many a simper-
ing Madonna !

A quarter of a million fugitives.

If any one now cares to work out a multiplication sum
in human misery, here are a few figures. The total
number of refugees has never fallen much below a quarter
of a million, the decrease caused by death having been
constantly supplied by new emigrations. Of these, the
number in Austro-Hungary, scattered along the whole
Slavonian, Croatian, and Dalmatian frontiers, is under-
estimated by the authorities at 115,000. The official
register of those in Montenegro and the part of
Herzegovina now in Montenegrin hands, sets them down
at 90,000; but this, I confess, I consider to be an over-
statement. On the borders of Servia there are about
40,000.

Mortality among Bosnian refugees.

As to the amount of mortality among them since
their arrival (the first comers have been here two full
years), it is difficult to obtain exact returns. The
death-rate has varied considerably, as might be expected,
in the different districts. Those who have sought refuge
in the rich Save valley have fared better than those amidst
the Dalmatian peaks ; and those who have found themselves amongst a ' Serb ' or Orthodox Greek population
have been better aided and sheltered by the inhabitants
of the country than those whose new neighbours have
belonged to the antagonistic creed of Rome. From
inquiries made in Slavonia and Croatia, I estimate the
mortality among the fugitives since their arrival at

something like 22 per cent. on that part of the frontier, the richest of all. Near Knin, on the worst part of the Dalmatian frontier, Miss Irby considers the proportion of deaths to be nearer 50 than 30 per cent. ; the native committees estimate it at 50. At one spot on the Bosnian-Dalmatian frontier—the miserable glen of Kamen, which I have already described, and where I have obtained accurate data,—the death-rate for the six months from the beginning of winter last, up to midsummer, had reached the terrible proportion of 40 per cent. In Montenegro and Serbia it is still more difficult to obtain trustworthy returns, but the refugees have certainly not fared better there than on Austro-Hungarian soil. From these calculations it results that 25 per cent. is a very moderate estimate of the average death-rate among the refugees since their arrival; and even this would give a total of 62,000 deaths. Deducting now 10,000 as the death-rate under normal circumstances during the same period, it will be seen that some 52,000 souls have succumbed on Christian soil to hunger and exposure and their attendant diseases. Those who have seen, as I have, new cemeteries in the wilderness where two years ago not a soul existed will hardly think this number an exaggeration. I believe it to be far below the mark.

Private charity and individual exertion might well recoil where an Empire and Principalities have failed ; and yet I wish that some of my readers who think such efforts hopeless, could have visited, as I have had the privilege of doing lately, the schools which the two English ladies, Miss A. P. Irby and Miss Johnston, have been founding for the refugee children. After seeing every moral mutilation that centuries of tyranny could inflict, aggravated and added to by the miseries of such an exile,

LETTER
XXI.

*Mortality
among
Bosnian
refugees.*

*Fifty-two
thousand
starved on
Christian
soil.*

*Miss Irby
and Miss
Johnston's
refugee
schools.*

who can go away without a feeling of despair for the
present generation of refugee Bosnia? Who might not
be tempted to doubt whether a future still existed for
these degraded pariahs? But the scene of the English
ladies' labours is indeed an oasis in the lengthening waste
of human misery. Pakratz, their head-quarters, is a
friendly little town in the Slavonian mountains, and has
been admirably chosen as a centre to work from, since
here, under the superintendence of Professor Josić, is
established the training school for schoolmasters of the
Serbs of Austro-Hungary, called the 'Preparandija.'

This Preparandija is an excellent institution, and it
might even afford a subject for reflection to some of our
smart writers, whose cue it is at present to 'write down'
the Serbs and other Slav rabble, that training colleges to
teach the art of teaching should exist among them. I
went over the Preparandija with Professor Josić, who
examined his class in my presence. He put a series of
questions to his pupils concerning the art of teaching, the
proper arrangement of a school, and so forth. It was
amusing enough to see one of the future schoolmasters
made to act the pedagogue while all the others transformed themselves into a class of children, and went
through their pothooks and spelling.

One feature in the teaching struck me especially.
When a child has made a mistake in his work he is to be
made to find it out himself, with the least possible help
from the schoolmaster. This pedagogic part is of course
only one of the subjects taught in the college, the various
masters having to pass in physiology, chemistry, geography,
music, and so forth ; but it is certainly not the least
valuable. Who would turn untrained nurses into a
hospital? And yet in how many English schools are

masters untrained in the 'art of teaching' let loose to experiment on the youthful *corpora vilia* !

In aiding Miss Irby's educational efforts among the Bosniacs the Preparandija has been invaluable. The excellent professors gave up the whole of their last vacation to teaching the masters that Miss Irby had found for her refugee schools, and very well they have taught them. Of course, the first difficulty that the ladies had to contend with was, how to get Bosniacs willing or in any way capable to be masters. Miss Irby may say in her own words how she and her fellow-labourer managed to find the first :—

'It was some weeks,' she writes, 'before we could find a teacher. The beginning was at length made in the following manner :—We were conversing with a Bosnian insurgent, one of those who had been living for some years in exile in Serbia, and had crossed the frontier into his own country at the beginning of the rising last August. He had now come over into Austria, most probably in order to recruit his band among his friends and relations. He was a fine tall man with a very striking countenance, and what the old Serbian song describes as the "glad, bright eye of heroes." While we were talking an old man came up and joined us. He was dressed like a Grenzer or Austrian borderer, in sheepskin jacket, military great coat, and blue trousers. "He is one of us," said the Bosnian, "and the very best among us all." After the unsuccessful rising in 1858 he settled in Slavonia, acquired land, built a hut, and was living with his children and grandchildren on the produce of his few cattle and crops. In reply to our inquiry about the Bosnian fugitives in his village, he told us that he had living in his hut a poor crippled young man who was absolutely destitute, and who did not receive the Austrian Government allowance because he had been assigned to a distant Catholic village

LETTER
XXI.

*Beginning
of Miss Irby
and Miss
Johnston's
schools for
the refugee
children.*
where he could not bear to go. The Austrian Government, with good reason, objected to the immense crowding of the Bosnian fugitives in the district of Pakratz, and was anxious to equalize their distribution along the frontier. " This poor cripple," said the old man, " was very clever, and had been a schoolmaster in Bosnia." Hoping that he would prove to be the very person we were seeking, we sent for him to come to us the next day. A more desponding, haggard-looking object I scarcely ever saw. We made him write before us, and read a Serbian psalm. He read with a feeling and expression rare in Bosnia; and we were struck with his singularly intellectual development of forehead. The next day we drove to the village of Kukunjevatz, where we heard it would be possible to obtain the old deserted school-house. By the courtesy of the Knez, or elder of the village, the arrangement was immediately made, the Knez offering to take the young schoolmaster into his house until a sleeping-place in the dilapidated building could be repaired. In two or three days the school was opened (March 6). The poor young man has displayed unusual skill and energy; the change in his appearance, now that he is earning his own bread in his own vocation, is very remarkable. He has already taught some of the elder boys to read, and they have received Serbian Testaments as a reward.'

Since this first beginning, in March 1876, the ladies have worked with such energy and success that they have now established 22 day schools; they have 23 school-masters and one schoolmistress, and very nearly 2,000 refugee children in their schools. The children are fed as well as taught; and Miss Irby has now set some of the elder lads, who have already learned to read and write, in the way of making their living by apprenticing them to various trades. I saw nine such apprentices at Pakratz, all doing very well; one apprenticed to a baker, another to a tailor, others to bootmakers, and so forth. One of these bootmakers could make four pairs of *opankas*, or native sandals, in a day.   Another scholar, a young insurgent, who so longed to learn to read and write that he had submitted to go to school with the children, now earns fifteen florins a month as a swineherd.   He lives in the forest, but he has managed to keep up his literary tastes, having taken with him quite a small library, some books of ' Piesme ' or Serbian heroic lays, a Testament, and writing materials ' to improve his hand.'   Yet in this case, as in the others, education seems to have given a greater capacity for the business of life ; so much so, that the lad's master declared the other day that ' there never was such a good swineherd.'

In company with the English ladies—to whom 30 miles in a springless cart is nothing of a day's journey— and Professor Josić, I visited several of the schools in the Slavonian villages, and was thoroughly initiated into their working.   Nothing struck me more than the amount of civilization and refinement that had been infused into the masters ; there was none of the dazed, stupid look of the raw Bosnian rayah.   It was quite a pleasure to watch the schoolmaster at Pakratz : teaching the children was so evidently a labour of love.   At the end of school several of the little ones went up to him and whispered their small confidences in his ear.   The children themselves did not seem a bit in a hurry for the end of school, though they might have been, for liberal hunches of bread made in Pakratz by one of the Bosnian apprentices were then distributed to them.   Quite rosy many of them looked—a cheerful contrast to what I have seen.   Each school was provided with a blackboard, there were globes to teach geography with, and the walls were bright with English coloured prints of New Testament subjects.

In several of the schools Professor Josić examined the children before me to see how they were being taught. The children passed very creditably in spelling, reading, writing, and simple arithmetic. The handwriting of one lad, who wrote on the blackboard at his Bosnian master's dictation, 'Heaven helps those who help themselves,' was quite a specimen of caligraphy. It was very pleasant to hear them repeat some of the New Testament parables, using their own language. In the parable of the Good Samaritan, for instance, the thieves were 'Haidutchi' (Haiduks), the Bosnian and South Slavonic brigands; the Levite was a 'parroch,' the Bosnian equivalent for 'parson' 'What was St. Paul before his conversion?' asked the Professor. 'A Pandour,' answered the child promptly,—the Pandour being a kind of frontier Zaptieh in Bosnia. Another boy was asked what was the meaning of 'neighbour' in the parable.

'Supposing, now, you were to see any one in difficulties, would you refuse to help him because he wasn't a true Serb, but an unbelieving Jew, or a Magyar, or a Turk?'

'Not a Turk !' said the lad, decisively.

'Oh yes, even if he was a Turk,' said another milder child.

At Novatz some of the children were asked why they had left Bosnia. 'Because the Turks robbed father and beat us,' answered one. And why did the Turks do that? After some consideration, the lad replied, 'Because it was their empire.' 'No,' broke in another little fellow impetuously—'not their land ; it is our land !' All the children clapped their hands at this answer.

Nothing took my fancy more than the spirit with which the children repeated parts of their national heroic lays that they had learned by heart. I think that they had been told to fold their arms while reciting, but one lad, when he came to a thrilling passage in the lay of Kossovo, unlocked his arms, and, throwing one hand behind him, pointed, with an energy of gesticulation all the more impressive from his previous calmness, at some imaginary actor in that national tragedy. It was quite natural : he so obviously had the hero before his eyes ; but I doubt if an English child would have done the same—just as I doubt whether any pure-blooded Anglo-Saxon is capable of fully understanding a Slav. Their imagination, their powers of realizing what is not patent to the eye—of converting ideas into realities—are something quite abnormal among European peoples.

The quickness with which the refugee children learn astonishes every one. ' I don't know how it is,' said a native of Pakratz to me, ' but these Bosnian children learn twice as quickly as ours.' Everywhere I find the same. It is just the same in Miss Irby's schools near Knin, on the Dalmatian frontier of Bosnia ; just the same among our little Herzegovinians in the Ragusan schools for which Mr. E. A. Freeman and Mr. W. J. Stillman have done so much. The children in Miss Irby's schools, from the age of six upwards, learn to read and write in the astonishingly short space of three months. They are helped, no doubt, in this particular by possessing a phonetic system of spelling, and the admirable Cyrillian alphabet ; perhaps if they had spelling such as ours to learn, with all their quickness many of them would have to return to Bosnia without being able to read. There is a hungering and thirsting after knowledge among these little ones which seems to me quite pathetic ! Packed together in their little school-rooms one could fancy them

Q

to be little birds waiting to be fed! I can imagine no more melancholy prospect than that these helpless, hungry fledgelings should be turned adrift to pass too many of them—as thousands of the refugee children have passed already—to the outer darkness of death, or, worse still, unreason. Yet that is what must happen unless fresh help comes from England ; for, including the housing, feeding, and clothing of 72 orphans that those kind ladies have on their hands, Miss Irby and Miss Johnston incur an average expense of £300 a month in order to keep up their schools.

Nobody who has seen them, I feel sure, can fail to love these Bosnian children. To whatever part of the country they belong, at whatever spot on the long frontiers you meet them, they are still the same ; there is the same quiet, homely expression ; there are the same neat little plaits that recall old German pictures ; the same quaint variations in the colour of the hair—it is a fact, that many of the children here have positively piebald pates— 'golden hairs amidst the brown,'—such as I certainly have not remarked anywhere else. And then too there are the same Serbian eyes, large and beautiful, sometimes a light hazel, which, in a sidelight, take a transparent lilac hue ; sometimes, and perhaps oftener, a pale sapphire. Pakratz is hundreds of miles distant from Ragusa, yet these are the same faces that one remembers among the little Herzegovinians there ; they might all belong to the same family—

> ' Facies non omnibus una ;
> Nec diversa tamen, qualem decet esse sororum.'

And this striking uniformity of type is but the external counterpart of an uniformity of character and temperament not less remarkable. The children behave here just as they behave at Ragusa; they never seem to quarrel there or here; there and here they have just the same capacity to learn; there and here each behaves just as his fellows, each repeats the same gestures. Individuality is at a minimum, but this sameness of character must naturally be of great aid to those who have to lead them. In an average English school there would be a much greater variety of type, physical, moral, and intellectual. Suppose the master is a pure-blooded Anglo-Saxon, he may have to deal with scholars whose blood is partly Celtic or partly Norman, or partly French, or of other nationalities. What rules of management can he apply to all? What universal key can he find to fit their character? He learns by painful experience that one child may starve on what is intellectual meat to another. But the Bosnian schoolmaster has to deal with a less mixed breed; when he understands how to teach one child he understands how to teach all. This sameness of type is really as true among the adults as among the children, and seems to me to have important political and social bearings in all South Slavonic lands, into which I cannot now enter, but which may, perhaps, be summed up as a capacity of being drilled.

I close this letter a long way off from the scene of Miss Irby and Miss Johnston's labours, but I wish my readers could catch a glimpse of the contrasts that return to me! There is a vision of girls who are hags before they are women; of human pigmies distorted by exposure and disease, and wasted away by hunger, staring the blank, stupid stare of idiotcy—a vision of the supreme corruption of the most beautiful; but, then, a vision of row on row of pretty, childish forms, neatly

LETTER
XXI.

*Uniformity
of type
among
Bosnian
refugee
children.*

ranged on their small school benches, neither starved nor naked ; of cheerful, fresh expressions—lashes quivering with the breath of a newly-awakened intelligence, as I have seen the tender sprays of a Bosnian forest stirred by the April breeze ; and a starlight of quick eyes twinkling forth from those half-dreamy child faces, like morning stars of a brighter life.   Then one feels that the hope of Christian Bosnia may not have set for ever !

APPENDIX TO LETTER XXI.

Virtual suppression of the Refugee Schools by the new Governor of the Croatian Military Frontier.

I HAVE already, in the course of these letters, been forced to allude to the hostile attitude which the Catholic and *Magyarizing* party in Croatia have thought fit to adopt with regard to the miserable Bosnian refugees who belong to the Greek Church.[1] Had I wished to enlarge on this disagreeable topic I might have accumulated instance after instance of the petty persecutions with which the Catholic governmental faction in Croatia take care to keep alive the enmity of their own Serbian subjects. I might have mentioned personal friends, men of learning and position, whose only crime was that they professed the Pravoslav religion and that they consequently sympathized with the oppressed Serbian nationality beyond the Turkish border, who have been dragged from their beds to prison on the denunciation ' of a Government informer,[2] and who, after suffering months of imprisonment without trial, and having had their most private papers ransacked, have been contemptuously set

[1] Although, as I have already pointed out, a large and respectable party amongst the Roman Catholics of Croatia regard these anti-Serbian manifestations with abhorrence.

[2] The technical name by which these modern *delatores* are known to the German-speaking bureaucrats is *vertraute Personen*—'confidential persons. The fear of again compromising some of the victims alone deters me from giving the names and the fullest particulars of these cases. The recent instance of Militić, however, would alone be sufficient to prove that there is no tool of despotic government borrowed by Metternich from Tiberius too vile to be made use of by the Constitutional tyranny of Hungary and its Croatian under-kingdom.

APPENDIX
TO LETTER
XXI.

*Miss Irby's
schools
practically
suppressed
by General
Philip-
povié.*

at liberty without being allowed so much as to know the specific charges against them or even to face their accusers !

It might, however, have been imagined that even among the Magyarizing officials of Croatia there would have been found sufficient respect for public decency to restrain them from extending their hostility to the two English ladies whose admirable work among the refugees has been recorded in the preceding letter. Unfortunately, however, such has not been the case. After annoying the two ladies with every petty persecution in his power, the new governor of the Croatian Military Frontier, General Philippović, has practically suppressed Miss Irby and Miss Johnston's refugee schools in Slavonia.

As the English ladies, in the pursuit of their work of relief on the still more destitute Dalmatian frontier in the neighbourhood of Knin, are not able during a good part of the year to superintend their Slavonian schools in person, it results that they would never have been in a position to keep them up had it not been for the invaluable and self-sacrificing services of the professors of the Serbian training school at Pakratz in undertaking to superintend Miss Irby's refugee schools in her own and Miss Johnston's absence. Professor Josić himself is a man of the highest character, greatly respected in the country, and has been for seven years and more director of the Serbian Preparandija for training schoolmasters at Pakratz. His assistant (Professor Despotović) bears the same high character. These two gentlemen, whose only crime is that they belong to the Pravoslav and not to the Roman Catholic religion, have now been prohibited from superintending the refugee schools which English charity had founded, and Miss Irby writes to me from Knin (February 16, 1878), that under the circumstances the schools must be closed and the unhappy Bosnian children turned adrift.

General Philippović has accomplished his object, and 'Croatian' and 'Magyar' interests have made themselves respected! But civilized Europe will shudder at such deeds ; and the student of history will point out that, as in the fifteenth century, Romish bigotry, by throwing Puritan Bosnia into the arms of the more tolerant Turks, opened the way for the Asiatic to the heart of Europe, so in this nineteenth century that same intolerance bids fair to escort the Russians in triumph to the Adriatic shores.

LETTER XXII.

POLITICS AMONG THE BOSNIAN BEGS.

Begun at Berbir, Turkish Bosnia : *November* 18.

THE world obtains passing insights into Bosnian affairs from two points of view, and from two points only. Now and then the cry of the rayah makes itself heard—even in the *salons* of 'society.' As to the most worthless of all aspects of the question—the state of Bosnia as surveyed from the standpoint of the present nominal governors of the province, the Osmanli bureaucrats—blue-books are crammed with it.

But Christian Bosnia is at present mostly to be found beyond its borders, and Osmanli Bosnia only exists on

LETTER
XXII.

*Bosnia to-
day neither
Ottoman
nor Chris-
tian.*
paper. Bosnia to-day is neither Ottoman nor Christian.
As week after week the dominant race of the Empire
pays to Russia that tax which of all others it is least
capable of supporting : the blood-tax of Ottoman man-
hood—as, day by day, intent on the forlorn hope of
Orkhaniè, Mehemet Ali calls off the few remaining
regulars that garrisoned this western corner of the Balkan
peninsula, till Northern Bosnia, at all events, is completely
drained of Ottoman troops—a silent Revolution, the progress of which I have already noted, has been working
itself out in this province.   By the force of circumstances,
Bosnia relapses into the state in which reforming Sultan
Mahmoud found her at the beginning of this century.

That work of Ottoman re-conquest which Mahmoud
began and Omar Pasha completed in 1851, is to-day
undone, with the exception of the mountain strongholds
where the insurgents still prolong, and will prolong, a
struggle ' deplored by diplomacy.   That old ruling caste
of Mahometan Slavs, which up to Omar Pasha's time
had preserved the feudal privileges and customs of the
mediæval Christian kingdom, for which at the moment of
Turkish conquest it had sacrificed its creed—the Bosnian
Begs and Agas—have stepped once more into their former
dominant position.

If there was peace to-morrow ; if by some miracle
' the integrity and independence of the Ottoman Empire '
were preserved, and the hand of Fate averted ; if the 'ring'
at Stamboul consented to introduce those reforms and
that impartial administration of justice of which the rayah
stands so much in need, the Ottoman would first have to
turn the forces which had escaped the Russians, against
the native, feudal, Mahometan aristocracy of Bosnia and
its retainers.

To-day the Begs are once more lords of Bosnia, and they know it. Their views and resolutions command at the present moment an importance which no other party in or out of the province—neither refugees, nor Serbs still resident in the towns, nor Roman Catholics, least of all the alien Ottoman bureaucracy—can claim for theirs. But of these views and resolutions, of Bosnia surveyed from the standpoint of the Mahometan nobility, the world at large knows nothing, or next to nothing. Haughty, reserved, hating the alien in every form, conscious of their strength, perhaps over-confident of it, biding their time, they do not deign, like their subtle Osmanli rivals, to manipulate European diplomacy and take consuls in tow. My readers may remember that not long ago, owing to a singular combination of circumstances, I was able to present them with what, without great pretension, I may call the only authoritative declaration of policy on the part of the Begs that has as yet reached the European public. The s ions of the great Kulenović family, who expressed their opinions to me so frankly at Kulen Vakup, could not be persuaded that my visit was unconnected with a desire on the part of the English Government to put itself in direct relation with themselves as the rightfully dominant element in Bosnia. They were frank to me because I spoke to them without the intervention of official Turks, in their communication with whom they are naturally most guarded. Since then I have recently, by less direct though trustworthy channels, obtained some further revelations as to the political attitude of the Bosnian Begs, which can hardly be without their value at the present moment, though it may not be advisable to allude too precisely to the when, where, and how of such experiences.

LETTER
XXII.

*The Begs
again
masters of
Bosnia.*

LETTER
XXII.

*Two parties
among the
Begs.*

*The Old
Bosnian
party.*

The course of events has brought to light two distinct parties among the Bosnian Begs. One of these, which I may call the Old Bosnian party, by far the larger of the two, is composed of the more fanatic and irreconcileable elements among the Mahometan nobles. The other is more moderate, and leans to a policy of conciliation towards the rayah.

The ideal of the Old Bosnian party is Bosnia as it existed before Omar Pasha succeeded in curbing that haughty oligarchy which had succeeded under a Mahometan guise in preserving to modern times the full spirit and practice of feudalism. The alien Osmanli bureaucracy which Omar Pasha succeeded in setting up in Bosnia, and all the centralizing innovations of the 'New Turks,' including the sham Constitution, is to be ruthlessly swept away. To the Sultan personally—the Czar, as he is always known to these Slavonic Mahometans—this party is loyal enough ; but they are willing to accept him rather as a suzerain than as a master, and any Vizier whom he may appoint, as in the old days, to be governor of the province must sink into his old position as a shadow of a shadow. As to the rayah, the reply given me by Mahomet Beg Kulenović—like other members of his family, an adherent of this Old Bosnian party—faithfully reflects its inflexible determination. The rayah is to remain a rayah still.

The man who is becoming more and more the recognised head of this Old Bosnian party, and whose influence throughout the length and breadth of the province is at present greater than that of any other, deserves more than a passing notice. In the last desperate struggle of the old Bosnian aristocracy against Omar Pasha, which was fought out in the bare and

mountainous angle of the province known as the Kraina
or Turkish Croatia, the adherents of the *ancien régime*
were headed by a certain Najib Aga.

In the battle of Bihacs, Najib Aga, with many other
of the principal Begs, fell into the hands of the Ottoman
commander, and was transported to Asia. The greater
part of his lands were also confiscated, but he was
afterwards allowed to return to Bosnia. There, however,
he again fell under suspicion, was summoned to Serajevo,
and, if report speaks truly, was there poisoned.

His son, Féim, had been taken away in early youth,
and sent to Constantinople, there to be brought up as a
true Osmanli, and to be cut adrift from all Bosnian
associations. His teachers, to all appearance, succeeded
admirably, and Féim, now Effendi, had become a most
promising specimen of a ' New Turk,'—a man of the
salons, affecting Parisian manners and costume, and
steeped in the newest corruption of Stamboul.

Féim Effendi might now be reasonably considered a
safe man by the Divan, and was allowed accordingly to
return to his native province and take possession of what
remained of his patrimony.

There is scarcely a rayah refugee from the country
round Banjaluka, where Féim resided, who has not his
bitter experience of the arts by which he now set himself
to increase that patrimony. This polished gentleman,
with his European fashions and easy, affable manner—
the very man to win a consul's confidence—stands con-
victed of more insatiable extortion and refined cruelty to
the rayah than any other tyrant landlord in Bosnia.
Féim Effendi did not, indeed, ride ' nadjak ' in hand
among his Christian serfs, robbing and mutilating, at the
head of Bashi-bazouk retainers, as fierce, fanatic Begs of

*Féim's tool,
the Der-
vish.*

the old school have done when the fit seized them or the
long-suffering rayah turned recalcitrant.

No ! Féim Effendi had not gone to school at Stamboul
for nothing. The worst crimes that are laid to his charge
he accomplished by means of middlemen. His chief
tool in these transactions has been a certain Dervish,
Fezlia by name, who has all the Vakufs or lands belonging
to the principal mosque in Banjaluka under his control.
This man, like Féim himself, has gained his knowledge
of men and things beyond the limits of the province
where he now resides. He was born in Fezzan, and has
visited most parts of the Ottoman Empire. A mutual
compact was soon struck between the two men. Féim
wanted land to exploit, Fezlia wanted patronage to enable
him to practise his extortions with impunity, and the
Christian rayahs of the Vakuf were pillaged between
them in the most barbarous manner.

*System of
false accu-
sations.*

Whenever a rayah seemed to have something worth
pillaging, the usual plan of these villains was to concoct
a false accusation against him. The poor man paid what
he could to be let alone, but if the sum was considered
insufficient, the false accusation was turned to account,
zaptiehs were sent to pounce upon him, and the refractory
rayah was thrown into a Banjaluka dungeon. There at
least it might have been imagined the rayah found
himself in the hands of the officers of justice ; but it was

*Tortures
applied to
rayahs.*

not so. In the cell itself a variety of tortures were
applied, with the alleged object of extorting a confession
of the crime, but really to extract more money. One
of the most usual tortures in vogue with Féim's apparitors
was to set the victim in a wooden cage which obliged
him to preserve a standing posture, and to leave him
there for days at a time, with heavy iron weights round

his neck. This torture, I am assured, is extremely painful, all the more so as during this time the prisoner is
without food. In Bosnia, as formerly in England,
prisoners are dependent for their sustenance on public
charity, and in Banjaluka, where the chief prison is
above a city gate, the prisoners obtain food by letting
down a basket through a hole in the floor, and whining
to the passers-by below.

I need not write in detail of other tortures applied
on the spot, in a more rough and-ready fashion by the
zaptiehs and other instruments of our Effendi and Dervish,
of men 'smoked' in pigsties, or tied naked to trees in
the depth of winter, with a freezing douche of water
thrown over them at intervals. It is enough to say that
there was no form of cruelty and extortion known to the
old feudal lords of Bosnia that was not practised by
Féim's agents. Meanwhile, this 'perfect Turkish gentleman' was amassing considerable sums, and with his
wealth was daily increasing his influence in the province.
Till the present troubles began he completely commanded
the confidence of the Osmanli governors of the province,
and was esteemed in every way a 'New Turk.' The
troubles began, and Féim's attitude became more
doubtful. It was observed that his relations with the
native aristocracy were more intimate, but, on the other
hand, when the new 'Constitution' was proclaimed,
Féim showed that he at least was on the side of ' enlightened reform' by getting himself elected member for
Banjaluka, the scene of his oppressions and infamies.
Féim became 'member for Banjaluka,' and as such might
be esteemed a friend of the new Ottoman Constitution.
But the troubles continued, the Russian war broke out,
the Bosnian Begs were beginning to awake to a con-

LETTER
XXII.

*Féim
assumes
leadership
of Old
Bosnian
party.*

sciousness of their power. Féim began to lay aside the mask. He ceased to be even nominally the ally of the Osmanli alien ; he began to take the place to which by birthright as well as by talent he was entitled as a leader of the native Bosnian aristocracy, and to-day he poses as the avowed head of the Old Bosnian party among the Begs.

This Old Bosnian party is, as I have said, largely leavened with religious fanaticism, and indeed, one of its chief adherents, a certain Sarcher Beg Djinić, is reckoned a kind of saint in Bosnia. He has built a shrine for himself near Banjaluka, and is the prophet and soothsayer of the party.

Thus the Begs, at whose head Féim stands, adopt an uncompromisingly intolerant attitude towards the Christians. But recent events have been bringing to light, even among the old Mahometan nobility of Bosnia, a party more moderate in its views, less fanatical, and inclined to take a juster view of the situation. It is the happiest sign of the moment that this party among the Begs—I may speak of it as the Moderate party—is daily on the increase, though still by far the larger number of the Begs are on the more irreconcilable side. At the head of the Moderates stands a certain Djinić, a relative of the Mahometan saint already mentioned as one of Féim's chief henchmen. The progress of this more liberal party is due to a variety of causes. The great impoverishment of the landlords, owing to the flight of their Christian serfs beyond the frontier, and the immense destruction of property ; the increasing consciousness that Turkey is fighting a losing battle against Russia, and perpetual rumours of the imminence of an Austrian occupation of Bosnia, have convinced

many of the Begs that the old order of things must be
changed, and that it is impossible at this time of day to
change it by going back to the feudal *régime* which
existed before Omar Pasha re-conquered Bosnia for the
Ottoman.

There are thus many symptoms on the part of this
more moderate party of an inclination to seek some basis
of compromise, and compromise more especially with
the Serbian or Greek Church elements of Bosnia and its
border-lands. Begs near Berbir have been making private
overtures to induce their refugee serfs to return, promising
each 'house community' a dozen acres of land, to be
held in perpetuity, but demanding three days' service
weekly on the Begluk, or property of the lord. Returning rayah refugees have, however, met such a fate lately
from the more fanatical among the Begs and from Turkish
officials that overtures far more liberal than these would
have no prospect of success.

There is no doubt that even the more moderate
among the Begs would preserve their old privileges if
they could ; but they begin to perceive that if they do
not set their own house in order, others will do it for
them. Thus there is no doubt that Djinić and his party
would, like the others, prefer that Bosnia should remain
in some form a vassal state of the 'Ottoman Czar.' But
many of them are beginning to doubt the possibility of
the Sultan retaining even a distant suzerainty over Bosnia,
and are asking themselves the pertinent question, 'If we
must bow before the Giaour, shall Bosnia be Austrian or
Serbian ?' And to this question their usual answer is—
'Bosnia shall never be Austrian !' An Austrian occupation and eventual annexation of Bosnia—which I for one
regard not only as the most probable solution of the

LETTER
XXII.

*Repug-
nance to
Austrian
annexa-
tion.*

present difficulty, but as the only solution within the
sphere of practical politics—is regarded by the majority
of Bosnian Begs and by all the orthodox rayahs with an
intensity of detestation which it is almost impossible for
the outsider to conceive of. As to the 'orthodox' rayah it
is useless attempting to argue the question with him ! On
this subject they are all fanatics. ' If Austria takes Bosnia,'
said one of the most intelligent among the refugees to me,
' Germans and Jews will get the land.   There will be no
real freedom.   If we must be slaves, we had rather be
the slaves of our own nobles ; they at least speak our
tongue.   But Austria or Hungary would destroy our
nationality ; they would do us more harm in 50 years than
the Turks in 500.' ' We have a proverb in Slavonia,'
another Serb, a native cf that Hungarian province,
remarked to me, ' the Turk sucks the rayah's blood ;
our Government soaks ours away with cotton wool.'

*Rapproche-
ment
towards
Serbs
among
Moderate
Begs.*

An intense feeling of nationality, shared in Bosnia by
both Mahometans and ' Serbs ' (though less conspicuous
among the more intellectually degraded Roman Catholics),
lies at the bottom of this repugnance to absorption by
Austro-Hungary ; and the natural outcome of this is a
tendency on the part of the Begs (the less fanatical, that
is, among them) to seek some kind of union with the
Serbian States—either Danubian Serbia or Montenegro—
as an alternative. I have evidence that in 1859 a most
remarkable convention was actually signed between the
Begs then desirous of freeing themselves from the
Ottoman dominion and the Slavonians and Croats of
Greek faith on the other side of the Save, then conspiring
against the hated yoke of Austria. What was possible a
few years since can hardly be impossible to-day.

It is, moreover, not only this national feeling, but a

certain shrewdness of perception as to their own interests as a caste, which lead the Begs to prefer union with Serbia to union with Austria. They know well enough that Serbia is too small and weak to reduce them to the level of ordinary subjects ; they see the probability even that Bosnia once tacked on to Serbia, Serbia would rather become an appanage of Bosnia than the reverse. And this correct instinct of the ruling caste seems to me to be a fatal argument against such an arrangement, even if Austro-Hungary were for one moment to permit of it. Before the discordant elements of Bosnia can be welded into one whole—as a preliminary to the revival in that sect-distracted country of any genuine national life—the application of a very real *force majeure*, in which this haughty, fatalistic, ruling caste should see the unmistakable decree of Kismet, seems to me a primary necessity. And that is precisely what Serbia cannot supply.

But the most striking symptom of the present tendency among the Begs to make friends with the Christian Mammon as the day of reckoning approaches is the manifestation of a tendency to return themselves to the faith which their forefathers abjured.

Elsewhere I have alluded to the possibility of the Mahometan Bosniacs under certain circumstances returning to the Christian fold. I have already introduced my readers to a district once Bosnian and Mahometan, but which, coming under Austrian rule, has re-accepted Christianity. We seem now on the eve of witnessing such a re-conversion on a large scale in Bosnia, and, extraordinary as the fact may seem, a careful study of the history of the country will go far to explain the phenomenon.

R

LETTER XXII.

Serbia too weak to annex Bosnia.

Bosnian Mahometans returning to Christianity.

LETTER
XXII.

That the Bosnian Nobles prefer their Caste interests to those of Islâm.

The nobles of Bosnia, whether Christian or Mahometan, seem always to have valued their interests as a caste more highly than the creed they professed. Their tyranny has, on the whole, been more the tyranny of a caste than a creed. At the time of the Turkish conquest of Bosnia, the forefathers of the present Begs renegaded for the most part from a Puritan form of Christianity, and accepted the creed of their conquerors rather than sacrifice their possessions. There is, indeed, no prospect of such a severe alternative being placed before the Bosnian Begs at the present time, but there can be no doubt that, even if it be for the sake of their social position, many of the Begs, if they must bow before the Giaour, will accept his creed. For them to-day, as at the moment of Turkish conquest, the chief anxiety is as to their position as a noblesse. Their rank secured, their future, political and religious, becomes quite a secondary consideration.

Remark of a leading Beg.

' Come Swabian, come Muscovite,' remarked old Beg Grosdanvić the other day to a friend of mine, ' I don't care what happens. I have got my old rolls and patents of nobility given my forefathers by our Christian kings, and I shall be a Beg still ! '

No doubt the Begs have at different periods since the Turkish conquest made great profession of their Mahometan faith, and Bosnia is the very Goshen of Mahometan old believers. But I doubt whether this religious Conservatism has not been more a weapon of policy than an evidence of deep conviction. Most of the nobles who at the end of the fifteenth century renegaded to Islâm, did so only as a temporary shift. Like the crypto-Catholics, to be met with to-day by the

thousand in Albania, they remained Christians, heretical
Christians, be it observed, at heart, though outwardly
conforming; and many of the great Bosnian families
have not even at the present day lost this transitory idea
of their religion.

Coming events cast their shadows before them. *Recent in-*
Some of the lesser Begs and Mahometan merchants have *stances of re-accepta-*
already begun to get themselves baptized. A friend of *tion of Christi-*
mine, a Bosnian merchant, perhaps the most prominent *anity by*
among the refugees, has within the last few days received *Bosnian Mahome-*
visits on Austrian soil from five Mahometan merchants *tans.*
of Novi and Priedor, who asked him to stand godfather
to them. He consented, and they have all been baptized,
changing their Mahometan names to Christian; Hassan
being known henceforth as Milan, and so forth.

My friend also received a more important visit from *Declara-*
one of the most moderate of the great Begs, and an active *tion of a great Bos-*
supporter of Djinić's party—Rustan Ali Begović, who *nian Noble.*
resides near Banjaluka. My friend, alluding to the new
converts to orthodox Christianity, asked Rustan what his
intentions were, and whether he thought of being baptized.

'Not yet,' replied the Beg; 'but when the time comes
and the hour of Fate shall strike, I will do it in another
style. I will call together my kinsmen, and we will
return to the faith of our ancestors as one man. We
would choose to be Protestants, as are the English; but
if need be, we will join your Serbian faith. Latins we will
never be! If we go into a Roman Church, what do we
understand? But if, on the other hand, we go into one
of your Pravoslav churches, we know what is said. My
family has never forgotten that they were once of your
faith, and they were made Turks by force. In my castle

there is a secret vault, and in that vault are kept the ancient Christian books and images that my forefathers had before the Turks took Bosnia. I remember once my father looked into it, then closed it up and said " Let them be ; they may serve their turn again." '

LETTER XXIII.

A BOHEMIAN STATESMAN ON THE EASTERN CRISIS
AND THE FUTURE OF ILLYRIA.

Prerogative position of Chesks among Southern Slavs. Conversation with Bohemian statesman. His views on an Austrian annexation of Bosnia. Austria and the Slavs. The attitude of Bohemia. My reasons for wishing to see Illyria re-united under one sceptre and Austro-Hungary merged in it. Desirableness of an autonomous Bulgaria. A Cheskian re-settlement of the Balkan Peninsula. Anglo-Austrian alliance criticised. A Bohemian view of the Magyars.

Prague : *November 25.*

OHEMIA is something more than the most flourishing province of Austria. The Chesks may claim at the present moment to represent something more extensive than the limits of their historic kingdom. Although differing somewhat in language from the Serbs and Croats, they are Slavs, and the most cultured representatives of the family. The very points in which they differ from the other Slavs of the South, their well-defined geographical limits, their history, their language, the fact that the higher grade of culture on which they stand renders them superior to the religious differences which still distract Serbs and Croats—all this gives them a certain prerogative position among the Southern Slavs. Prague is the Slavonic capital of Austria, just as Vienna is the German, or Buda-Pesth the Magyar. Prague is the representative of something greater than the official capital of the Empire represents. Vienna may be a dead pleasure city, but Prague is throbbing with national life. Prague is the eye of the Slavonic intelligence from the Adriatic to the Lower Danube, from the Ægean to the Giant Mountains.

My conversation with a Bohemian Statesman.

I find myself in the Cheskian capital, led there by a desire to obtain the Bohemian views as to the possibilities of the present situation, and especially as to the future of Bosnia, from a leading Bohemian statesman. The expressions of opinion with which I was honoured may have an interest, not only as coming from a statesman of European standing, but as being a representative utterance on the Eastern Question from the Cheskian point of view ; and as my informant was desirous that these views should be placed before the English public, I will make no apology for giving my readers the substance of my conversation. I have ventured to add my own share of the dialogue, as I am not able to subscribe to all my Bohemian friend's conclusions.

Austrian occupation.

I had been alluding to the long postponement of Austrian action on the side of Bosnia in spite of the complete military preparations and of confident statements on the subject made by distinguished personages. 'Still,' he replied, 'you may regard it as a moral certainty that Austria will occupy Bosnia. It is true that the Hungarians—the Magyar dominant caste of Hungary, that is— are dead against it, partly from a disinclination to do anything disagreeable to the Turks, partly from a fear of new accessions of Slavonic strength to the monarchy. But so far as Russia is concerned there would be no opposition. The whole matter was settled between

Austria and Russia long ago; and you may rest assured that the scheme has received the Russian sanction. I cannot, of course, speak definitely about the arrangement; but I believe there is a full understanding that Austro-Hungary is at liberty to take the whole of Bosnia and Northern Herzegovina up to the Narenta Valley. The annexation of Bosnia is, and always has been, a pet object with our Emperor. On that point I can speak positively from personal knowledge. And, after all, as regards Magyar public opinion, it is true it runs very strongly against the project; but Magyar public opinion is very liable to sudden changes. I don't think the wishes of the Court will be seriously opposed in Hungary, and with the King's weight thrown into the scale, and Bosnia annexed to the Hungarian Crown, the measure may suddenly become popular even among the Magyars. You see the Magyar nobility is not so sure that it may not find allies among the Mahometan aristocracy in Bosnia; they still stand in much the same relation to the Slavs this side of the Save as the Begs do to the Bosnian rayahs. You have asked me what I think will be the probable course of events. You have not asked me what I, as a Chesk, as a Slav patriot, would prefer to see. Frankly, I do not desire to see Bosnia annexed by Austro-Hungary. First, because, if it was annexed to the Hungarian part of the Monarchy, the Magyars would crush all nationality out of the country; they are much better hands than the Turks at doing that! Secondly, because, if Austria annexed Bosnia, the whole expense of the new administration would fall on our side of the Leitha; and what with road-making and railway-making and generally developing the resources of the province, the amount of capital that Bosnia would swallow up

*Mineral
and other
wealth of
Bosnia
urged as a
reason for
Austrian
occupation.*

*Chesh view
that Bosnia
should be
Serbian.*

would be enormous—far more than we are in a position
to afford.'

'But as to that,' I urged, 'surely foreign capital will
come to your aid in developing the marvellous resources of
the country as soon as they are generally known. English
capital has only been deterred hitherto from working, for
instance, the rich quicksilver mines of Crescevo by
Turkish mal-administration. Just consider the wealth
that the two most civilized peoples that have had anything to do with Bosnia—the Romans and Ragusans—
drew from it ; the Romans, if I remember rightly, got
50 lb. weight of gold out of those regions daily, and the
Ragusans in the middle ages paid 300,000 ducats yearly
for the lease of some gold-fields. And as to the Magyars,
they may have the will to denationalize Bosnia ; but have
they the power? Their rule, on the contrary, seems to
evoke every latent spark of nationality on the part of
their Slavonic subjects.'

'They may not eventually succeed in crushing the
national life out of the Bosniacs,' he answered, 'but we
know too well what it it is to suffer even a generation of
intellectual torture and political mutilation; and we cannot wish the Bosniacs to endure such a fate, even for a
limited period. No ; Bosnia is a Serbian State, and
Serbian Bosnia should remain. Surely you, as an Englishman, ought to admit that the wishes of the population
should be respected ! If Bosnia is to be attached to any
State, she must be attached to Serbia.'

'But is it not in the interests of the Serbs and of all
Southern Slavs,' I asked, 'that Bosnia should go to
Austria ? Would it not ensure the preponderance of the
Slav element in the Monarchy, and secure the future of
Austria as part of a great South Slavonic State ?'

'Oh, that is the old story! As if we had not a
Slavonic majority in Austria-Hungary already. Believe
me, we do not need any new accession of strength to
assert our position. To-day, as you know, we are
gagged ; but we can bide our time. Here, in Bohemia,
with three-fifths of the population belonging to our
Cheskian nationality, we are put in a miserable minority
at the elections by a manipulation of the electoral districts which gives places where there are 30,000 Germans
greater representation than other districts where there
are 100,000 Chesks. You know our resolve to hold
aloof from Parliament till this iniquitous state of things is
brought to an end. An "Opposition" on strike—that
must seem odd to English ideas! But it may happen
that we know our own interests best. We can bide our
time. Austria has ill-treated us ; but Bohemia is too
rich a country to indulge in a revolt. We shall simply
wait, and when the time comes, as come it will, when
Austria has need of us, and an appeal is made to the
loyal Chesk nationality—well, we shall not respond.
That is all. And as to Bosnia, what new strength would
it give us? A paltry half-dozen votes or so! Certainly
no cultured minds to aid us in our struggle against Ger-
manization.'

'But anyhow,' I interposed, 'half-a-dozen votes are
better than none ; and the question is not so much what
Bosnia is as what Bosnia may be. Besides, you do not
seem to reckon in the secondary effects of such a step
as affecting the prosperity and importance of Slavonic
provinces at present under Austro-Hungary. Illyria
was once a centre of European commerce. Siscia, Sir-
mium, and Salona were once world-cities ; but in those
days Illyria was under one Emperor. To-day, however,

LETTER
XXIII.

*Self-con-
fidence of
Austrian
Slavs.*

*Commer-
cial
advantages
of an
united
Illyria.*

LETTER
XXIII.

*Commer-
cial
advantages
of an
united
Illyria.*

Croatia and Dalmatia are cut off from the continent behind them by political barriers; their commercial development is stifled by artificial means. With Illyria some way re-united, your Croatian and Dalmatian emporia may grow bigger than Vienna itself; your provinces may become tenfold more populous; the whole centre of gravity of the Monarchy may change.'

'There is something in what you say,' he replied; 'but, on the whole, Bosnian commerce must flow mainly into the Danubian commercial basin, and in a far less degree towards the Adriatic. Belgrade rather than Siszek seems to me to be the commercial emporium of the future. There can be little doubt that the great line of communication between East and West will be a railway running from Belgrade through Pristina and Salonica.'

'But the Siszek line,' I remarked, 'is at any rate begun; nor does that consideration much affect the question, for Serbia must of course eventually aggregate itself to the rest of Illyria. The great necessity is that Austria should become the nucleus of a new South Slavonic State, embracing at least the whole Serbian area; that the empire of the Hapsburgs should cease to be a geographical expression, and should become a nation; that forced —as it must be eventually by the Germans—to retreat on the South and East, heterogeneous Austria should be merged in a Slavonic Illyria. You, on the contrary, speak of Serbia annexing Bosnia. Do you really suppose that the Austro-Hungarian Government would tolerate that for a moment?'

' They may have to put up with it !' my friend replied with warmth. ' Rest assured that if Serbia were to annex Bosnia to-morrow, Austria could not raise a' finger to prevent it ! How could Austria prevent it? Declare war against Serbia? The Government knows well enough that there are some things which the Slav majority of the Monarchy would not tolerate, and a war against Serbia or against Russia is one of them. Such a war would mean the disruption of the Empire. If Austria does occupy Bosnia, it will be in virtue of an agreement with Russia and with the Czar's permission. As to our Government actively interfering against Russia, or any alliance with the English Government for that purpose, that is out of the question. If the foregoing considerations were not enough, there is one all-sufficient answer to such rumours—the Russo-German convention.'

'So far as we are concerned,' I observed, 'it is hard to see what interest we have in hindering the development of South Slavonic States in the Balkan Peninsula. They would become the surest bulwark against Russian aggression on the side of Constantinople. Even were the new State weak at first, it would be at least a better ally to us than Turkey, for the simple reason that the Turks, as in the case of the Bulgarian massacres, are liable just at the critical moment to commit some revolting deed of savagery, which turns the English people away from them in shuddering abhorrence! No, Lord Strangford and Mr. Finlay, the two Englishmen who have made the deepest study of those lands, were both agreed that the establishment of a South Slavonic power was the only barrier that could prevent the ultimate seizure of Constantinople by Russia. And if Austria takes Bosnia, and acquires a dominant position in the West of the Balkan Peninsula, there will be no danger of Russia domineering in an autonomous Bulgaria. A free Bulgaria would be led by most obvious interests to lean on the Illyrian Power to her West. I have even thought,' I added,

LETTER
XXIII.

The impotence of Austria.

Advantages to England of rise of South Slavonic power.

'that at no distant date Stamboul itself might become
the Bulgarian capital. As it is, the Bulgarian colonists
have been drawing nearer and nearer to it every year ;
there is, or was, a large Bulgarian population in the city
itself ; and over half the students in the most civilizing
institution in the place—the Robert College—were
Bulgarians.'

'God preserve Bulgaria from such a capital !' he said.
'It would poison the whole State. I look upon Stamboul
as the Capua of empires ; it is the native city of the
Fanariotes, the gathering-place for the scum of Europe.
Constantinople may be a Bulgarian possession, but let
them fix their capital at Adrianople—anywhere but there !

Interests of Southern Slavs NOT *anti-English.*

You are right in supposing that there is no danger to English interests in the autonomy of Bulgaria or other South
Slavonic States. It is the absurdest fallacy to suppose
that any of us are desirous of coming under the yoke of
Russia. It is you English, who, by supporting Turkish
misrule, have been simply making Russia a present of
paramount influence among the South Slavonic populations of the Balkan Peninsula ! What a marvellous

A Christian re-settlement of Balkan Peninsula.

opportunity your Government has at the present time for
resettling the whole of the Balkan Peninsula on a durable
basis ! The whole matter might be settled with Russia in
half an hour. Bulgaria, Servia, Bosnia, Albania to be free
States, and Greece to be given Thessaly and half Epirus.
With Turkish dominion transferred to Asia Minor, the
question of the Bosphorus would settle itself ; the great
difficulty at the present moment is that one State holds
both shores of the narrow Straits, but with the Turks
only on the Asiatic shore the Straits would be *ipso facto*
neutralized. Your Government, however, will persist in
propping up the Turks.'

'Perhaps,' I said, 'it would be fairer to call our attitude anti-Russian than pro-Turkish. England, as Lord Beaconsfield once remarked, is "a great non-European Power." Our Government seems to regard the question rather from the Asiatic standpoint; but for that very reason we have little direct interest in the Balkan Peninsula itself. It is not so much because a free Bulgaria or an enlarged Serbia would injure us that we fill the waste-paper basket of Belgrade with diplomatic admonitions; we do it rather out of friendship for Austria. We say a word against South Slavonic liberation on the Danube in order that Austria may say a word against Russian aggrandizement on the Asiatic side, where she has no interests. And yet,' I continued, 'though I have travelled from one end of the Empire to the other, I have never quite made out what "Austria" is. I have talked with Germans, Magyars, Slavs, Italians, Viennese; but a "good Austrian—*ein guter Oesterreicher*," I have nowhere discovered.'

'Nor has anybody else!' he replied. 'Your diplomatists are well enough informed as to the views of the German and Magyar politicians of Austria-Hungary. They see dualistic Austria as she is, and overrate her power. They certainly do not command the confidence of our party, of the Slavonic majority of the Monarchy.'

'I was speaking with a Magyar,' I remarked, 'the other day, and he seemed to think that very little count need be taken of Slavonic opinion in the matter. In his opinion the Slavs were quite an inferior race.'

'That is really a little strong even for a Magyar!' exclaimed my Bohemian friend. 'Why, the greatest men the Magyars can boast of were all foreigners by birth, and mostly Slavs; their greatest poet, Petrosy, is a Serb,

whose real name is Petrović.   Vambéry is the German
Bamberger.   Kossuth was a Slovak ; his peculiar genius,
his enthusiasm, his whole character are Slavonic.   The
Magyars have their high qualities, but they have produced
no literary talent.   Like the Turk, the Magyar is Turanian,
and he has just the virtues and defects of the Osmanli.
I remember once a French traveller who had been many
years in Egypt telling me that the commonest Turk was
capable of commanding a regiment of Arabs or Egyptians.
Let him be never so ignorant, all that was necessary was
to give him an officer's grade, and he kept discipline and
command.   The Arab might be a man of much higher
culture, of much higher mental capacity, but he never
made such a good officer as the Turk.   Well, that opened
my eyes to a parallel.   The Magyar is among the Slavs
just what the Turk is amongst these Africans and Arabs.
He knows how to command.   A single Magyar can order
about ten Slavs.   This inability to command, to govern,
to maintain discipline, is our chief defect as a race.   Nor
will I deny the Magyar many social virtues.   He has a
dignified and courteous manner, and he is hospitable ; so
is the Turk ; but, like the Turk, he is incorrigibly idle.
He has not the slightest aptitude for business.   Most of
the great Magyar families are ruined—their debts are
notorious.   Even the Hungarian State seems incapable
of controlling its accounts—witness the gigantic railway
swindles.   It is this inherent disqualification on the part
of the Magyars for finance that was one of the great objections on this side of the Leitha to allowing them to
have their way on the " Bank Question."   A Magyar
cannot even carry his own harvest; he has to employ
Slovaks—a Cheskian race.   The wealth of the country is
rapidly passing away from the ruling castes on these ac-

*Want of
qualities
of govern-
ment
among
Slavs.*

counts. Wherever in Hungary you see a well-kept farm, you may be sure that the owner is either a German or a Jew, or one of our people. There is a very large Bohemian population now in Hungary.

'The Magyars say—and there is hardly one of their race that is not imbued with the idea—"We will either govern an Empire or fall to the ground." Well, in nine-teenth-century Europe masterful pride is not enough to secure dominion ; the race which works wins. To-day the Magyars are a small dominant caste governing a hostile population. In gazetteers you will find that there are 5,000,000 Magyars in Hungary, and some 10,000,000 of other nationalities. These figures are untrue. The Magyars are in reality an even smaller minority than this ; but in the census papers every one who can under-stand their language—be he Serb or Rouman, German or Slovak—is reckoned in. The domination of that mi-nority will die a natural death ; but the Magyars need not fear that they will be ill-treated if they are merged eventually in a Slavonic State. We are not a revengeful race.'

LETTER XXIII.

Magyar domination doomed.

LONDON : PRINTED BY
SPOTTISWOODE AND CO., NEW-STREET SQUARE
AND PARLIAMENT STREET

THROUGH BOSNIA AND HERZEGOVINA ON FOOT

DURING THE INSURRECTION, AUGUST AND SEPTEMBER 1875.

With a Historical Review of Bosnia, and a Glimpse at the Croats, Slavonians, and the Ancient Republic of Ragusa.

SECOND EDITION. WITH A MAP AND 58 ILLUSTRATIONS.

London, LONGMANS & CO.

OPINIONS of the PRESS.

'A walk through Bosnia last autumn, in the disturbed state of popular feeling, with no guide but a map, and no protection but an autograph letter from the Governor-General, subject to the annoyance of being stoned as a Giaour, and scimetared by Bashi-Bazouks as a Servian incendiary, was an exciting enterprise. Mr. EVANS is a describer of no ordinary power. We could not wish for a fuller or more vivid picture of all the externals of Bosnian life, the houses and dresses, the fauna and flora. A great part of the book is occupied with descriptions of landscapes, and these are done with all the enthusiasm and knowledge of an artist. . . . The book, as a whole, is one of the freshest and most opportune and instructive books of travel that have been published for some time.' EXAMINER.

'Mr. EVANS has published a work which at the present time no intelligent Englishman can overlook.' ENGLISH INDEPENDENT.

'This well-written, interesting, and seasonable book discusses the north-western districts of Turkey in a scholarly and lucid style, with the pen of a competent, if not a well-known writer, to whom description is clearly no hard or irksome task, and who displays judgment and original thought in the exercise of his literary calling.' PALL MALL GAZETTE.

'In this rambling, scrambling, and altogether most delightful book, we have the prose poetry of Christopher North in the best passages of his *Noctes Ambrosianæ*. . . . From an interesting historic narrative he passes on to deal swashing blows at the tyrants of the Bosniacs and Herzegovinians of a kind that ought to please the soul of Mr. Freeman, to almost lyrical descriptions of female beauty, or to pictures of intensely artistic scenery, the fidelity of which would be acknowledged by Mr. Ruskin.' OBSERVER.

'Whether you regard the book as one of travel only, or as one having a special interest at this time because of its political bearings, it deserves the closest attention. There is nothing in his descriptions of the penny-a-lining style; he writes only that which is necessary for the right understanding of his subject, and he adorns it with an amount of information which is as useful as it is pleasant to read. Mr. EVANS has, besides, sound artistic tastes and a ready pencil, and the result is that he gives you in the course of his book little sketches of singular excellence. . . . If for nothing else, the book would be valuable for the introductory chapter, which contains an historical review of Bosnia which is deeply interesting. It is a delightful book in all respects.' SCOTSMAN.

S

' Of this book we can say, as the Author does of Ragusa, " it far surpassed our most sanguine expectations." . . . Wherever he goes he carries with him the eye of an artist and the memory of an historian. His historical review of Bosnia seems to us a model of what such an essay should be ; it sets the conversion of the Mussulman population of Bosnia to Islâm in a novel and interesting light. . . . Frenchmen are generally affected by prejudices which may not unfairly be described as either sentimental or conventional, in favour of Christianity in general and Roman Catholicism in particular. From such prejudices our English author is quite free. . . . It would, perhaps, have been difficult to choose a route which, without ever going twice over the same ground, touches so many places interesting to the historian. . . . Descriptions of the most interesting city of Ragusa, and the country round it, serve to close the book with an artistic abruptness worthy of an ode of Horace.' ACADEMY.

' It is not plain to us whether the "Slavonic Mahometans" or the Christian populations have Mr. EVANS's most profound sympathies. His book is valuable for its candour and calmness. . . . One of the most interesting chapters in the book is devoted to the old military frontier, originally the outwork of Christendom, " the political sea-wall of her provinces, painfully reclaimed." The old order of things, of which Mr. EVANS gives a vivid description, which divided the border provinces among Slavonic house-communities, . . . has not quite passed away. . . . For strangeness that excites the imagination there is nothing in this book of out-of-the-way travel to compare with the expedition which the Author announces thus :—"To cross the military frontier is to survey a phase of society so primitive that it was already antiquated when the forefathers of the English sate among the fens and forests of the Elbe-lands ; it is to wander beyond the twilight of history, and to take a lantern into the night of time." The description of the still existing communistic homesteads, illustrated by a very quaint drawing, is exceedingly interesting. . . . When Mr. EVANS diverges into antiquarianism we enjoy the book particularly. He draws a beautiful picture of Siscia in her days of grandeur and commercial importance. . . . The late Mr. Mortimer Collins, in one of his witty *vers de société*, made a young lady, after some attention to the talk around her, say to her partner at a ball, "Who is the Herzegovina ?" It was not an extreme satire on the popular ignorance and indifference little more than a year ago. Mr. EVANS's work answers the question in detail, with lingering pleasantness and dainty divergence into picturesque tracks and historical bypaths, for which we thank him heartily.'   SPECTATOR.

' We cannot but congratulate Mr. EVANS and ourselves that he has lived to tell the tale.'   ARMY AND NAVY GAZETTE.

' Mr. EVANS's book is a very able, instructive, and readable one. . . . That such a state of servility on the one hand and barbarous injustice on the other should exist at the present day in Europe, is a disgrace to humanity.'   MORNING POST.

' There is not a dry page in this fascinating and well-told story of travel.'   WHITEHALL REVIEW.

' Mr. EVANS does not hesitate to denounce the abuses and cruelties of the corrupt Turkish administration. Yet he betrays no vehement hatred of Turkey, and his only anxiety seems to be lest the Mohammedan party in Bosnia should be unfairly dealt with in the event of a triumph of Panslavism. . . . It is pleasant to share the Author's frank enjoyment of the landscape, changing from day to day, as he and his companion rambled up the fertile Bosnian vale, stopping here and there to sketch an ancient ruined castle, a group of pilgrims on the road or at the shrines, a view in some village street, a picturesque bit of rock, or a woodland glade. The night they passed amidst the gathering of the Roman Catholic worshippers at the mountain sanctuary near Comusina was a piece of genuine highland life alone worth the toil of their journey on foot from the banks of the Save.' SATURDAY REVIEW.

'A volume so full of 'meat,' of picturesque description and condensed information, is a rare apparition among modern books of tours. At home alike among the Grenzer communities of the Austrian borderland, the wandering colonies of Wallachs and Bulgarians, the native Christians and old conservative Mahometans of Bosnia ; ready to sleep in the open air and make his way from point to point across the woods and water-courses of a genuine Bosnian ravine, Mr. EVANS possesses in a more than ordinary degree the power of presenting to the reader, in a few graphic touches, the scenes and inhabitants of these romantic lands.' GRAPHIC.

'His descriptions of the beautiful landscape scenery, fertile plain, forest, and mountain, which is traversed in going up the course of the river Bosnia, and the sterner aspect of the Herzegovinian highlands, are very impressive. . . . The night encampment of an assembly of Roman Catholic peasantry in the highlands at the religious festival of Comusina is almost like a scene of romance in " Waverley." ' ILLUSTRATED NEWS.

'This is a most opportune contribution to the geography, customs, and history of a country which has suddenly emerged from the dimmest obscurity into the full glare of European observation.' GUARDIAN.

'Mr. EVANS repaired last year to the least known and most neglected part of Europe, though it lies within a few days' journey of the course of the Danube and the shores of the Adriatic. He took with him the qualifications of an accomplished traveller—experience of foreign lands, a multiplicity of languages at command, a store of historical and antiquarian knowledge, even of extinct sovereigns and races, a taste for natural history, which singularly enlivens his pages, a keen eye for the picturesque, a ready pencil, a good deal of humour, a bold heart and ready hand in emergencies, and, above all, a stout pair of legs and a hardy constitution, which enabled him to tramp over hills and valleys scarcely trodden by man or beast, to live on the food of a savage, and to sleep as well on the hillside as in a Bosniak *Han.* Here are abundant materials for one of the most agreeable and instructive volumes of travel that we have had the good fortune to meet with, and Mr. EVANS has not failed to make the best of his opportunities. But his good fortune did not end here. He started on his journey in total ignorance of what he was to meet with. As he advanced into the country, the natural beauty of these provinces, the simplicity of their inhabitants, their past history and their present condition, under a weak and incapable g vernment, awakened in him sympathies amounting to enthusiasm ; and before he left it a popular and political movement had broken out around him, which seemed to be the harbinger of brighter and better days to a downtrodden race, and which, as it has since turned out, was of the gravest moment to the Ottoman Empire itself and to all the powers of Europe. As the traveller quitted Serajevo, on a gloomy evening in August, the city stood out in lurid light above the mist and darkness that enshrouded its base, an emblem of its portentous position. "It is the begining of the end," said one of the foreign consuls to them. . . . A year has passed, and the cloud has spread to the dimensions of a tempest. . . . In this book we find a vivid and sympathetic picture of the origin of the contest, drawn by an eyewitness, full of the just and generous sympathies of a young Englishman.'   EDINBURGH REVIEW.

'Many volumes of travel have been published which profess to describe the aspects of those South Slavonic lands in which the insurrection against the Turkish power has now for more than a year been aflame ; but we have not met with any that deserves to be compared with the book which lies before us. Mr. EVANS combines a variety of qualities, every one of which contributed its share to the excellence of his work, but which, even taken singly, are not too commonly found among writers of travel, and in well-harmonised union are still more rare.   Sound scholarship, wide historical and archæological reading, an intimate previous knowledge of other Slavonic populations, and an appre-ciation of the peculiar merits of the Slavonic character, prepared Mr. EVANS for an investigation into the state and prospects of Bosnia, which was the more valuable because it had been projected long before even the first outbreak in Herzegovina, and was carried out without any idea that the troubled scenes amid which it was conducted involved the large political issues subsequently apparent.   But other travellers with similar advantages of knowledge and pre-possession might have missed the most important of Mr. EVANS's observations. To have passed through the Slavonic provinces of Turkey in a travelling carriage, along the main roads, from city to city, and to have been the guest of Pasha after Pasha, would have been the ordinary fate of the English traveller, and such an experience would have revealed little or nothing of the character and condition of the rayahs.   Mr. EVANS, to the amazement of the Turkish officials, and not a little to their embarrassment, made up his mind to penetrate across the country on foot, and to see close at hand the common life of the Christian peasants.   In this purpose he persevered, in spite of the remonstrances and menaces of puzzled and suspicious Turks, and his success has secured us a most important mass of testimony bearing upon that phase of the Eastern Question which Europe can no longer put aside.   Moreover, a refined and educated taste has enabled Mr. EVANS to reproduce for the benefit of his readers the sensations of pleasure aroused by grand or tender scenery, by historical associations and dim suggestions of antiquity, by those beauties of nature in tree and flower, and even insect life, that escape the careless eye.   For Mr. EVANS is something of a botanist and an entomologist as well as an antiquary and a scholar.   He is as ready to call our attention to interesting mountain forms, to the delicate beauty of the flora, and to the moths and butterflies that revel among these blossoms, as to a trace of Roman inheritance in the form of a jar, or to an apposite allusion in Claudian or Ausonius.   His style, it must be added, is vigorous and well sustained, often pleasantly touched with humour, and some-times approaching to eloquence.   Few indeed will take up Mr. EVANS's volume who will decline to read it through, and even those who feel no active curiosity about Slavonic society, or who turn from the Eastern Question as an interminable tangle of inconsistent theories, cannot refuse to interest themselves in this record of travel through scenes that have now obtained for themselves a permanent place in history.'   THE TIMES.

For EU product safety concerns, contact us at Calle de José Abascal, 56–1°,
28003 Madrid, Spain or eugpsr@cambridge.org.

www.ingramcontent.com/pod-product-compliance
Ingram Content Group UK Ltd.
Pitfield, Milton Keynes, MK11 3LW, UK
UKHW010346140625
459647UK00010B/873